Peace Works

Peace Works

The Citizen's Role in Ending the Cold War

David Cortright

WESTVIEW PRESS

Boulder • San Francisco • Oxford

Copyright © 1993 by Westview Press, Inc.

Published in 1993 in the United States of America by Westview Press,Inc., 5500 Central Avenue, Boulder, Colorado 80301-2877, and in the United Kingdom by Westview Press, 36 Lonsdale Road, Summertown, Oxford OX2 7EW

Library of Congress Cataloging-in-Publication Data
Cortright, David, 1946–
   Peace works : the citizen's role in ending the Cold
War / David Cortright.
      p.   cm.
Includes index.
   ISBN 0-8133-1881-5 (HC). — ISBN 0-8133-1882-3 (pbk.)
   1. Peace movements.   2. Cold War.   I. Title.
JX1952.C659   1993
327.1'72—dc20   93-20431
                                                                        CIP

Printed and bound in the United States of America

⊗ The paper used in this publication meets the requirements of the American National Standard for Permanence of Paper for Printed Library Materials Z39.48-1984.

10   9   8   7   6   5   4   3   2   1

Contents

Acknowledgments

This book is the collective work of many people, and I am deeply grateful to all who helped to make it possible.

The greatest credit goes to John J. Gilligan, the first director of the Institute for International Peace Studies at the University of Notre Dame and former governor of Ohio. Gilligan brought me to Notre Dame following my tenure at SANE and SANE/Freeze and strongly supported the writing of this book. Enormous thanks are also due to George Lopez, director of undergraduate studies at the institute and chair of the Program for Research and Writing on Peace and International Cooperation at the John D. and Catherine T. MacArthur Foundation in Chicago. Lopez actively encouraged my work at Notre Dame and provided important assistance in obtaining the financial support that made it possible. Robert Johansen, Senior Fellow at the Institute for International Peace Studies, offered valuable guidance and constant inspiration. Polly Carl, a graduate of the institute, served as my editorial and production assistant during the summer of 1990 and provided extremely helpful advice and encouragement throughout the research and writing process. Vienna Colucci also provided research support. Several graduate students at Notre Dame read and critiqued the manuscript as part of a colloquium at the university. They included Katy Brown, Catherine Hill, Dani Leis, Michael Mann, Svetlana Morozova, Laura Schwingel, Jackie Smith, Anna Snyder, Fran Teplitz, Diava Vaskeviciute, and Karsonya Wise. Dolores Michael typed most of the manuscript, and Rita Kopczynski, Midge Holloran, Rosemarie Green, and Ann Miller helped with administrative support.

Several scholars and activists read all or parts of the manuscript and provided suggestions for improvement. They included Cindy Buhl, Bill Callahan, Gene Carroll, Charles Chatfield, William Sloane Coffin, Frances Farley, Cynthia Maude Gembler, Marc Hardy, John Isaacs, Jennifer Leaning, Michael Mawby, Marilyn McNabb, David Meyer, and Glen Stassen. Advice and assistance were also provided by Chad Dobson, Mary Kaldor, Robert Musil, Marla Painter, Marcus Raskin, Jo Sedeita, and Duane Shank. I am especially grateful to the dozens of activists and public officials who agreed to be interviewed for this work.

Financial support came primarily from the John D. and Catherine T. MacArthur Foundation Program for Research and Writing on Peace and International Cooperation. Funds also were provided by Rockefeller Family Associates, the Samuel Rubin Foundation, Hilda Mason, and the Town Creek Foundation.

A special word of tribute is due to my wife, Karen Jacob, who encouraged me during the long hours of research and writing and inspired me with her achievements. Deep thanks also go to Patricia Cameron Cortright and my children, Michael, Catherine, and James.

To all who provided insight, inspiration, and support for this book, I gratefully acknowledge your assistance.

David Cortright

1
Making History

The beginning of the end of the Cold War came in 1987 when the United States and the Soviet Union signed the Intermediate-Range Nuclear Forces (INF) Treaty eliminating all intermediate-range nuclear weapons. The treaty heralded a dramatic improvement in East-West relations and a new era of demilitarization and political change in Eastern Europe.

What caused these momentous events? Two sharply differing interpretations have been offered. When the INF Treaty was signed, Randall Forsberg, founder of the Nuclear Weapons Freeze Campaign, declared, "This is a victory for the peace movement."[1] Secretary of State George Shultz countered that "if we had listened to the freeze movement there never would have been an INF treaty."[2] President George Bush frequently claimed credit for winning the Cold War and found it necessary on numerous occasions to deny the influence of the peace movement. In the 1992 presidential debates, he declared, "We never would have got there if we'd gone for the nuclear freeze crowd. "[3]

Who's right? Did the peace movements of the United States and Europe create a political climate conducive to arms reduction and U.S.-Soviet cooperation? Or are former Reagan administration officials correct in asserting that "peace through strength works"? What about the sweeping changes that transformed the former Soviet Union? Were these the result of internal dynamics or a response to military pressures from the West?

The stakes in this debate are high. If one accepts the peace-through-strength interpretation, the implication is that "hanging tough pays off" (to paraphrase historian John Lewis Gaddis).[4] According to this view, missile deployments and military buildups can help to secure the peace, and continued weapons development is necessary to create bar-

gaining chips for future arms reduction. With its faith in military solutions, the hardline interpretation also implies a greater readiness to use
force in international affairs. If military confrontation could force the
Soviet Union to "cry uncle," as Ronald Reagan once phrased it, the
same approach can be applied to other world trouble spots—in Iraq, Panama, or elsewhere. This is not just an academic debate but a vital question about the nature of foreign policy and the proper U.S. role in
global affairs.

The interpretation offered by the peace movement is very different.
According to this view, the road to peace is through military restraint
and international cooperation. The pressures that brought an end to
the Cold War were peaceful and democratic in nature, not military, and
the sources of change in the Soviet Union and Eastern and Central Europe were primarily internal, not external. Credit for ending the Cold
War belongs to those who struggled for freedom from within, not those
who brandished weapons from without. Peace was achieved in spite of,
not because of, the arms buildup.

The alternative view also holds that ordinary people can play a central role in making history. Peace movements are legitimate players in
foreign policy, and citizen action can be an essential force for peaceful
change. Where conventional history credits the decisions of a few, usually men, in determining world events, this perspective gives voice to
the unnamed millions who participate in the great social movements
that shape the course of human affairs. It recognizes the Europeans and
U.S. citizens who struggled for peace and an end to the war system as
the true architects of the post–Cold War era.

This book is not a dispassionate examination by a detached observer; rather, it grows out of personal experience and a lifetime of commitment to peace activism. My experiences in the peace movement began when I was an antiwar soldier during the Vietnam War and have
continued to the present. In fact, I have been personally involved in
many of the campaigns described in these pages. From 1978 to 1987, I
was privileged to serve as executive director of SANE. During that time,
I was an active participant in the nuclear freeze movement, the stop
MX campaign, the June 12, 1982, rally in New York's Central Park, citizen diplomacy at the Reagan-Gorbachev summits, the Central America
solidarity movement, and many other efforts. I had a front-row seat for
one of the most dramatic periods of peace mobilization in U.S. history.

In this book I have attempted to answer that most important but difficult of questions: Was it all worthwhile? Did the peace movements of

the 1980s have an impact? Those of us involved in the freeze movement believed that our efforts would have an impact, but it was more a matter of faith than certainty. When government leaders seemed to ignore our efforts or claimed to be unaffected by them, it was hard to maintain that faith. We yearned to know if we were really having an impact, and if so, what strategies and tactics worked best. These were the questions that motivated this study. I wanted to determine as precisely as possible what, if any, influence our efforts had on decision making within the White House and Congress. During the course of my research, as politicians and scholars began to debate who won the Cold War, I realized that I would have to go beyond assessing the impact of a social movement and attempt an interpretation of this dramatic turning point in world history.

The term "peace movement" refers not only or even primarily to the organized activities of specific groups like SANE/Freeze or the Women's International League for Peace and Freedom. Of course, such groups are essential to the movement, but the movement extends far beyond traditional peace organizations to include people of all walks of life who commit themselves to the prevention of war. This broadly cast net includes physicians who warn of the medical consequences of nuclear war, members of Congress who work for arms control, artists who help to shape an antinuclear culture, religious leaders who raise a moral voice for peace, scientists who question the wisdom and feasibility of new weapons, and countless others who contribute in ways large or small to the public outcry against war. Movements cannot be neatly compartmentalized, especially when they are as broad as the peace upsurge of the 1980s. Many different tendencies and political approaches, some at odds with one another, coexist within the same movement, but all contribute directly or indirectly to political pressure for arms restraint. This expansive and holistic framework is essential for understanding the full impact of peace activism.

The methodologies for assessing peace movement influence are necessarily imprecise. Social movement analysis is not a quantitative science. It would be extremely difficult to prove that a particular government action, such as the decision to begin strategic arms talks, resulted from specific activist pressures from the nuclear freeze movement. Yet certain causal relationships can be traced. Documentary evidence on Reagan administration decision making is becoming increasingly available in published memoirs of former White House officials, and I have conducted a series of interviews to supplement these. Although the leading decisionmakers generally deny that they were influenced by the peace movement, all acknowledge its presence and most admit that public pressures constrained White House policy to some degree. A careful reading of these sources, combined with a close examination of the historical record, reveals several important instances of peace-movement influence on Reagan administration policy.

My approach focuses to a large extent on indirect means of pressure because I believe that peace movements often have a greater impact on the general political climate than on specific policy changes. To define these indirect influences, I emphasize two key mechanisms of social change—the role of public opinion and culture and the impact of the legislative process.

In the first half of the book, Chapters 2 through 6, I discuss political culture and the pressures that influenced public opinion in the 1980s. The many diverse manifestations of peace activism—grass-roots organizing, public education, religious involvement, media communications, and so on—helped to create a new public awareness of the nuclear threat and increased political pressure for arms reduction. In Chapter 2, I examine the emergence of the nuclear freeze movement. Chapter 3 describes the Nobel Prize–winning efforts of the Physicians for Social Responsibility, and Chapter 4 explores the involvement of churches and the religious community. I turn to the important but often overlooked realm of media and popular culture in Chapter 5, and in Chapter 6, I analyze the changes in public opinion. Chapter 7 shows how these changes in the political climate specifically influenced decision making within the White House.

The second half explores how peace pressures influenced the outcome of specific policy debates. In Chapter 8, I describe the struggle of the West European peace movement against Intermediate-Range Nuclear Forces. I look at the campaign against the MX missile in Chapter 9, and in Chapters 10 and 11 I examine the Strategic Defense Initiative (SDI) and nuclear testing. Chapter 12 focuses on the sources of perestroika and new thinking in the Soviet Union, revealing ways in which Western peace movements may have helped the process. Chapter 13 extends the analysis to U.S. Central America policy, and Chapter 14 gives a scorecard summarizing peace movement impacts.

The story begins with the rise of the nuclear freeze movement.

2
The Nuclear Freeze

The day dawned cool and gray. On Central Park West, only a few cars upset the rare quiet of an early Saturday morning. The songs of morning birds, undisturbed by the roar of traffic, filled the springtime air. The idyllic calm would soon be shattered, though, for on this day— June 12, 1982—nearly 1 million people would throng to New York's Central Park for the largest political demonstration in U.S. history.[1]

Participants had trekked from every part of America and from around the world to demand an end to the arms race and commemorate the opening of the United Nations Second Special Session on Disarmament. From Boston and the cities of New England came a peace train, specially rented for the occasion, that was packed with thousands of freeze activists. From dozens of states came more than a thousand chartered buses. Feeder marches poured in from Brooklyn, Harlem, and other parts of New York. International delegations arrived from Japan, Europe, the Soviet Union, Zambia, Bangladesh, and many other countries.

The official demands of the June 12 march were to halt the arms race and fund human needs, but the press referred to it simply as the nuclear freeze rally. Media reports put the crowd size at 500,000 to 700,000,[2] but the official rally committee (of which I was part) estimated 1 million. In fact, it was impossible to determine the exact number, for the park itself and the main thoroughfares of downtown Manhattan were clogged with demonstrators trying to reach the rally site.[3] One thing was certain: It was the largest peace rally ever to take place on U.S. soil. Many marchers that day wore tags reading "I made history." Indeed they did, as the giant rally gave voice to an unprecedented social movement for peace and an end to the nuclear madness.

The June 12 rally was more than a political event. It was a cultural and social phenomenon that succeeded despite, not because of, the official rally committee. Planning for the rally had begun nearly a year before, but the organizing meetings were plagued with constant divisions over what the demands should be, who would speak, how much music to include, even where the march would take place. In fact, just a few weeks before the march, the rally committee nearly broke down completely, and it was only through the pastoral intercession of the Reverend William Sloane Coffin, senior minister at New York's Riverside Church, that a measure of civility was restored to the planning process. As the day of the rally approached and the committee faced the daunting challenge of providing security for the expected throng, the New York City Police Department stepped in and wisely offered to take charge of crowd control. New York's finest performed superbly that day as peace activists and police officers worked together to manage the huge crowds that jammed central Manhattan.

The June 12 rally succeeded because the peace movement and the nuclear freeze enjoyed overwhelming public support in the early 1980s. Vast numbers of U.S. citizens were concerned about the nuclear threat and wanted to "do something" for peace. The rally gave expression to these feelings and became a cultural happening. FM radio stations and local news programs promoted it like a new product. Rock stars and Hollywood celebrities volunteered their services and clamored to participate. Two nights before the rally, rock concerts featuring James Taylor, Jackson Browne, Linda Ronstadt, and Billy Joel were held at Nassau Coliseum on Long Island to promote and raise money for the demonstration. On June 12 itself, these stars were joined by Bruce Springsteen, Joan Baez, Rita Marley, Susan Sarandon, Peter, Paul and Mary, and many others. As the program began, Orson Welles arrived in a huge limousine that pulled right behind the stage area. A short time later, a hush of excitement swept the backstage area as Yoko Ono discreetly arrived on foot but declined an invitation to be introduced on stage. Among the more than seventy speakers scheduled to address the crowd that day were Dr. Benjamin Spock, freeze founder Randall Forsberg, Congressmen Ron Dellums (D-CA) and Ed Markey (D-MA), and such veteran peace activists as David Dellinger, Cora Weiss, and Seymour Melman.

On June 6, a companion rally and peace festival was held at the Rose Bowl in Pasadena, California. "Peace Sunday" brought about 90,000 people to the stadium that day to hear political speeches and performances by musical artists. Among the performers were Graham Nash,

Stevie Nicks, Stephen Stills, Stevie Wonder, Jesse Colin Young, and Donovan. The speakers included Muhammad Ali, Delores Huerta, the Reverend Jesse Jackson, and Petra Kelly, founder and leader of the Green Party of West Germany. Also speaking at the peace rally that Sunday was Patti Davis, youngest daughter of Ronald and Nancy Reagan. The message in California was the same as in New York: Freeze the arms race and fund human needs.

The California and New York rallies were reflections of one of the largest grass-roots populist movements in U.S. history. Like the proverbial prairie fire, the nuclear freeze swept across the United States and implanted itself in every part of society. In the process, public consciousness was transformed, a new political climate was created, and government policy responded, first with a change in rhetoric and finally with policies that led to arms reduction. Although the nuclear freeze as a specific proposal to halt the arms race was never adopted, the larger social movement it spawned had an enormous impact in paving the way for an end to the Cold War.

Nuclear Clouds

The massive wave of peace activism that erupted in the 1980s was a direct response to the extremist, right-wing military policies of the Reagan administration. Although the emergence of the freeze concept predated the inauguration of Ronald Reagan, the inflammatory rhetoric and radical policies emanating from the White House fanned the flames of antinuclear revolt and gave a decisive boost to peace organizing.

As *Time* magazine editor Strobe Talbott has observed, "Reagan and his administration came into office not really wanting to pursue arms control at all."[4] The president and his advisers believed that the United States had been weakened militarily by arms control treaties. During his political career, Ronald Reagan had opposed every previous arms control agreement. He had spoken out against the 1963 Limited Test Ban Treaty, opposed the 1968 Nuclear Nonproliferation Treaty, attacked the Strategic Arms Limitation Talks (SALT) I and the Anti-Ballistic Missile Treaty, and campaigned against SALT II. He had even opposed the innocuous Peaceful Nuclear Explosions agreement negotiated by Gerald Ford in 1974.[5] As peace activists quipped at the time, Ronald Reagan had never met an arms control agreement he liked. The administration's dismissive view toward arms control was perhaps best captured in 1983 remarks by Pentagon official Richard Perle to Richard Starr, the departing U.S. negotiator at the deadlocked conventional arms talks in Vienna, which had languished for fifteen years without agreement: "Congratulations! You obviously did a good job because nothing happened."[6]

In Reagan's Manichaean vision, the Soviet Union really was an evil empire. It could never be trusted to negotiate in good faith and would only respond to brute force. Former White House Counselor Martin Anderson paraphrased the president's philosophy, conveyed to his aides in private, as follows:

> The Soviets will stop only when they realize that we are willing to go all out in an arms race. ... If we release the forces of our economy to produce the weapons we need, the Soviets will never be able to keep up. ... Only then will they become reasonable and willing to seriously consider reductions in nuclear arms.[7]

Secretary of State Alexander Haig reported in his memoirs that Soviet officials were eager to begin negotiations as soon as the new administration entered office but that the White House refused:

> The Reagan administration was not prepared to go ahead with this process. ... Instead the President decided ... to build and deploy the MX missile, develop the ... Trident II submarine, and ... build the B-1B bomber and further expand cruise missile capability. With this ... Reagan would feel able, eventually, to propose a new round of Strategic Arms Reduction Talks.[8]

Defense Secretary Caspar Weinberger made the same point in testimony before the U.S. Catholic Bishops Committee in 1982: The administration could not begin substantial negotiations until after the United States had "rearmed" (i.e., completed the Reagan military buildup), a process he estimated would take about eight years.[9] A similar comment was made in May 1981 by Paul Nitze, cofounder of the Committee on the Present Danger, shortly before he was appointed to serve as the administration's senior negotiator on Intermediate-Range Nuclear Forces. When asked about the prospects for arms control negotiations at a conference at the Lawrence Livermore National Laboratory in California, Nitze answered that there could be serious arms control talks "only after we have built up our forces." When asked how long that might take, Nitze replied, "ten years."[10]

The administration backed up these beliefs with action. Immediately upon taking office, Reagan launched the largest peacetime military buildup in U.S. history. The military budget grew from $130 billion in 1979 to nearly $300 billion in 1985, an increase of more than 50 percent above inflation.[11] The government's rhetoric and declaratory statements escalated along with the military budget. Navy Secretary John Lehman proclaimed a new doctrine of deploying naval forces near Soviet territory and threatening nuclear strikes against the Soviet heartland. Secretary of State Alexander Haig talked of a "nuclear warning shot" in Europe.[12] A Pentagon report disclosed in the *New York Times* instructed the military services to prepare for "prevailing" in a "protracted" nuclear war.[13] The president himself spoke of the possibility of limited nuclear exchanges.[14] The administration's loose talk of nuclear war struck terror into the hearts of many people. Here was a government that was proclaiming for all to hear that it would not shrink from the use of military force, including nuclear weapons, to impose its will.

Seeds of Opposition

A clarification of terms is necessary at the outset. In this study, the term "nuclear freeze movement" is used in a broad and inclusive manner. The phrase refers not just to specific groups within the official Nuclear Weapons Freeze Campaign but also to the full range of organizations working for an end to the arms race. Many tactical and political differences existed among the thousands of local and national citizens' groups engaged in these issues. Some espoused radical disarmament, and others pursued more limited arms control aims. Some practiced civil disobedience, and others employed more conventional tactics. Whatever their particular emphasis, though, nearly all backed the proposal for a bilateral halt to the arms race that was issued by Randall Forsberg in March of 1980. The idea of the freeze provided unprecedented visibility and coherence to the peace movement and helped to attract millions of new supporters.

The early organizing that led to the creation of the Nuclear Weapons Freeze Campaign grew out of peace movement efforts to link the growing public concern about nuclear power with the escalating dangers of the nuclear arms race. In 1978, Pam Solo of the American Friends Service Committee and Mike Jendrzejcyk of the Fellowship of Reconciliation founded the Nuclear Weapons Facilities Task Force to support antinuclear organizing in communities adjacent to the Department of Energy's major nuclear weapons production sites. The task force reflected mounting citizen opposition to nuclear power plants (most visible at Seabrook, New Hampshire, and Diablo Canyon in California) and increasing concern about the nuclear arms race. It connected these issues through demonstrations and protests at nuclear production sites such as Rocky Flats in Colorado, Barnwell in South Carolina, the Lawrence Livermore National Laboratory, and elsewhere.

Another early manifestation of the movement that challenged nuclear policy in the 1980s was the Women's Pentagon Action. In November 1980, more than a thousand women descended on the Pentagon for a series of demonstrations and sit-ins demanding disarmament and an end to the war system. A similar mobilization was held a year later. The Women's Pentagon demonstrations were significant for two main reasons. First, they articulated a feminist peace perspective linking rejection of hierarchy with peace and nonviolence. Second, they signaled a new level of feminist peace activism. Women had always been key players in the U.S. peace movement, especially at the grass-roots level, but in the 1980s their involvement intensified. In thousands of local groups throughout the country, women took the lead in educating citizens about the nuclear threat.

The accident at the Three Mile Island nuclear reactor in Pennsylvania in March 1979 gave a decisive boost to the antinuclear cause and accelerated the organizing that led to the freeze. Public faith in nuclear technology dropped, and a visceral fear of radiation spread through society. (Seven years later, the far more catastrophic accident at the Chernobyl reactor in Ukraine had a similar, probably greater, impact on Soviet public opinion.) Antinuclear sentiment, already on the rise, increased and became more generalized. The worsening Cold War atmosphere at the time only added to these fears. The public mood was ripe for a creative approach to overcoming nuclear anxiety.

The intellectual preparations for this political awakening were already under way. Peace organizers seeking a winning proposal to spark grass-roots activism and liberal senators frustrated at the SALT II debate in Congress were gravitating toward the idea of a nuclear moratorium, a mutual halt to the testing and deployment of nuclear weapons by both the Soviet Union and the United States. This idea of a U.S.-Soviet nuclear freeze had first been proposed in the early 1970s by Gerard Smith, chief U.S. arms negotiator for the SALT I Treaty. The concept was raised again and developed in more detail by Richard Barnet of the Institute for Policy Studies in the spring 1979 issue of *Foreign Affairs*.[15] Similar ideas were emerging in Massachusetts within a research collective known as the Boston Study Group, which had just published an important book, *The Price of Defense*. The moratorium concept was also floated by members of an American Friends Service Committee delegation visiting the Soviet Union that summer.

The first formal action on the idea came in June 1979 when Senator Mark Hatfield (R-OR) introduced an amendment to the SALT II Treaty (with cosponsorship from Senator George McGovern, D-SD) calling for a U.S.-Soviet freeze on strategic nuclear weapons deployment.[16] Although the Hatfield-McGovern amendment, like SALT II itself, died when Jimmy Carter withdrew the treaty in the wake of the Soviet invasion of Afghanistan, the idea of a mutual freeze attracted growing interest. Underlying all of these initiatives was a common dissatisfaction with the terms of SALT II, which would allow continued nuclear build-ups on both sides, and concern about mounting right-wing efforts to accelerate the arms race and scuttle arms limitation altogether. Activists and policymakers alike were searching for a simple, unequivocal proposal for ending the arms race that could break through the militaristic atmosphere gripping Washington and inspire a new wave of citizen participation for peace.

In early 1980, these common threads came together in one of the most remarkable political documents of the decade, the "Call to Halt the Arms Race." The Call was principally the work of Randall Forsberg, director of the newly founded Institute for Defense and Disarmament Studies in Brookline, Massachusetts, and a member of the Boston Study Group. A native of Alabama and graduate of Barnard College in New York, Forsberg had spent seven years in Sweden working at the prestigious Stockholm International Peace Research Institute, SIPRI. A former schoolteacher, Forsberg began at SIPRI as a typist but advanced to become an editor and researcher. She also became an extremely well-informed and sophisticated expert on the problems of disarmament. Returning to graduate study in the United States at the Massachusetts Institute of Technology, Forsberg focused on ways of applying her scholarly abilities to the concerns of peace activists. Her aim was to craft a set of intermediate policy proposals that could unite traditional peace groups with ordinary citizens in a common campaign for ending the arms race.[17]

The resulting Call to Halt the Arms Race (later published as a feature article in *Scientific American*) combined the emerging proposal for a nuclear moratorium with a rigorous analysis of U.S. and Soviet nuclear arsenals.[18] The freeze proposal articulated by Forsberg was breathtakingly simple yet profoundly significant in its political implications. It read: "The United States and the Soviet Union ... should adopt a mutual freeze on the testing, production, and deployment of nuclear weapons."[19] With this modest formulation, Forsberg and the emerging nuclear freeze organizing team sparked one of the largest peace mobilizations in history.

The freeze proposal captured the public imagination as no other idea in the history of the atomic age had. It did so precisely because of its uncomplicated and direct message. The way to stop the arms race, it said, is just to stop. The deployment, testing, and production of all nuclear weapons should cease immediately on both sides. Here was a simple yet elegant proposal that cut through the confusing technical jargon of the arms race and the often conflicting claims about which side was ahead. Suddenly, the problem of the arms race and the growing danger of nuclear war seemed resolvable.

The greatest value of the freeze from a political perspective was its accessibility to the average citizen. It was "user friendly." You didn't need a Ph.D. in physics or a degree in international relations to understand and accept the logic of the freeze. It was eagerly embraced by a public anxious for a way out of the worsening nuclear dilemma. This popular appeal of the freeze was perhaps its most revolutionary aspect. Previously an obscure and highly technical field reserved for experts, nearly all of them white males, nuclear policy making now became the province of ordinary citizens. The debate over nuclear weapons and military strategy was thus radically democratized. The discussion of nuclear policy was removed from the cloistered boardrooms of the Pentagon and taken to the village square. The freeze was more than a specific proposal for ending the arms race. It was an assertion and a demand by ordinary citizens for a say in the most vital of all issues, the survival of the human race. By democratizing the debate on war and peace, the freeze movement educated and empowered millions of people to work for the prevention of nuclear holocaust. Cardinal Joseph

Bernardin of Chicago captured the significance of this contribution in a 1990 speech at the University of South Carolina:

> The characteristic that set the 1980s apart ... was the degree of public engagement in the [nuclear] policy debate. ... The nuclear freeze movement was the most visible symbol of this broader public discussion. In retrospect, its significance lies less with the specific proposal than with its capacity to draw ordinary citizens into an argument that had always affected them but had hardly ever included them.[20]

Grass-roots Beginnings

True to its democratic character, the first effective organizing for a nuclear freeze occurred at the grass-roots level. National organizations such as the American Friends Service Committee and Clergy and Laity Concerned organized meetings in Washington to discuss the idea of a national freeze campaign, but except for the publication and circulation of the initial Call in April 1980, not much was done to implement the plan. An effort was mounted in the summer of 1980 to introduce a freeze resolution at the Democratic National Convention in New York City, but party leaders rejected it, although nearly 40 percent of the delegates voted in favor of the resolution when it was brought up on the floor.[21] Although many leading activists and arms control experts endorsed the freeze, most were occupied with other matters (such as the growing anti-MX campaign) and paid little attention to the freeze.

If national groups were slow to pick up on the new concept, the reaction at the local level was very different. Community activists immediately saw the value of the freeze—its accessibility to ordinary citizens—and began to organize on its behalf. The most successful of these efforts, the example that would set the standard for similar drives all across the country, took place at the Traprock Peace Center in Deerfield, Massachusetts. Eastern Massachusetts may have been the intellectual birthplace of the freeze, but it was in the more conservative western part of the state that the organizing strategies were developed and perfected.

A key figure in this initial campaign was Randall Kehler, a veteran peace activist and founder of the Traprock Peace Center. Born in Scarsdale, New York, and a graduate of Phillips Exeter Academy and Harvard University, Kehler had been radicalized, like others of his generation, by the Vietnam War. When confronted with the military draft, he had refused to cooperate with the Selective Service System and instead went to work for the War Resisters League. Kehler was later convicted for draft resistance, and he spent twenty-two months in federal prison at La Tuna, New Mexico. His commitment to peace was only strengthened by his prison ordeal, however, and he remained actively involved in local and national peace issues throughout the 1970s. In 1979 Kehler participated in some of the early planning meetings for the Freeze Campaign. He also closely followed the efforts of Senator Hatfield to attach a freeze amendment to the SALT II Treaty. At the Traprock Center, Kehler and his colleagues decided to put the freeze on the ballot as a nonbinding referendum in three western Massachusetts state senate districts. The ballot resolution called upon the president to negotiate a mutual freeze with the Soviet Union and to redirect federal funds from the military to human needs.

In early 1980, Kehler, Frances Crowe, and other organizers began a year-long campaign to educate local citizens about the nuclear arms race. They collected the 6,000 signatures required to qualify the referendum for the ballot, obtained endorsements from prominent politicians (the most important was local Republican Congressman Silvio Conte), and launched a vigorous voter education and turnout drive prior to election day.[22] When the votes were counted on November 4, the freeze had won by a wide margin: 94,000 voters, 59 percent of the electorate, had endorsed the freeze, while 65,000 had opposed it. The latter were in rural districts that in the same election voted heavily for Ronald Reagan. The freeze thus showed its ability to win voter approval even in the face of a conservative electoral tide. On an election day in which the right wing celebrated huge victories nationwide, the returns from western Massachusetts signaled the beginnings of a new political force that would soon challenge the prevailing trends.[23]

As news of the success in western Massachusetts spread, the idea of a freeze campaign gained momentum. Contributions began to flow to the freeze organizing committee. One of the first came from Massachusetts businessman Al Kay, a pioneer in the development of personal computers and a former top designer with Apple Computer. In March 1981, more than 300 people from thirty-three states gathered for the founding national conference of the Freeze Campaign at Georgetown University in Washington, D.C. The assembled participants decided that a new organization should be formed to promote the freeze concept. It was also agreed that the new group, to be called the Nuclear Weapons Freeze Campaign, would be different from other national peace organizations. The Freeze Campaign was to be more of a network than a formal, top-down organization. Its philosophy and structure were almost entirely grass-roots oriented. Strategy and policy for the new movement would be set not by elite experts or a national staff, but by an annual meeting in which all local freeze activists could participate. This annual congress would be the highest decision-making body of the campaign. The National Committee, composed of representatives from each state, would act as a kind of board of directors between annual conferences. To reinforce this grass-roots emphasis, the national office would be located not in Washington, D.C., but in St. Louis, Missouri, in the heartland of the country. In fact, the central office was called a clearinghouse, not a headquarters, again making the point that this was to be a loose coalition, not a rigid hierarchy. As its first national coordinator (the title "executive director" was shunned), the campaign selected Randy Kehler. Keenly sensitive to grass-roots concerns, Kehler was the perfect choice to head the new campaign.

Even before Kehler and his staff could set up the new clearinghouse offices in St. Louis (the doors finally opened in December 1981), local activists raced ahead with the freeze idea and began organizing campaigns all over the country. In Massachusetts, Connecticut, New York, Pennsylvania, Maryland, Ohio, Illinois, Minnesota, Wisconsin, California, and elsewhere, statewide campaigns sprang up. Nowhere did the freeze catch on more rapidly than in New England. In the finest tradition of American democracy, organizers in Vermont and New Hampshire brought the freeze proposition to local town meetings. Here in the cradle of American democracy, ordinary citizens assembled in town halls and village squares to debate and vote on the nuclear arms race. By early 1982, more than 440 towns in Vermont and other parts of New England had voted to endorse the freeze.[24]

Not just in New England but throughout the country, people brought the freeze proposal before local governments and all manner of organizations and associations. By 1982, the freeze had been endorsed by 11 state legislatures, more than 200 city councils, and 40 county governments.[25] Support for the freeze also poured in from prominent academic scholars and former government officials. More than 150 national organizations endorsed the freeze, including the U.S. Conference of Mayors, the Young Women's Christian Association

(YWCA), and the American Nurses Association.[26] Religious leaders also lent their support. Half of the U.S. Roman Catholic bishops personally endorsed the freeze. Also supporting the freeze were the National Council of Churches, the major Jewish religious bodies, and nearly all the mainline Protestant denominations.[27]

Among the endorsing organizations were twenty-five of the largest trade unions in the United States, including the International Association of Machinists, United Auto Workers, United Food and Commercial Workers, the National Education Association, and the Service Employees International Union. These endorsements from big labor came in part because of the crucial support of William Winpisinger, the progressive president of the machinists' union. They also resulted from the tireless efforts of retired United Food and Commercial Workers Vice President Jesse Prosten. Prosten had been a spirited fighter for labor rights and an opponent of Cold War politics for more than forty years. An early organizer in Congress of Industrial Organizations (CIO) drives of the 1930s and a leader of the Amalgamated Meat Cutters and Butcher Workmen of North America for many years, Prosten spent his retirement years befriending and counseling young activists in the peace movement and using his lifetime of contacts and experience to win union endorsements for the freeze. In contrast to the Vietnam era, when organized labor often opposed peace protests and hard-hat workers attacked demonstrators, the Freeze Campaign enjoyed substantial trade union support. This was an important advance for the peace movement and another sign of the broad social support for the freeze.

Millions of people jumped on the freeze bandwagon in 1982 and lent their support to the burgeoning peace movement. The Freeze Campaign launched a nationwide petition drive that met with immediate success. In June 1982, 2.3 million signatures were presented in New York at the U.S. and Soviet missions to the United Nations. In the spring of that year, the Freeze Campaign in St. Louis reported some 20,000 volunteers working in 140 offices in 47 states. Organized freeze activity was counted in 326 congressional districts.[28] Local freeze groups formed in hundreds of communities as the new movement rapidly swept the nation.

The freeze movement sparked a new sense of citizen involvement, not just in the campaign itself but in many other peace and antinuclear groups. The result was an unprecedented increase in peace activism and a huge jump in membership and fund-raising. Many new groups were formed during this time, and nearly all of the traditional national peace organizations saw their memberships and budgets grow dramatically. One study put the total number of local and national peace groups in 1985 at 8,000.[29] At Physicians for Social Responsibility, membership rose from just a few hundred in 1979 to 30,000 at the end of 1984.[30] Donors to the Council for a Livable World jumped from a low point of 7,500 in the late 1970s to 100,000 in the mid-1980s.[31] Perhaps the greatest growth occurred at SANE, where membership rose from barely 4,000 in 1977 to more than 150,000 in 1986. Never before in American history had support for nuclear disarmament been so widespread. Nuclear freeze organizing penetrated every part of society, every walk of life, and nearly every community. The movement to end the arms race was gaining powerful momentum, and it was about to embark on a spectacular demonstration of its nationwide political support.

A National Plebiscite

Jo and Nick Sedeita were longtime social activists who, like so many others in 1980, were searching for a way to turn their nation and the world back from the brink of nuclear confrontation. Eating lunch at their home in Los Angeles that December, the Sedeitas noticed an article in *The Nation* describing the recent campaign in western Massachusetts. The victory for the nuclear freeze in rural Massachusetts seemed to offer a ray of hope in an otherwise gloomy tide of political reaction. Feeling a sudden rush of excitement, Nick exclaimed, "Maybe we could do that here in California." Jo thought for a moment and also began to see the light, "Yeah, why not? This is a kookie, avant garde state. It just might work."[32] Soon the indefatigable couple threw themselves into a two-year drive to place the nuclear freeze on the state ballot. The freeze had been born in the venerable traditions of New England town democracy, but the wave that captured national and international attention came from the trend-setting state of California.

Jo and Nick Sedeita were no strangers to statewide political campaigns. In 1968 they had spearheaded an innovative effort to win first place on the California Democratic primary ballot for antiwar candidate Eugene McCarthy. According to state rules, the candidate turning in petitions first would receive the top position on the ballot, usually good for about 5 percent of the vote. Aiming to collect the more than

300,000 required signatures literally overnight, the Sedeitas organized midnight petition-gathering parties in some 500 communities on the first day of official campaigning. The petition drive was a huge success, and the McCarthy campaign shocked the political establishment in California by turning in its signatures first and winning the top spot on the ballot. The Sedeitas hoped to replicate this success in winning a spot for the freeze on the 1982 ballot. As Jo later described it, "My address book was still hot."[33] Working from their kitchen table, the Sedeitas set about the task of reactivating their network of contacts up and down the state. Tirelessly phoning and writing friends and colleagues, they steadily won support for the idea of a statewide ballot on the nuclear freeze.

One of the first places the Sedeitas went for help was to their local Unitarian church. The members of the liberal congregation enthusiastically endorsed the campaign, and when a church leader observed that the effort would cost money, the congregation voted to make an initial contribution of $1,500. Soon other donations began to pour in and the Sedeitas were able to expand their outreach and create a formal organizing committee. Headquarters for the campaign moved from their kitchen table to modest offices in North Hollywood, and from here Jo Sedeita coordinated a growing army of local volunteers and activists.

The most important early convert to the fledgling California Freeze Campaign was Los Angeles businessman Harold Willens. President of the Factory Equipment Corporation and a former Marine Corps officer, Willens was on the board of directors of the Center for Defense Information in Washington, D.C., and had been a mover and shaker in California liberal politics for years. He and Jo Sedeita had worked together on previous political campaigns in California, and although their styles were very different (she the energetic grass-roots organizer, he the reserved power broker) they had learned to respect each other. Willens needed no persuading on the urgency of the nuclear war issue, and he quickly recognized the exciting potential of a freeze referendum in the nation's largest state. As he said at the time, "This campaign ... can be a match to strike sparks all around the country."[34] Willens enthusiastically agreed to join the campaign and become its state chairman. Before long, his calls to the rich and famous in Hollywood and elsewhere in the state produced a steady flow of contributions. Eventually, more than $1 million was raised for the California campaign. Willens hired media producer Bill Zimmerman and his political consulting firm to manage the campaign and develop a public relations effort for it. In early 1982, a direct mail and advertising program was launched on the theme: "Only one person can prevent a nuclear war. You."

Although the business executives, celebrities, and professional campaign managers recruited by Willens were important to the referendum effort, the heart and soul of the campaign were the thousands of volunteer activists who flocked to join the movement. In Jo Sedeita's words, "People were willing to give of themselves, to drop everything and spend 10–12 hours a day working for the freeze because they felt they were saving the planet for their children and their grandchildren."[35] In California, as elsewhere in the nation, this was not only a time of great fear but also of hope. This new citizens' movement to end the nuclear madness gave many a sense of optimism and purpose. The bickering at meetings, the long hours of standing on the street corner to gather petition signatures, the weekends spent at political gatherings rather than at the beach—none of it seemed to matter to the thousands of committed people joining this crusade to prevent nuclear holocaust.

The official petitioning to qualify for the ballot began just before Thanksgiving in 1981. As with the McCarthy campaign in 1968, the plan was to gather as many signatures as possible in the first few days. Again, hundreds of petition parties were held in communities throughout the state. As before, the signature gathering went extremely well, and the campaign was able to submit more than 700,000 valid signatures, nearly twice the number required.[36] By spring 1982, the California campaign was riding a wave of rising popularity and support.

The Sedeitas were also promoting the idea of a freeze referendum not just in California but throughout the country. In March 1981, they traveled to Washington to attend the founding conference of the national Nuclear Weapons Freeze Campaign. There, they reported on their plans for California and met with freeze organizers from other states interested in the same idea. Back in California, Jo received many late-night calls from activists around the country eager to learn about the California experience and how to put the freeze on the ballot in their city or state. Eventually, freeze referenda campaigns were mounted in nine states and the District of Columbia and in more than thirty major cities and counties. The California model was being applied throughout the country. A quarter of the American electorate would be voting in an informal nationwide referendum on the nuclear arms race.

It was at this time, in early 1982, that political experts in Washington suddenly "discovered" the freeze. Balloting in the small towns of New England had been easy to ignore, but a referendum in the nation's most populous state demanded attention. When the respected Field poll in California showed the freeze leading by a 2-1 margin, and as word of similar referenda in other states began to spread, the political establishment stood up and took notice. The pundits who had only recently celebrated the Reagan revolution were now dumbfounded. Here was a grass-roots peace movement with wide public support challenging the very foundations of administration policy. The political landscape seemed to be shifting. The freeze movement, barely a year old, was catapulted to the center of national attention.

The White House certainly took notice of the freeze movement and quickly launched a nationwide public relations counteroffensive.[37] California was the major target of this campaign, and in the weeks prior to the November vote, a steady stream of administration officials and retired military officers paraded through the state and saturated its media markets. Initially facing no opposition, the Freeze Campaign now found itself under attack. Thrown off balance, the campaign saw its support in the polls begin to erode. The freeze received another setback in the final days of the campaign when a celebrity television debate between freeze supporter Paul Newman and conservative spokesman Charlton Heston went badly. Newman had been very helpful in generating political and financial support for the campaign, but his performance as a freeze debater was disappointing. He came off at first as nervous and withdrawn and then as combative while Heston retained a cool self-assurance throughout. Newman may have won the debate on the facts, but the all-important image he conveyed was of a campaign on the defensive. With popular support declining, freeze organizers were glad that the election came when it did. If the campaign had gone on another couple of weeks, they feared, the freeze might have lost.[38]

In the end, the freeze referendum in California won by a 52-48 margin. While the results were closer than organizers would have liked, the victory was nonetheless sweet. It had come in the face of fierce opposition from the Reagan administration and in an election where conservative Republicans swept statewide races for both governor and U.S. senator. The freeze referendum was the only ballot initiative in California that fall to win voter approval.

Freeze referenda won not just in California but throughout the country (see Table 2.1). Only in Arizona did voters reject the freeze. Everywhere else—in seven other states and the District of Columbia and in some of the nation's largest cities—the freeze won handily. In New Jersey, the freeze won by a whopping 76-24 margin. In Chicago and Philadelphia, it received 75 percent of the vote. Across the nation, 18 million Americans voted on the freeze that fall, with 10.7 million, or 60 percent, voting in favor. As Congressman Ed Markey (D-MA) observed:

> It was the closest our country has ever come to a national plebiscite on nuclear arms control. Within a very brief time the freeze had taken education at the grass roots and translated it into political muscle at the ballot box, delivering to the White House a resounding vote of no confidence in its nuclear buildup.[39]

The Legislative Embrace

The Freeze Campaign managed to fend off the attacks of its right-wing opponents more successfully than it survived the embrace of its friends on Capitol Hill. No chapter in the saga of the freeze is more tangled than its encounter with the U.S. Congress. For those who championed the grass-roots independence of the movement, the votes in Congress were premature and ultimately counterproductive.[40] For those who worked on Capitol Hill for arms control, the freeze debate showed the strength of the peace movement and had a significant impact on Reagan administration policy.[41] To a degree, both interpretations are correct. The manner in which the freeze came before Congress did indeed rob the movement of some of its potential influence. Yet the highly public debate on the issue and the ultimate passage of the resolution in the House of Representatives conveyed a sense of mounting political opposition to the Reagan military buildup. From a strictly legislative point of view, the campaign to stop the MX (described in Chapter 9) probably accomplished more, but the freeze debate was important nonetheless.

Politicians like to lead a parade, and thus it was neither surprising nor unusual that elected officials sought to jump out in front of the nu-

TABLE 2.1   Nuclear Freeze Referenda, 1982

	Percentage		Votes	
	Yes	No	Yes	No
States				
Arizona	41	59	262,012	379,759
California	52.5	47.5	3,778,331	3,414,987
Massachusetts	74	26	1,221,710	437,905
Michigan	58	42	1,508,659	1,159,263
Montana	56	44	—	—
New Jersey	76	24	1,780,862	575,527
North Dakota	58	42	113,523	80,765
Oregon	61.5	38.5	572,000	357,586
Rhode Island	59	41	161,852	112,011
Selected Cities				
Chicago	75	25	404,173	135,325
Denver	62	38	93,630	56,981
Philadelphia	75.5	24.5	231,787	75,149
Washington, D.C.	70	30	77,521	33,369
Total Nationwide	60	40	10,729,922	7,120,915

Source: Nuclear Weapons Freeze Campaign.

clear freeze bandwagon. In early 1982, as the sensational discovery of this new populist movement shook Washington, members of Congress suddenly began to pay attention. As Ed Markey phrased it, "Political reality finally hit as the million people showed up in Central Park. That demonstrated that the issue had razor sharp edges at the grass roots."[42] For arms controllers, this new movement seemed like manna from heaven, a potent new political force that might help tame the excesses of the White House. Perhaps the freeze might restrain the nuclear buildup and force the administration to negotiate with the Soviets.

Other less lofty motives were also at work. Politicians seeking higher office sought to tap the legions of volunteers associated with the new movement. The freeze had become something of a "motherhood issue," as Jo Sedeita put it, and politicians seeking office were eager to wrap themselves in the righteous mantle of concern about nuclear war. The Freeze Campaign was gradually transformed by this process. What began as a pure grass-roots movement for disarmament was turned into an instrument of conventional politics.

The first legislator to act on the freeze was Ed Markey, a third-term Democratic congressman from the working-class suburbs north of Boston. Charismatic and activist-oriented, Markey was a vigorous opponent of nuclear proliferation who came to realize, in his words, that "the biggest problem with nuclear power is nuclear bombs."[43] Markey quickly saw the value of the freeze movement emerging in his home state, and in January 1982 he directed his staff to begin crafting legislation. This was just weeks after the Freeze Campaign clearinghouse was opening its doors in faraway St. Louis and well ahead of the political timetable that the campaign had set for itself. The original intention, as articulated in early freeze strategy papers, was to focus on public education and movement building before jumping into the legislative fray.[44] The train was already leaving the station on Capitol Hill, however, and freeze leaders were powerless to stop it. On February 10, 1982, Markey and twenty-eight cosponsors formally introduced the first nuclear freeze resolution in the U.S. Congress.

These early efforts in the House were soon eclipsed by the decision of Senator Edward Kennedy (D-MA) to introduce a similar resolution in the Senate. As an aide to Kennedy said, "The Senator just wanted to … harness all that energy, and bring it to Washington instead of letting it go."[45] On March 10, 1982, to the accompaniment of great media fanfare, Kennedy announced his decision to introduce the freeze resolution. The senator's press conference was the lead story in news reports all across the country. The freeze was now on the front pages, and the issue quickly moved to center stage in Washington politics.

Kennedy's sponsorship may have brought many benefits (greater visibility, broader political support, more legitimacy), but it also created problems. Chief among these was the identification of a potentially broad and universal issue, preventing nuclear war, with a specific candidate and political party. Kennedy at the time was actively preparing for a presidential bid, and he clearly hoped that his leadership on the freeze would boost his candidacy. At the Democratic midterm convention in Philadelphia that summer, the auditorium was flooded with placards that read "Kennedy: Nuclear Freeze." This was fine for the senator's campaign but disastrous for the freeze movement. The freeze became increasingly associated with the senator from Massachusetts and the Democratic party. The fact that Republican Senator Mark Hatfield was a cosponsor did not alter the perception that the freeze was primarily a Democratic issue. As Kennedy and his staff sought to capture the freeze, a broader political appeal became increasingly difficult.

From the very outset, the legislation crafted by Kennedy, Markey, and others in Congress fell far short of the political goals set by grassroots freeze leaders. The biggest problem was the use of a nonbinding resolution. Instead of asking Congress to use its power of the purse to cut off appropriations for nuclear weapons, the Kennedy-Markey bill merely conveyed a sense of opinion. Another weakness was that the resolution called not for an immediate halt to the arms race but for the United States and the Soviet Union to "decide when and how" to freeze. Slippery legislative phraseology thus replaced the original call for an immediate freeze. These provisions were then further watered down through a tortuous and labyrinthine legislative debate. The final resolution that passed in the House in May 1983 bore little resemblance to the original Call to Halt the Arms Race. The leader of the floor debate was Representative Clement Zablocki (D-WI), chairman of the House Foreign Affairs Committee and a political moderate at best. His aides told a reporter that the point of the legislation was "not to freeze the testing, production and deployment of nuclear weapons ... but to tell the President that they wanted something done on arms control. "[46] For these politicians, the freeze was not a specific proposal for ending the arms race but a symbolic statement of concern for arms control. In such a climate, opponents of the freeze had a field day, and qualifying clauses were steadily added to the legislation. The language in the resolution increased from a simple 16-line statement in the original Markey version to a 152-line monstrosity fifteen months later. By the time the House approved the freeze resolution on May 4 by a lopsided 278-149 margin, the legislation had lost coherence and political focus.

When freeze staffers and friendly members of Congress celebrated their victory that night in Ed Markey's office, the champagne left a bitter aftertaste. True, the House of Representatives had endorsed the nuclear freeze: Newspaper reports the next day read "Congress Passes Nuclear Freeze." The congressional deliberations on the issue legitimized the freeze and provided an important indicator of deepening political opposition to the Reagan military buildup. The public would interpret the vote as yet another slap at White House policy. The victory was a hollow one, though, for the resolution that had passed was practically devoid of meaning. The language had become so convoluted that Representative Leon Panetta (D-CA) could tell his colleagues in the House: "Whether you are a hawk or a dove ... you can interpret anything you want in this resolution."[47] The original nuclear freeze proposal was thus sacrificed to political expediency and linguistic obfuscation.

Even more devastating was the shock three weeks later when the House voted in favor of the MX missile. Many of those who had voted for the freeze resolution turned around and approved renewed funding for the MX. This repudiation of the freeze message was the result of maneuvering between the White House and moderate Democrats led by Les Aspin (D-WI), as described in Chapter 9. The result was a deep sense of dejection among many peace activists. As Ed Markey described it, "The impact of that vote was to make the grass roots cynical. The sense of idealism, of clout and accomplishment, was lost. On the eve of what could have been a substantive win against the MX, the Aspin coalition snatched defeat from the jaws of victory."[48]

Despite the trials of dealing with Congress, the grass-roots freeze movement remained an important presence in U.S. political life. In Ohio, Illinois, Maryland, Massachusetts, and a dozen other states, formidable statewide organizations were created and extensive peace education programs were launched. Although public attention to the freeze itself ebbed after the high water mark of 1982–1983, the organized peace movement continued to grow for several years. In the coming years, its focus would shift to other issues—the MX, Star Wars, the nuclear test ban, and the war in Central America—and its impact would continue.

3
Prevention

A Voice of Healing

Jennifer Leaning grew up in the mid–Hudson River valley region of New York State in the orchard and dairy farm country near New Paltz. Bright and socially concerned from an early age ("I worried about population growth and conservation"[1]), Leaning graduated from Radcliffe in the 1960s during the height of the Vietnam antiwar movement. Like others of her generation, she became active in efforts to bring the war to an end. Spending a year in Africa as a volunteer during undergraduate studies had sparked her interest in population and public health concerns, and she spent two years at the Harvard School of Public Health, where she earned a master's degree in population studies. While there, Leaning began to be fascinated by the work and training of clinical medicine. After a year of premed studies, Leaning was admitted to the University of Chicago Pritcker School of Medicine and began the long and arduous journey to become a physician.

During her medical training and residency in Boston in the late 1970s, Leaning gravitated toward emergency and disaster medicine: "This kept me in touch with my original interest in public health. I also felt that this was an area of medicine that was unquestionably necessary and of benefit to the public."[2] It was this interest in emergency medicine that led Leaning to become concerned about the threat of nuclear disaster. The turning point for her was the accident at the Three Mile Island nuclear power plant in Pennsylvania in 1979 and the chilling realization of what a nuclear meltdown could mean for public health. With her concern for the medical effects of nuclear disaster, Leaning soon crossed paths with like-minded doctors in the Physicians for Social Responsibility movement.

Physicians for Social Responsibility (PSR) had been founded in 1961 to deal with the growing concern about the health effects of atmospheric nuclear testing. During most of the 1970s, the group was dormant, but at the end of the decade it was reactivated under the charismatic leadership of Dr. Helen Caldicott. An Australian by birth, and based during these years at the Children's Hospital Medical Center of the Harvard Medical School, Caldicott combined her professional concern for the health of children with an abiding fear of the potential consequences of nuclear disaster. As she later explained, "What was the point of keeping these children alive for another five, ten or twenty years ... when during this time they could be vaporized in a nuclear war?"[3] Possessed by a driving sense of responsibility to save the children of the world and blessed with enormous energy and a forceful personality, Caldicott became the catalyst for a worldwide crusade to shake people out of their complacency. In the early 1980s, she set out on a whirlwind tour of lectures and speaking engagements. She crisscrossed the country many times and appeared on hundreds of television and radio programs. At one point Caldicott even went to the White House for a personal meeting with Ronald Reagan. Although she was unable to shake the president's deeply held beliefs, she inspired thousands of doctors and ordinary citizens to follow in her footsteps in a new public awakening for peace.

Caldicott was also an organization builder, and it was in a series of meetings in her sitting room that PSR was reborn. Initially, the fledgling new organization focused on nuclear power. In an ironic twist of fate, the group placed a full-page advertisement in the *New England Journal of Medicine* that appeared on March 29, 1979—the day after the reactor accident at Three Mile Island. The remarkable coincidence of the advertisement and the reactor accident brought a flood of inquiries. PSR headquarters, operating out of a basement cubbyhole in the office of Cambridge pediatrician Richard Feinbloom, was suddenly inundated with membership applications. One of those who decided to join was Dr. Jennifer Leaning.

As the proselytizing of Caldicott and her colleagues expanded and public alarm about the arms race increased, the physicians' movement grew rapidly. Membership in PSR multiplied from just a few hundred physicians in 1979 to 30,000 by the mid-1980s.[4] A new international organization, International Physicians for the Prevention of Nuclear War (IPPNW), was also founded. Cochaired by Dr. Bernard Lown from the United States and Dr. Evgeni Chazov from the Soviet Union (Chazov was the personal physician and cardiologist of Leonid

Brezhnev and also ministered to Yuri Andropov and Konstantin Chernenko), IPPNW organized among health professionals in the Soviet Union and dozens of other countries and sponsored international forums on the medical consequences of nuclear war.

The Bombing Run

Although PSR was concerned initially about nuclear power, the doctors quickly shifted their focus to the threat of nuclear war. As Jennifer Leaning explained, "The more we looked into the nuclear dilemma, the more evident it became that the real problem was nuclear weapons."[5] By the end of 1979, prevention of nuclear war had become the overriding mission of PSR and the doctors had launched a major campaign to educate the public about the dangers inherent in the escalating nuclear arms race. PSR's educational program centered on a remarkable series of medical symposia on the consequences of nuclear war. Originally conceived by Dr. Eric Chivian, a psychiatrist at Massachusetts General Hospital, the symposium program was designed to educate the medical community and the general public about the terrifying realities of nuclear weapons. The first symposium took place in February 1980 at the Harvard Science Center and was cosponsored by the Harvard Medical School and the Tufts Medical Center. The program was thickly laden with testimony from medical experts, scientists, and former government officials who analyzed the physics of the bomb, recounted the devastation of Hiroshima and Nagasaki, assessed the grim state of U.S.-Soviet relations, and described the potential consequences of a nuclear attack on the local community.

Jennifer Leaning was one of the organizers of the Harvard symposium, and for her and others in the audience, the impact was overwhelming. "It was inexorable," Leaning recalled, "as much an emotional experience as an intellectual one." Leaning continued:

> I remember well that first symposium at the Harvard Science Center. It was a crisp, bright, sunny winter weekend. But inside the auditorium, the atmosphere was somber: Hundreds of people sat stunned in the darkened lecture hall as professors and scientific experts read from prepared texts and presented slides on overhead projectors. As you sat there hour after hour listening to all of this information, you felt an enormous sadness, but also an enormous anger, that we could be so close to doing something so unspeakably insane.[6]

In one presentation, Dr. Howard Hiatt, dean of the Harvard School of Public Health, described the enormous effort required to treat just one serious burn patient, which could often take hundreds of hours of skilled medical care and large quantities of plasma and other supplies. Noting that a nuclear attack on a large city might produce hundreds of thousands of such injuries, Hiatt demonstrated that any hope of treatment was impossible, the very idea preposterous. Other speakers gave similar presentations, and before long the relentless barrage of horrifying information brought many to tears. As Jennifer Leaning confided, "It was a good thing that the lecture hall was darkened."[7]

The medical symposium held at Harvard was followed by another in New York in September 1980 and was then repeated in dozens of cities all over the country during the next three years. Initially, the conferences were sponsored by the national office of PSR (in cooperation with the Council for a Liveable World), but soon local chapters of PSR began to organize their own events. In all, more than thirty conferences were held: In addition to those in Boston and New York, symposia were held in San Francisco, Seattle, Los Angeles, Washington, Miami, Detroit, Minneapolis, San Diego, Atlanta, Philadelphia, Pittsburgh, Cleveland, Baltimore, Denver, Salt Lake City, Albuquerque, Chapel Hill, Stanford, Sacramento, Portland, Bangor, Trenton, Madison, Spokane, Rockford, Albany, and Montreal. Once the conference series began, it was so successful that it took on a life and momentum of its own. Thousands of medical professionals and concerned citizens would pay a hefty admission fee to attend a symposium. At the Los Angeles conference in October 1981, for example, 2,900 people paid and 1,500 had to be turned away for lack of space. Two thousand people participated in the conference in Salt Lake City, and more than 900 attended in Albuquerque. In many cases, the symposium would help to activate the local peace community and lead to the creation of a PSR chapter. During the symposium campaign, the number of local PSR chapters grew from a handful in 1980 to more than 150 in 1985.[8]

A factor that contributed greatly to the credibility and success of the PSR symposia was their official cosponsorship by prominent medical schools and state medical societies. These were not merely peace movement gatherings but officially accredited medical conferences. This meant that physicians and other medical professionals attending could obtain academic credit toward their continuing medical education (CME) requirements. The significance of this official sponsorship

should not be overlooked. Given the traditionally conservative leanings of the medical profession, these endorsements from organized
medicine were quite extraordinary. As a former PSR staffer observed la-
conically, "Doctors are not liberals." Normally, doctors would not be
expected to become antinuclear crusaders or to go out on a limb for a
controversial cause.[9] The fact that medical authorities endorsed the
symposia was a testament not only to the effective organizing of PSR
but to the mood of the times. Concern about nuclear war and the escalating arms race had permeated every part of society and had even
reached into the traditionally conservative hierarchy of the medical
profession.

The core of the medical symposium, and the part that often had the
greatest emotional impact, was a description of what nuclear war
would mean for the local community. "We did a bombing run on the
community," said Leaning. "Our goal was to show exactly what the impact of a one-megaton bomb would mean for the places where we
live."[10] In an attack on Boston, for example, more than 2 million people would die. In the immediate impact zone, up to 1.7 miles from
ground zero, nearly everything would be totally destroyed and 98 percent of the people would die instantly. Downtown Boston and the people in it would cease to exist. In the secondary impact zone, out to a radius of 3 miles, 50 percent of the people would die instantly and nearly
everyone would be blinded or injured. This would bring the devastation out past Logan Airport and into Brookline, Somerville, and other
suburbs. Continuing out to a radius of 5 miles, well into Watertown,
Quincy, and outlying communities, 5 percent of the people would die
and nearly half would be injured in fire storms.[11] Such information, repeated in meticulous detail for dozens of cities, had a powerful impact
on people and made the threat of nuclear war seem very real and immediate.

An Awakening of Public Opinion

The grim message of the PSR medical symposia reached far beyond the
university lecture halls where they were held. Thanks to the extensive
public relations efforts that accompanied each conference, the physicians were able to bring their cry of alarm to tens of millions of Americans. In nearly every major media market in the United States, the PSR
bombing run was a major news story. Wherever they were held, the

medical symposia were usually covered in front-page stories in the major daily newspapers. Local and regional television and radio coverage was also extensive. Network television affiliates often aired stories before the symposium and then carried live reports from the conference site on the day of the event. Conference speakers and PSR leaders were booked on local talk shows and interview programs before, during, and after the conferences. In New Mexico, for example, speakers were placed on fifty-five of the state's fifty-seven broadcast news outlets.[12] The medical symposia also spawned numerous follow-up articles, editorials, and letters to the editor in the newspapers. The physicians' peace movement thus saturated local and regional media markets throughout the country.

The influence of the medical symposia spread in other ways as well. At the San Francisco symposium, filmmaker Ian Thierman made an important documentary, *The Last Epidemic,* which was subsequently distributed as a video throughout the country and shown thousands of times by PSR chapters and local peace groups.[13] During the symposium campaign, Helen Caldicott and other PSR leaders held meetings with the editorial boards of the *New York Times,* the *Washington Post,* the *Miami Herald,* the *Boston Globe,* and many other major papers. The medical symposia also resulted in the publication of important scholarly articles in leading medical journals, including the *Lancet,* the *Journal of the American Medical Association,* and the *New England Journal of Medicine.*[14]

The PSR medical symposium campaign was one of the most successful public education efforts in the history of the U.S. peace movement. The physicians' campaign was a decisive event in shaping public awareness during the early 1980s. In 1982, Dr. Jonas Salk evoked this sense of a fundamental change in public consciousness in his opening remarks to the PSR medical symposium at George Washington University Medical Center in Washington, D.C. The world-famous immunologist spoke of "a signal in the air" that symbolized the transition of civilization from one epoch to another. Through greater understanding of the nuclear peril, Salk suggested, humankind was beginning to understand the folly of war and was thereby reaching toward a new level of maturity. He expressed the hope that the information presented through the PSR symposia would help Americans "immunize ourselves against evolutionarily disadvantageous thinking."[15]

An even more significant acknowledgment of the physicians' peace movement came in 1985, when IPPNW received the Nobel Prize for

Peace. The governors of the Norwegian Nobel Committee lauded the physicians for their "considerable service to mankind ... creating an awareness of the catastrophic consequences of atomic warfare." The citation went on:

> The committee believes that this in turn contributes to an increase in the pressure of public opposition to the proliferation of atomic weapons and to a redefining of priorities with greater attention being paid to health and other humanitarian priorities. Such an awakening of public opinion as is now apparent both in the East and the West, in the North and the South, can give the present arms limitation negotiations new perspectives and a new seriousness.[16]

The Nobel Committee thus acknowledged the physicians' efforts as an important factor in generating public pressure for arms limitation. By bringing scientific authority and professional prestige to the cause of preventing nuclear war, the physicians contributed significantly to the transformation of public consciousness and cultural values during the 1980s.

Many of the individuals who attended the PSR symposia went on to make important personal contributions to the shaping of public consciousness. Prior to the New York forum in 1980, for example, Dr. Henry Abraham invited *New Yorker* writer Jonathan Schell to attend the medical symposium. Schell was so moved by what he saw and heard that he wrote an influential series of articles for the magazine. These articles were later published in his book *The Fate of the Earth.* In the overflow audience at the Los Angeles Forum, there was a group of television writers who later wrote a script on the medical effects of nuclear war; it eventually became an episode of a popular television program, the "Lou Grant Show." Others in attendance at the Los Angeles symposium contributed significantly to the making of the television movie "The Day After," one of the most widely viewed programs in television history.[17]

Perhaps the greatest impact of the symposium campaign was on the physicians themselves. It is hard to comprehend, many years later at a safer time in history, the effect that these programs had on those who experienced them. For many, attending the symposium was a life-transforming event that produced profound emotional distress but also sparked an intense commitment to social activism. Jennifer Leaning described how a physician colleague reacted to that first medical symposium at Harvard:

> As he drove home that bright, sunny February, passing through the New-
> ton suburbs and admiring the trees and beautiful houses, he was sud-
> denly possessed by the weight of what he had heard that day and burst
> out crying. The concentric circles reaching out from ground zero kept ap-
> pearing in his mind, and all he could see were the blast and fire storms
> and radiation destroying everything around him. Here was a grown man,
> a physician familiar with a wide range of emotions and human suffering,
> yet overwhelmed by the prospect of what could happen in a nuclear
> war.[18]

Out of such agonizing realization came not only sorrow but also moti-
vation and a sense of purpose. The doctor in Boston and thousands of others like him were moved to the depths of despair, but they were also compelled to act for peace.

Jennifer Leaning summed up the conversion that she herself experienced:

> As I got in touch with the moment of jeopardy facing humankind, I felt
> compelled to act. I was reminded of the rabbi's challenge we learned as
> children: "If I am not for myself, who will be for me? If I am only for my-
> self, who am I? If not now, when?" I felt called to take action and hoped
> that as a medical doctor I could motivate others to act as well. I never
> could have done it alone, though. It was the feeling of strength in being
> with others that made it possible.[19]

Preparing for Armageddon

The public's existential encounter with the nuclear threat in the 1980s had many ramifications. It nurtured the nuclear freeze movement and fostered political resistance to menacing new weapons systems, such as INF missiles in Europe, the MX, and the Strategic Defense Initiative (SDI). The public's nuclear phobia also spelled trouble for the Reagan administration's plans for civil defense. More than any other nuclear program, civil defense depends on the cooperation of the public, and to be effective, it requires massive public participation and volunteer effort. In the 1980s, this support was not forthcoming, and White House attempts to prepare the nation for nuclear war flopped.

In 1980 and 1981, *Los Angeles Times* reporter Robert Scheer conducted an extraordinary series of interviews with Ronald Reagan, George Bush, and other members of the administration. What Scheer discovered in these sessions—later published in the book *With Enough Shovels: Reagan, Bush and Nuclear War*—was that top government leaders held the startling belief that a limited nuclear war was possible. From his discussions with the president, Scheer concluded that Reagan "believes that a nation sufficiently well-prepared can survive and win a nuclear war."[20] In October 1981, the president publicly admitted as much when he stated that nuclear weapons could be fired at troops in the field without causing an all-out nuclear exchange. George Bush was even more adamant than Reagan in his interview with Scheer. He asserted that nuclear war was survivable and, referring to the view that there could be no winners in a nuclear war, stated emphatically, "I don't believe that." The future president went on to describe how a country could win a nuclear war: "You have survivability of command and control, survivability of industrial potential, protection of a percentage of your citizens, and you have a capability that inflicts more damage on the opposition than it can inflict upon you."[21]

To give credence to this outlook, it was necessary not only to build up offensive weapons like the MX but also to increase defensive preparations, which meant a greatly expanded civil defense program. Both components—greater offense and an enhanced defense—were essential to the Reagan/Bush program. Civil defense was not a minor sideshow but a central part of the psychological shadow boxing of nuclear strategy. Acquiring an ability to survive nuclear retaliation would convince the Soviet Union that the United States was prepared to fight a nuclear war. In turn, the United States's threat to use nuclear weapons in a crisis would be more credible. The Reagan administration (and the Carter presidency before it) devoted a major effort to convincing the American people that, as a December 1980 civil defense publication stated, "With reasonable protective measures, the United States could survive nuclear attack and go on to recovery within relatively few years."[22]

In early 1982, the administration announced plans to spend $4.3 billion over a seven-year period to build a network of new bomb shelters and develop evacuation plans for the nation's major cities. The centerpiece of this new civil defense program was the Crisis Relocation Plan (CRP) of the Federal Emergency Management Agency (FEMA). This program, it was claimed, could save the lives of 80 percent of the American people in the event of nuclear attack. Almost from the moment it was announced, however, the Reagan plan ran into a storm of criticism. A *New York Times* editorial of April 3, 1982, labeled the idea of trying to survive a nuclear war "mad."[23] The *Times* asserted that whoever the "mastermind" of the civil defense plan was, he should be fired. As Robert Scheer pointed out, however, the person who championed the program and pushed it through the bureaucracy was none other than Ronald Reagan himself.[24] At a December 3, 1981, National Security Council meeting, the president overruled both the Joint Chiefs of Staff and the Office of Management and Budget to approve a major civil defense budget increase.[25]

Finding the Flaws

When Marilyn Braun took the job of director of Emergency Management for Guilford County, North Carolina, her main hope was that she would not have to talk to the press. A quiet person ("I'm a researcher type"[26]), Braun had previously worked in the Greensboro City Manager's office. She entered her new position expecting that her low-key style of hard work would produce results and avoid controversy. Braun was also honest, however, and had the misfortune of taking office just as the new Crisis Relocation Plan (CRP) was being imposed on local communities. Much to her dismay, Braun soon found herself at the center of a political tempest—as a reluctant celebrity in the cause of nuclear sanity.

Braun had no preconceptions for or against civil defense planning, and when the relocation plans arrived at her office she set about studying the documents in her usual careful and methodical way. She recalled:

> I felt initially that we could come up with at least a minimal defense plan that would work. I read all of our records going back to 1949. But the more I learned, the more I began to see a pattern of good intentions but faulty program designs. I also became disturbed by what I perceived to be highly deceptive information being given to the public by the government.[27]

Like hundreds of other local officials across the country, Braun came face to face with a CRP that was fundamentally flawed.

The first assumption in the CRP was that the United States would have a ten-day warning period in which to carry out the proposed evacuation plans. How and when such notification would come, however, was never specified. "All we were told was that there would be an increase in international tensions," Braun said. The evacuation plan assumed that the nation's major cities and population centers could be relocated to rural communities in three days. Everyone would respond to evacuation orders calmly and rationally, and no bottlenecks would develop. ("We were given films showing that people don't panic or loot."[28]) People who owned cars with even-numbered plates would drive out of the cities on one day, and those with odd-numbered plates would patiently wait and go the next day. Of course, all cars would be fully fueled, none would break down, and everyone would drive down the highways in an orderly fashion. As for the host communities in rural areas, they would welcome the hundreds of thousands of urban refugees with open arms and freely share their food, fuel, and shelter.

The utter absurdity of these plans was especially evident in the proposal for evacuating New York City. According to a plan commissioned by FEMA, more than 11 million people would evacuate the metropolitan New York area and travel to small towns in upstate New York and rural Pennsylvania.[29] Two million cars would flow smoothly along the tunnels and bridges leaving the city. How this was to occur without creating total gridlock on New York's already congested highways was not explained. As for the 4.8 million New Yorkers without automobiles, most would supposedly be flown out of the city, although the required passenger capacity would take more than half of all the jumbo jets in the United States. When these proposals came before the City Council of New York in the spring of 1982 (ironically, just before the giant June 12 rally), they were openly mocked.

Back in the more genteel environs of North Carolina, Marilyn Braun and the city officials of Greensboro tried to give the federal proposal the benefit of the doubt. The more they studied the plan, however, the more skeptical they became. When Braun presented the federal proposals to her Community Planning Committee, a diverse group consisting of representatives from the police department, the fire department, local universities, and the city government, the conclusion was unanimous: The plan could never work. Guilford County and the city of Greensboro rejected the federal government's civil defense proposal and refused to sign FEMA's evacuation plan.

FEMA officials may have expected a harsh reception in New York, but they were unprepared for the polite but equally negative reaction in Greensboro. They lashed out at Braun and called her "difficult and noncooperative." When she and her colleagues raised questions about government assertions at FEMA briefings, they were removed from the room. The conservative and unassuming Braun thus found herself in the unaccustomed position of feuding with federal officials. "It was a confounding experience. These things just don't happen here in Greensboro. We are used to more open exchanges." Although Braun ran into difficulties with federal officials, she enjoyed strong support at home. "We had tremendous community support, because the public knew we were square with them."[30]

Local newspapers reported extensively on the dispute between Guilford County and FEMA, and soon word of the controversy spread to the national press as well. The Associated Press called for an interview, and stories appeared in the *Washington Post* and numerous other papers. "NBC Nightly News" did a story, and ABC's "20/20" ran a feature. Braun was even called to testify before Congress. Her hope for anonymity now totally shattered, she was also contacted by officials in nearly 100 other communities and by dozens of citizen's groups. Soon Braun was traveling all over North Carolina and the country, speaking to local officials and citizen activists on her now standard topic, "The Myth of Civil Defense." Marilyn Braun was never comfortable with this celebrity status and often felt uneasy and embarrassed at newspaper editorializing that described her as a rebel: "We weren't trying to cause trouble; we were merely searching for the truth. We always tried to keep this on a scientific level. For us it was not a matter of liberal versus conservative, or Northern versus Southern, but a question of rational versus irrational."[31]

Prevention, not Protection

The drama over the CRP in Guilford County was repeated in hundreds of communities across the United States during the 1980s. Since the plan required the cooperation of more than a hundred evacuating cities and several hundred smaller host communities, civil defense became a potent grass-roots issue. Hundreds of cities and towns faced the challenge of investigating and debating how to survive World War III.

This process was occurring just as the PSR medical symposia were taking place around the country. Local government officials were thus hearing two radically different messages: The federal government wanted them to prepare to survive a nuclear war, but medical professionals were saying there could be no defense against nuclear weapons. Not surprisingly, PSR members played an active role in community debates on the CRP and contributed significantly to the mounting public skepticism. Once again, Jennifer Leaning played a prominent role in these efforts, coauthoring an important critique of civil defense, *The Counterfeit Ark,*[32] and working with local officials in numerous communities.

One of the first cities to reject civil defense planning was Cambridge, Massachusetts. When City Council members David Wylie and Saundra Graham learned in March 1981 of FEMA's plans to evacuate the city's 100,000 residents to nearby towns in rural New England in the event of nuclear war, they scoffed at the proposal and demanded a public hearing. PSR members and other local peace activists provided information and political support for the officials, and Helen Caldicott and other antinuclear leaders testified at the public forum. The City Council voted not only to reject the FEMA plan but also to produce and distribute an alternative publication, "Cambridge and Nuclear Weapons." The eight-page booklet, distributed to every household in the city, urged residents to become active in educational efforts to end the arms race and argued that the only protection against nuclear war "would be for nations with nuclear arms to destroy those arms and renounce their use."[33]

News of the Cambridge City Council's action quickly spread, and hundreds of other communities requested copies of their booklet and adopted similar approaches to the civil defense debate. All over the country, cities and towns voted not only to reject the FEMA plan but also to encourage local public educational efforts on the prevention of nuclear war. PSR members and other peace activists used these debates to build coalitions and broaden their involvement in local political affairs. In Boston, New York, Chicago, San Francisco, Sacramento, and dozens of other major cities, peace activists succeeded in persuading local governments to reject the CRP. In all, more than 300 cities and towns, nearly half of those addressing the plan, rejected FEMA's relocation proposals. In several instances, entire state agencies rejected CRP, including Arizona, Massachusetts, and Maine.[34] In some communities, the civil defense plan initially slipped through quietly without public notice, but citizen activists then forced it back into the limelight. In Boulder, Colorado, for example, county officials had initially approved the FEMA plan, but when local residents learned what had happened, they demanded a public hearing. In March 1982, 1,000 people jammed a local auditorium to voice their opposition to civil defense. Not a single witness testified in favor. Faced with this overwhelming public opposition, the county commissioners voted unanimously to reject the relocation plan and agreed to sponsor a program of public education on preventing nuclear war.

This growing resistance at the community level was reflected in widespread skepticism on Capitol Hill. When the White House's huge civil defense budget increases were presented to Congress in 1982, the normally pliant Senate Armed Services Committee slashed the request by 40 percent.[35] Congress supported FEMA's budget requests for natural disasters and civil emergencies but consistently cut the agency's requests for evacuation planning to protect against nuclear war. As a result of this congressional skepticism, itself a product of citizen opposition at the grass-roots level, the White House was never able to obtain the funding increases it requested. The proposal for a vastly expanded network of blast shelters was rejected, and the plans for nuclear war evacuation were substantially scaled back.

For the peace movement, the government's retreat from its extravagant plans for civil defense was an important victory. Precisely because civil defense was so central to the Reagan strategy of military confrontation, the campaign to derail the plans dealt a major blow to administration policy. By discrediting the administration's claims about surviving a nuclear war, the peace movement helped the public understand that the only protection against nuclear war is its prevention.

4
God Against the Bomb

Onward Christian Soldiers

For centuries, bishops beyond measure have stood with a cross in one hand and a sword in the other. From the time of the crusades to the more recent struggle against "Godless communism," church leaders often have sanctioned the call to arms. War was seen as a justifiable and sometimes even favored instrument of God's will. Of course, a pacifist tradition also existed, embodied, for instance, in the Mennonite, Brethren, and Quaker churches. A commitment to peace and nonviolence has also been kept alive within the Roman Catholic church and mainline Protestant denominations. In more recent decades, in response to the horrors of war and repression in the modern world, peace and social justice have become dominant themes in religious doctrine. Christian social teaching has become an important source of moral guidance in the struggles for peace and social equality.

Thus it was neither surprising nor out of character when the Roman Catholic church and major Protestant denominations issued declarations in the 1980s supporting the goals of the peace movement. Nearly every major religious organization in the United States raised its voice for peace and disarmament, and many explicitly criticized the policies of the Reagan administration. The churches issued pastoral letters, conducted educational campaigns, held conferences, organized vigils, joined in lobbying campaigns, and in some cases even supported demonstrations and nonviolent civil disobedience. The theological basis for this commitment was simple: God alone has the authority to end life on this planet, while human beings have only the power. The religious community became an essential part of the movement to end the nuclear arms race. In the hearts of millions of Americans, God was on the side of peace and against the bomb.

Of all the influences for disarmament during the 1980s, the involvement of the churches was perhaps most important. Surveying these developments for the influential journal *Foreign Affairs* in 1983, Bruce Van Voorst saw the involvement of the churches as "to some extent an irresistible force in American affairs."[1] Given the scale of the religious challenge, Van Voorst observed, "No government in Washington can afford not to pay attention; no statesman can be indifferent to the debate."[2] As we shall see, the Reagan administration paid close attention to the religious debate, especially that of the Roman Catholic bishops. White House officials correctly saw that the deep misgivings of the religious community could seriously erode public support for their military policies. While it is impossible to measure such things quantitatively, the involvement of the churches clearly had an enormous influence on the political climate of the country and contributed greatly to public pressures for peace.

The religious engagement was particularly important in creating a mass constituency for peace. The Roman Catholic bishops explicitly aimed to broaden public understanding of the nuclear issue and actively involve the human community in the search for peaceful solutions. Pope John Paul II declared in his "World Day of Peace Message" in 1982 that "peace can be firmly constructed only if it corresponds to the resolute determination of all people of goodwill. Rulers must be supported and enlightened by a public opinion that encourages them or, where necessary, expresses disapproval."[3] The U.S. Catholic bishops felt it necessary to express such disapproval and read the pope's message as "an appeal to form public opinion." Their hope was that an aroused public could "indicate the limits beyond which a government should not proceed."[4]

The participation of the churches cast a "mantle of respectability" over the peace movement and gave new legitimacy to discussions of disarmament.[5] When religious leaders spoke out for reversal of the arms race, it became easier and more acceptable for others to express similar views. The backing of the religious community made peace a mainstream issue and gave credibility and momentum to the disarmament movement. The enhanced legitimacy arising from this support strengthened peace activism and helped to generate the political pressure that ultimately led to a change in nuclear policy.

By the Riverside

In the religious community as in other sectors of society, participation in the nuclear debate was not purely spontaneous but resulted from the initiative and conscious effort of dedicated individuals. Long before mainstream institutions became involved, a prophetic minority stepped forward to raise alarms about the increasing danger of nuclear war and urge a more active commitment to peace. The Sojourners religious community in Washington, D.C., led by Jim Wallis, played a crucial role in the founding of the nuclear freeze movement. One of the most eloquent of these early voices was that of the Reverend William Sloane Coffin, the former chaplain of Yale University who in 1977 had begun a ten-year term as senior minister of the prestigious Riverside Church in New York City. A longtime social activist and veteran of both the civil rights and Vietnam antiwar movements, Coffin came to his new position at a time of deepening concern about the threat of nuclear war. One of his first acts upon arriving at Riverside was to establish a disarmament program. To direct the program, Coffin turned to his old friend and colleague from the antiwar movement, Cora Weiss. A veteran activist in her own right and an early member of Women's Strike for Peace, Weiss brought tremendous talent and energy to the Riverside program. Together, Coffin and Weiss were a winning team, and they contributed greatly to the building of the new disarmament movement.

Beginning in the fall of 1978, Riverside organized annual conferences for disarmament. These became landmark events in awakening public consciousness and encouraging citizen activism. Held in Riverside's majestic sanctuary on Manhattan's upper west side, the conferences brought together clergy, lay activists, policy experts, and elected officials from all over the country. The focus was a process of learning and empowerment that Weiss termed "education toward action."[6] The first event in December 1978 drew more than 1,500 people from nearly forty states. Each year thereafter for the next decade, similar large-scale conferences were held.[7] The last and perhaps grandest of the Riverside conferences was held in 1987, the year before Coffin left the church to become president of the newly merged SANE/Freeze organization in Washington. The conference focused on the links between disarmament and development and the struggle for freedom in South Africa. Featured speakers were the Reverend Alan Boesak and African National Congress leader Oliver Tambo, who appeared together on the same platform for the first time. Nearly 4,000 people jammed into Riverside to cheer Tambo and Boesak and support Coffin's call for an end to apartheid in South Africa. In addition to these large annual conferences, the Riverside program sponsored monthly forums entitled "Coffee: Grounds for Discussion" featuring prominent peace advocates from the United States and around the world.

These events in New York helped inspire the creation of similar peace programs in other churches and communities. "That was our goal," said Coffin, "to start something that would then be picked up elsewhere. The creation of the disarmament program at a prestigious church like Riverside made it easier and more respectable to address such issues in local pulpits."[8] Within months of the first conference in New York, similar events were held in Kansas, Massachusetts, Oklahoma, and Maine and a dozen more were scheduled in other states.[9] One major program was created in the image of Riverside in Pasadena, California (the Interfaith Center to Reverse the Arms Race) and another in Princeton, New Jersey (the Committee for Nuclear Disarmament). Weiss found herself called upon not only to direct the Riverside program but to assist ministers and lay activists in creating similar programs elsewhere. "Ministers would come up to Riverside," Weiss recalled, "and we would sit together in the cafeteria and go over the details of how to get started: organizing conferences, raising funds, the whole business."[10] Before long, instead of inviting people to New York, Coffin and Weiss found themselves traveling to other cities to attend church-sponsored disarmament events. Coffin crisscrossed the country during his tenure at Riverside and even more intensely as president of SANE/Freeze. He gave tirelessly of his eloquent gift of speech on these tours, and he was thanked frequently, not only for his inspiring words but also for his initiative in creating the Riverside disarmament program. He recalled, "In my travels around the country, many times ministers said to me, you have no idea how much it helped to have Riverside take the lead on these discussions. It made it easier for us to follow along."[11] The Riverside disarmament program was vitally important in sowing the seeds of peace activism within the religious community.

Couscous and Marmalade

Dedicated individuals in the Roman Catholic Church also played a key role in prompting the greater commitment to peace. Perhaps the most important catalyst for peace was the pacifist organization Pax Christi. Though its membership and budget were small, Pax Christi had a major influence within the Catholic community during the 1980s. At the time of the writing of the bishops' Pastoral Letter on War and Peace, for example, 57 of the 280 Catholic bishops in the United States were members of the organization.[12] The president and spiritual mentor of Pax Christi was Thomas Gumbleton, the auxiliary bishop of Detroit. Soft-spoken and gentle in manner, Gumbleton was nonetheless a fierce opponent of war and a passionate advocate for peace and justice. Gumbleton was perhaps the key figure in the 1980s in focusing church attention on the danger of nuclear war and pressing the hierarchy to speak out for peace and reversal of the arms race.

Often overlooked in the male-dominated world of the Catholic church is the contribution of women. Nuns and female lay workers played a central role in Pax Christi and other peace initiatives within the Catholic community and were often the organizers who did the work and carried out the church's social commitments. "Behind every right thinking Catholic bishop" joked William Sloane Coffin, "stands a nun with a two-foot-long knitting needle jabbed between his ribs."[13] One of these needlers for peace during the 1980s was Sister Mary Evelyn Jegen, a medieval scholar and college professor who became the first national coordinator of Pax Christi and served in that position during the critical period of the writing of the pastoral letter. Jegen and her Pax Christi colleagues were instrumental in shaping the pastoral letter and mobilizing the church community, both within the hierarchy and at the grass-roots level.

A key example of this behind-the-scenes influence came in March 1981 when seventeen bishops wrote to then archbishop Joseph Bernardin asking that the newly formed Committee on War and Peace* address a series of fundamental questions on the morality of nuclear weapons policy.[14] That letter, which played an important role in defin-

---

*Members of the bishops' committee included Bernardin, Gumbleton, Daniel Reilly of Norwich, Connecticut, George Fulcher of Columbus, Ohio, and John O'Connor of the Military Ordinariate. The principal assistant to the bishops was Father J. Bryan Hehir.

ing the issues addressed by the bishops' committee, originated in a meeting coordinated by Jegen with bishops Carroll Dozier of Memphis, Walter Sullivan of Richmond, and Gumbleton. Dozier, a longtime advocate of social justice and civil rights, had urged that a few of the bishops get together, but it was Jegen who made it happen and who circulated the letter among other bishops for support. The purpose of the letter, according to Jegen, was to "make sure the right kind of questions were asked and that one of our own would be appointed to the committee."[15]

When Gumbleton was named to the bishops' committee, one of his first acts was to get together with Jegen to plan strategy. Jegen said:

> Before the first committee meeting, Tom and I met at a McDonald's in Detroit. He picked me up at the Greyhound station and we went in for a coke. We sat there together drawing up a list of scripture scholars and women to have testify before the bishops. We wanted to make sure that the input to the committee would be broad and that there would be women represented in the thinking of the pastoral.[16]

Throughout the deliberations of the bishops, Pax Christi kept up what Jegen described as "a kind of running dialogue, a lobbying action." As each draft of the pastoral letter appeared, the organization issued commentaries and reflection papers urging the strongest possible commitment to disarmament.

Jegen's partner in these efforts, the woman she described as "my godmother in the peace movement," was Eileen Egan, a veteran of the Catholic Worker movement and a longtime associate and disciple of Dorothy Day. Egan and Jegen would meet in Egan's apartment and plan how to bring particular issues before the bishops' committee. Jegen recalled:

> When we had an idea that we wanted in the pastoral, we would say, let's try to find a priest on our side who will present it for us. We would do all the footwork. We'd write the letter and even type it and then ask someone to sign it. If you're terribly mad on the whole feminist agenda, you might say no, I won't do it. But we were more concerned about what we saw as the big questions. That's just the way it works in the church.
>
> We had fun over this. In our playful way Eileen and I founded a society, ESO, the Evangelical Society of Outflankers. When we got together we

even had our own ritual food: couscous and ginger marmalade. You do these things to keep up your morale.[17]

In this way, Jegen and her colleagues brought key issues before the bishops' committee.

Others were stoking the fires of debate within the church in more provocative ways. In June 1981, Archbishop Raymond Hunthausen of Seattle gave a speech in which he condemned the Trident missile-firing submarine, to be based in nearby waters, as the "Auschwitz of Puget Sound." In August, Bishop Leroy Matthiesen of Amarillo, Texas, denounced production of the neutron bomb and other nuclear weapons at the local Pantex plant and urged parishioners working at the complex to resign their jobs and seek employment in more peaceful pursuits.[18] These were shocking statements, coming as they did from the leading Catholic prelates in heavily defense-dependent areas, and they signaled a growing ferment among Catholics and other religious people against the mounting threat of nuclear war.

The Bishops' Challenge

Roman Catholics have constituted the largest religious denomination in the United States since before the Civil War. More than 50 million Americans profess to be Catholic, and although many do not practice the faith actively, nearly all are heavily influenced by the culture and social milieu of the church. Through its more than 18,000 parishes and 9,000 schools, the Roman Catholic church exerts a powerful influence not only on members of the flock but on the entire society. Of course, members of the church do not march in lockstep behind their bishops. Indeed, many Catholics ignore the directives of the hierarchy and display considerable skepticism toward the teachings of the church. This is especially so on matters of sex and personal morality. Polls show, for example, that a majority of Catholics oppose the church's rigid positions on birth control. Nonetheless, the church's teachings and moral statements do have influence, and even the most hardened agnostic pays attention when the bishops invest themselves in a major policy declaration. With its vast network of churches, schools, and universities and its access to the mass media, the Catholic church has powerful means of communicating its beliefs. When the energies of the bishops are intensely focused on a particular message, as they were in the early

1980s on nuclear disarmament, the impact is felt not only within the Catholic community but throughout society.

This is especially so when the judgment of the church is controversial and when it directly challenges established government policy. The pastoral letter, entitled *The Challenge of Peace: God's Promise and Our Response,* was issued in May 1983. It challenged the very foundations of U.S. nuclear policy and specifically opposed key elements of the Reagan administration's military buildup. The following is a summary of the major policy recommendations of the letter.[19]

- The bishops declared their support for "immediate bilateral agreements to halt the testing, production and deployment of new nuclear weapons systems." (§191)

- They endorsed a policy of no-first-use and condemned nuclear warfare: "We do not perceive any situation in which the deliberate initiation of nuclear warfare, on however restricted a scale, can be morally justified. … We judge resort to nuclear weapons to counter a conventional attack to be morally unjustifiable." (§150, §153) This statement not only challenged Reagan administration policy but also the very foundations of North Atlantic Treaty Organization (NATO) doctrine.

- The pastoral letter explicitly rejected the administration's rhetoric: "There should be a clear public resistance to the rhetoric of 'winnable' nuclear wars, or unrealistic expectations of 'surviving' nuclear exchanges, and strategies of 'protracted nuclear war.'" (§140) The bishops made a similar judgment against a central element of Reagan/Bush political strategy: "The quest for nuclear superiority," they said, "must be rejected." (§188)

- The bishops endorsed a comprehensive test ban treaty and urged "removal by all parties of short-range nuclear weapons." (§191) They also opposed "prompt hard-target kill" weapons that may be perceived as threatening a first strike. (§190) In the footnotes to this section, they specifically mentioned the MX and Pershing II missiles as possibly fitting this category.

- In perhaps the most important but also most ambiguous section of the pastoral letter, the bishops questioned the fundamental principles of nuclear deterrence. Since they condemned even retaliatory strikes that threaten innocent life, opposed any initiation of nuclear war, and were highly skeptical of so-called "limited nuclear war," the bishops seemed to be saying that any use or even threatened use of nuclear weapons is impermissible. The most logical conclusion would have been that deterrence itself, which is based on the threat of such use, must be rejected. The pastoral letter hedged on this point, however, and offered instead a "strictly conditioned" acceptance of nuclear deterrence. The bishops stated, "We cannot consider [deterrence] adequate as a long-term basis for peace" (§186) and concluded that "nuclear deterrence should be used as a step on the way toward progressive disarmament." (§188)

To Halt or Curb?

By far the most contentious part of the debate over the pastoral letter was whether it should endorse the nuclear freeze. The bishops focused enormous attention on the single word "halt." Right-wing groups correctly pointed out that although the original draft did not explicitly mention the freeze, its call for a halt to the testing, production, and deployment of nuclear weapons meant the same thing. The press had also interpreted the draft as an endorsement of the freeze. Conservative forces thus lobbied intensively to delete the word. Within the bishops' committee, this challenge was led by its most conservative member, John O'Connor, the auxiliary bishop of the Military Ordinariate who was later elevated to cardinal. Just as Gumbleton led the charge for pacifist views on the Left, O'Connor was a constant defender of military interests on the Right. Throughout the deliberations of the drafting committee, O'Connor and other conservatives in the church community kept up intense pressure on Bernardin and the other bishops. By early 1983, as they were preparing the third draft of the pastoral letter, Bernardin and the majority within the committee agreed to compromise, hoping that a tactical retreat on the question of the freeze might allow greater attention to the statement's more fundamental thesis regarding the unacceptability of using nuclear weapons. The committee decided to substitute the weaker word "curb" for "halt." The decision proved to be a major political blunder, however, for right-wing groups quickly seized on the concession as a sign of diminished support for the nuclear freeze. Newspapers across the country headlined: "Bishops

Back Off Freeze Idea."[20] The nuclear freeze resolution was coming to a vote at that time in the House of Representatives, and Reagan administration supporters, led by Congressman Henry Hyde (R-IL), used the bishops' retreat to urge rejection of the freeze resolution.

Faced with this unintended interpretation of their verbal retreat, and pressured from within the church community by Pax Christi and other peace advocates, Bernardin and the committee reversed their decision. In April, just before release of the final draft, they voted to change the language back from "curb" to "halt." When the full conference of bishops met shortly thereafter to review the draft for the last time, the decision to keep the word "halt" and thereby uphold support for the nuclear freeze was approved overwhelmingly. Even bishops who otherwise had doubts about the freeze proposal joined in the vote against "curb" to make it clear that they did not endorse administration policy. Not just on the question of "halt," but on numerous other key provisions, the final votes of the bishops' conference in May 1983 strengthened the pastoral letter and sharpened its criticisms of Reagan administration policy.[21]

When the final vote was taken, the conference of bishops endorsed the revised and strengthened pastoral letter by an overwhelming 238-9 vote—a 96 percent margin of approval. This extraordinary endorsement surprised and stunned nearly everyone, including Gumbleton and the other Pax Christi bishops who had done so much to initiate and sustain the process. It was a tremendous victory for the forces of peace. The influential Christian journal *Commonweal* called the pastoral letter a "watershed event" not only for the Catholic church but for society as a whole.[22] George Kennan wrote in the *New York Times* that the bishops' letter was "the most profound and searching inquiry yet conducted by any responsible collective body into the relations of nuclear weaponry, and indeed of modern war in general."[23]

Into the Media Limelight

Bernardin and the members of the committee writing the pastoral letter were keenly aware of the significance of their task, and they made sure that the drafting process was as open and meticulous as possible. The writing of the letter took nearly two years and required fifty-five separate meetings. The committee took extensive testimony from both peace advocates and military experts, including leading Reagan administration officials such as Defense Secretary Caspar Weinberger. Bernardin and his colleagues also sifted through an enormous volume of commentary from fellow church officials and the public. Responses to the first draft of the pastoral letter, for example, extended to more than 10,000 pages.[24] Despite their busy schedules, the bishops on the drafting committee gave freely of their time. Except for Fulcher, who was hospitalized for part of the time, none of the bishops missed a single meeting.[25] This was especially extraordinary for Bernardin, who during this time was selected as archbishop of Chicago and elevated to cardinal. The seriousness of the bishops and the thoroughness of their methodology contributed greatly to the authority and importance of the pastoral letter.

In June 1982, as the bishops gathered to review the first draft of the letter, word of its contents began to leak to the press. Gumbleton had talked in public about the emerging document at a meeting of the Catholic Theological Society of America in New York, and reporters had quickly picked up the story. On June 19, the *Washington Post* gave a report under the headline "Nuclear Weapons Use Immoral, Bishops State." The *Post* article was subsequently picked up and carried by newspapers all over the country. Shortly thereafter, the *National Catholic Reporter* also ran a story and printed the full text of the draft. Suddenly the bishops' debate was out in the open for all to see. For the next year, the publicity surrounding the bishops' deliberations was extraordinary, far beyond anything the church had encountered in previous pastoral statements. Literally thousands of newspapers and broadcast stories reported on the pastoral letter, many of them highlighting the bishops' differences with Reagan administration policy. As a "real world event" generating press coverage of antinuclear issues, the Catholic bishops' letter was one of the most significant events of the decade.

After the initial barrage of coverage in the summer of 1982, press attention continued and intensified. Each nuance of language or editing change became the subject of scrutiny and press debate. When the bishops met in Washington to review the second draft in November 1982, the event became a media circus. The prelates were blinded by a phalanx of television klieg lights and mobbed by 300 news reporters. The *Washington Post* and other newspapers ran front-page stories, and the bishops' meeting was reported on network television. Bernardin was featured on the cover of *Time* magazine.[26] The comic strip *Doonesbury* also got into the act, as the Reverend Sloane (modeled after

William Sloane Coffin) was depicted writing a pastoral letter of his own. Even the popular late-night television show "Saturday Night Live" joined in, as the "Weekend Update" reporter joked that the bishops shouldn't have trouble with having weapons but not using them since, after all, they've been practicing celibacy for centuries.

The Administration Responds

Within the White House, the bishops' pastoral letter was no laughing matter. Senior officials recognized the serious challenge posed by the letter, and they became increasingly concerned as the document took shape. "This was very important to us," admitted Robert Sims, the senior National Security Council press officer at the time.[27] To address the "problem" of the bishops, a high-level group was assembled. This group was spearheaded by National Security Adviser William Clark, a devout Roman Catholic who as a young man had studied for the priesthood, and also included his fellow Catholics John Lehman, secretary of the navy, Ambassador Vernon Walters, and Chief of Naval Operations James Watkins. Admiral John Poindexter, whose wife was studying for the Episcopal priesthood, also participated in the group. The president's men may have felt, as Shakespeare's Henry II said of Thomas à Becket, "Who will rid me of this troublesome priest?"[28] Attempting to alter the opinions of the Catholic bishops, however, was an extremely delicate matter, and not something that could be accomplished with the usual means of political pressure and intimidation. As Sims put it, "We tried to handle this one with kid gloves."[29]

As soon as the first draft of the pastoral letter was published and its sharply critical tone became evident, the administration swung into action. In July 1982, Clark wrote to the prominent Catholic columnist Clare Boothe Luce complaining of the letter's contents: "I am troubled in reading the Pastoral Letter to find none of the serious efforts [of the administration] at arms control described or even noted in the text."[30] Clark took particular exception to the bishops' endorsement of no-first-use of nuclear weapons. At the same time, however, Clark attempted to interpret the bishops' letter as supportive of Reagan administration policy. "On the subject of overall nuclear deterrence strategy, then, I find that the position recommended by the Pastoral Letter is remarkably consistent with current U.S. policy."[31] This was a tactic the White House would attempt with each new draft of the pastoral letter.

If they could not persuade the bishops to change their views, White House officials hoped they could at least obfuscate the issue by claiming that the letter endorsed administration policy. The effort failed, however, for the differences between administration policy and the views of the bishops were too great. Try as they might, White House officials could not turn a dove into a hawk.

The administration also attempted to go over the heads of the bishops by appealing directly to the pope. It was no accident, for example, that Clark's letter to Clare Boothe Luce was subsequently forwarded to Apostolic Delegate Archbishop Pio Laghi. In October 1982, prior to the bishops' national conference, Vernon Walters was dispatched to Rome for an audience with Pope John Paul II. Columnists Rowland Evans and Robert Novak reported on Walters's "unannounced papal audience" under the headline "Will Pope Stop Nuclear Heresy?"[32] The veteran diplomat was in Rome, according to Evans and Novak, to enlist the pope's help in "blunting the attack" of the U.S. bishops. Unfortunately for the White House, its lobbying effort proved a flop. If administration officials had studied Vatican teachings, they would have realized that opposition to the arms race had been an important theme of Catholic doctrine for decades. An attempt to enlist papal support for Reagan administration nuclear policy was bound to fail. The fact that the White House had to go so far in its futile bid for help is a reflection of how isolated the president's men were in their battle with the bishops. A few days later, Vatican delegate Laghi told the U.S. bishops in Washington that their pastoral letter "coincides remarkably well with Pope John Paul II's commitment to peace in the world and to authentic doctrines of the church."[33] Shortly thereafter, Bernardin was elevated to cardinal, the only U.S. bishop to be so honored at the time—hardly a sign of Vatican displeasure with his work.

Frustrated in their attempts to lobby the bishops, administration officials tried to take their case to the press but again failed clumsily. On the opening day of the bishops' conference in November, the *Wall Street Journal* carried an editorial piece by Lehman charging that the pastoral letter could undermine chances for arms control and have "immoral consequences." At the same time, National Security Adviser Clark wrote a letter to the bishops on behalf of the president and the cabinet complaining that the draft letter "continues to reflect a fundamental misreading of American policies and continues essentially to ignore the far-reaching American proposals that are currently being negotiated with the Soviet Union."[34] Clark also attempted again to portray the pastoral letter as an endorsement of White House policy: "The deterrence posture [of the United States] is judged in the pastoral letter as being morally justifiable." The letter was released to the press even before it reached the bishops.

Bernardin and his colleagues responded swiftly. With aplomb and studied understatement, Bernardin stepped before the microphones to comment on the White House letter. "The committee welcomes Mr. Clark's letter," said Bernardin, "although [we were] somewhat surprised to read it first in the *New York Times.*"[35] Pressed by reporters to respond to White House pressure, Bernardin replied, "We are not intimidated." The archbishop added, "We will see who is misreading whom in due time."[36] In the end, the White House gave up its efforts to challenge the bishops and tried to put the best possible face on a difficult situation. When the letter was released in its final form in May 1983, the administration downplayed its significance. Officials who only a few weeks before had attached great significance to the use of the word "curb" now sought to minimize the return to "halt" and the more critical tone of the document.[37] Ronald Reagan claimed that the bishops were attempting "to do exactly what we're doing."[38] Despite these attempts to obfuscate and gloss over the bishops' message, the pastoral letter was a clear and unequivocal rebuke to administration policy and a major boost for the cause of disarmament.

To the Grass Roots

In September 1982, the Catholic archdiocese of Washington, D.C., sponsored a conference on War and Peace in the Nuclear Age. Held at Gonzaga High School in downtown Washington near Capitol Hill, the convocation was part of a local educational program paralleling the national effort sponsored by Archbishop James Hickey. Expecting a crowd of perhaps 700, church organizers were stunned and a bit overwhelmed to see an overflow audience of 1,400 people jamming the school auditorium. Even more impressive was the character of the crowd. These were not radical students or long-haired activists but respectable middle-class parishioners: priests and nuns, representatives of church social action committees, educators, and ordinary churchgoing people. For many at the conference, including those who attended a workshop session at which I spoke, this was their first exposure to peace movement activity. I saw the beginnings of awareness and a commitment to action taking root right before my eyes. Many left the day's proceedings determined to take up these concerns in their local parishes. The Washington conference was a remarkable example of a broad-based movement in the making.

Another instance of church support for peace activism occurred earlier that year in Philadelphia when the Catholic archdiocese, led by its otherwise conservative prelate, Cardinal John Krol, became a sponsor of the Interfaith Witness to Stop the Nuclear Arms Race. Initiated in previous years by the Religious Society of Friends (Quakers) and clergy from other local churches and synagogues, the Interfaith Witness was suddenly catapulted to a higher level of visibility when the huge Catholic archdiocese threw its weight behind the event. The archdiocese produced radio spots advertising the Interfaith Witness and wrote letters to every priest and Catholic institution in the city urging participation. As a result, more than 15,000 people attended the candlelight procession and outdoor rally on the evening of March 26.[39] The program began with prayer services in the oldest churches and synagogues in the historic downtown area and then continued as people streamed onto Independence Mall, candles in hand, to hear Krol and other speakers call for an end to the arms race. "We must ask," declared Krol, "whether the nuclear arms race is a threat to our security and whether nuclear disarmament might not directly enhance our national security."[40] Silence was maintained throughout the ceremony, and people responded to the speeches not with applause but by holding aloft their lighted candles. Robert Musil, a participant in the event and the executive producer of SANE's "Consider the Alternatives" radio program, recalled the Interfaith Witness:

> It was a deeply moving and powerful event that galvanized Philadelphia around concern for the arms race. This is a very ethnic and religious city, and the involvement of a broad interfaith spectrum—Catholics, Protestants, Jews, Greek Orthodox—had a big impact. For the first time, many mainstream, ordinary Philadelphians were involved in the debate over nuclear war.[41]

Not just in Philadelphia and Washington, D.C., but throughout the country, the Catholic church's engagement in the arms debate at the national level had an important impact on local parish life. The sheer magnitude of the educational effort was staggering. Officials at the U.S. Catholic Conference estimated that more than 1 million copies of the pastoral letter were published and circulated.[42] Ed Doherty, an adviser to the Catholic Conference who assisted the bishops' committee, calculated in 1984 that educational programs on the pastoral letter were held in more than half of the nation's dioceses.[43] The teaching of the pastoral letter also reached into the extensive Catholic educational system. Catholic textbooks were adapted to include material from the pastoral, and in many dioceses peace themes were integrated into the curricula of parochial schools. Catholic colleges and universities went even further. More than 150 of these schools established peace education programs and offered courses or seminars on the findings of the pastoral letter.[44] At Notre Dame, the Institute for International Peace Studies was founded, where I wrote this book, and peace studies courses were introduced into the graduate and undergraduate curricula.

This widespread educational effort strongly influenced public opinion, especially within the church community. Polling information from the National Opinion Research Center analyzed by writer Andrew Greeley demonstrated that, in 1983, the percentage of Catholics believing that too much money was being spent on the military stood at 32 percent, the same figure as for Protestants. In 1984, after publication of the pastoral letter, the percentage of Catholics holding this belief jumped to 54 percent, while among Protestants it remained the same.[45] Here was strong evidence that the teachings of the bishops were having an impact on the understanding and awareness of U.S. Catholics.

Nonetheless, the church as a whole did not make a major effort to promote the pastoral letter, and as a result the full potential of the document was never realized. The Roman Catholic church, like other denominations, suffered from a phenomenon that the Reverend William Sloane Coffin has termed "resolutionary Christianity." An enormous effort goes into the formulation of a church statement, and although the intention is to make this only the first step in a long journey, so much intellectual and emotional energy is expended in the process that the next steps tend not to be taken.[46] In the case of the Catholic pastoral, the follow-up steps at the national level were minimal. At the U.S. Catholic Conference headquarters in Washington, D.C., the bishops created a tiny office known as the Clearing House for the War and Peace Pastoral Letter. The Clearing House had a two-person staff and a minimal budget and confined itself primarily to networking and exchanging information about educational resources. Even this modest effort was closed after a year, however, and local priests and church leaders were left on their own to interpret and use the pastoral letter. The significance of *The Challenge of Peace* could have been much greater had the church practiced what it preached and thrown its full weight behind a national peace education program.

Ecumenical Peace

The religious cry for peace during the 1980s was heard not just from Catholics but from all believers, especially Protestants. Indeed, most of the Protestant churches went further than the Catholics in condemning the very existence of nuclear weapons. The uneasy acceptance of deterrence that had characterized the Protestant tradition prior to the 1980s gave way in many instances to an explicit endorsement of disarmament. Not only the use but the very possession of nuclear weapons now became unacceptable. The American Lutheran Church and the Lutheran Church of America passed resolutions urging the elimination of nuclear weapons. The executive ministers of the American Baptist Church called the existence of nuclear weapons and the willingness to use them "a direct affront to our Christian beliefs."[47] At the World Council of Churches Sixth Assembly in Vancouver in 1983, the delegates adopted a statement of virtual nuclear pacifism: "We believe that the time has come when churches must unequivocally declare that the production and deployment as well as the use of nuclear weapons are a crime against humanity and that such activities must be condemned on ethical and theological grounds."[48]

Many pastoral letters were issued during the 1980s but none was more far-reaching in its condemnation of nuclear policy than that of the United Methodist church. The Methodist document, *In Defense of Creation,* went beyond the Catholic letter in a number of respects. It was more radical in its critique of nuclear policy and explicitly rejected not only the arms race but the whole concept of deterrence. Addressing the ambiguity left by their Catholic brethren, the Methodist bishops declared that nuclear deterrence "must not receive the Church's blessing even as a temporary warrant."[49] The Methodist statement also went beyond the Catholic letter in addressing the economic consequences of the arms race. According to the bishops, "justice is forsaken in the squandering of the arms race while a holocaust of hunger, malnutrition, disease and violent death is destroying the world's poorest peoples."[50] The Methodist policy recommendations included a comprehensive test ban, support for existing arms control treaties (a slap at the decision of the Reagan administration to exceed SALT II limits), a ban on space weapons, and no-first-use of nuclear weapons. The bishops also expressed specific opposition to the MX missile, Trident submarines and missiles, and Pershing II missiles (and their Soviet counterparts). Unfortunately for the Methodist bishops, *In Defense of Creation* received little press attention. It was released just as the nuclear disaster at Chernobyl occurred and was completely overshadowed in the media.

A number of Protestant denominations went beyond statements of belief and attempted to translate their words into action. The United Presbyterian church, an early endorser of the nuclear freeze, established a Peacemaking Program in 1980 that has continued ever since. Financed by a special collection each fall in Presbyterian churches throughout the country, the Peacemaking Program maintains a national staff at church headquarters in Louisville, Kentucky, and supports peace education programs both nationally and in local presbyteries. The National Council of Churches also launched a peace education program that continues to this day. Since 1983, the New York–based council has sponsored annual "Peace With Justice" week-long programs in hundreds of local churches. The National Council, the United Church of Christ, and other Protestant denominations also established peace advocacy programs, located either at the Interchurch Center in New York (irreverently referred to as the "God Box") or in the Methodist Building next to the U.S. Capitol in Washington, D.C. Many of these church offices participated in lobbying efforts and were actively involved in the campaigns for the nuclear freeze, against the MX, and for peace in Central America. The church social action offices are now a regular part of the peace movement presence on Capitol Hill and provide both stability and grass-roots clout for disarmament efforts in Washington.

The Jewish community also raised its voice for peace during the 1980s. Although many individual Jews were actively involved in the peace movement, the mainline organizations of Judaism tended to be more cautious. The one important exception was the Union of American Hebrew Congregations (UAHC), which represents approximately one-third of the Jewish community in the United States. Led by rabbis

Alexander Schindler and David Saperstein, the UAHC was an early supporter of the nuclear freeze movement and a vigorous supporter of local educational forums in synagogues and community organizations
all over the country. Although the UAHC was the most vocal of the Jewish groups, other, more conservative groups also spoke out against the
nuclear threat. In April 1982, the Rabbinical Assembly of America, the
largest of the three groups within Judaism, issued a statement endorsing the nuclear freeze. In February 1983, the Synagogue Council of
America, an umbrella group embracing all branches of Judaism,
adopted a resolution urging that the United States and the Soviet
Union "implement a bilateral mutual cessation of the production and
deployment of nuclear weapons," that is, a nuclear freeze.[51]

African-American Involvement

Most Americans, including many in the peace movement, are unaware
that African Americans as a group strongly support peace and nuclear
disarmament. As scholars Frances Beal and Ty dePass have written:

> A consistent thread that has been woven into black intellectual and polit-
> ical thought in the United States has been a pattern of ardent anti-
> colonial and anti-imperialist consciousness. From a historical perspec-
> tive, therefore, one of the strongest voices for peace within this country
> has come from the black community.[52]

Polls have consistently shown, and history confirms, that African
Americans are more likely than whites to endorse arms reduction, dis-
approve of higher military spending, and oppose wars of intervention,
whether in Vietnam or the Persian Gulf. The vote for nuclear freeze referenda in 1982 was highest in Washington, D.C., and other major cities
with large black populations. From the days of Frederick Douglass's opposition to the Spanish-American War to the protests by Malcolm X
and Martin Luther King, Jr., against Vietnam, African Americans have
long spoken out against war and military intervention. On Capitol Hill
the Congressional Black Caucus consistently has the best voting record
on issues of nuclear arms reduction.

Given the prominent role of the churches in African-American culture, one might expect that black churches would be a leading voice in
the disarmament movement. Although the commitment to peace is in-

deed strong, however, black churches tend not to be involved in the organized peace movement. During the 1980s, many black churches and religious leaders were supporters of disarmament, but their organizational energies and personal commitments were focused elsewhere—on the institutionalized violence of poverty and injustice within their communities. African Americans know that the arms race is dangerous and a waste of economic resources, but for many the threat of nuclear war is an abstraction compared to the more urgent challenge of day-to-day survival. Achieving economic and social justice here at home is the priority.

This difference in emphasis has made it difficult at times for the predominantly white peace movement to work well with African Americans. The Reverend William Sloane Coffin recounted the obstacles he encountered when attempting to enlist the black churches of nearby Harlem in his Riverside disarmament program in the late 1970s. The local ministers were very supportive and endorsed the goals of the Riverside program, but they chose not to become actively involved. "They would tell me, it's fine, Bill, what you're doing, that's great, but it's white man's stuff. We're not against it, but we're not going to get into it."[53] The Harlem ministers were focused instead on economic and social survival, on stopping the war in their communities caused by crime and poverty. Nor were they convinced by Coffin's point that an end to the arms race would mean more money coming into cities and communities such as Harlem. Blacks had not seen a "peace dividend" after World War II, Korea, or Vietnam, and they were not expecting one from the end of the Cold War. It wasn't until well into the Reagan era, when money was being taken directly out of human needs programs and put into the arms budget, that black preachers began to speak out and become more actively involved, according to Coffin. When they did, they had a natural constituency ready to support their call for peace and reversal of the arms race.

At the national level, a number of black ministers played a prominent role in the peace movement. The Reverend Joseph Lowery, president of the Southern Christian Leadership Council, was a cochair of Clergy and Laity Concerned and was involved in numerous peace campaigns. Perhaps the most active black leader for peace during the decade was the Reverend Jesse Jackson. An early endorser of the nuclear freeze, a sponsor of Jobs with Peace, and a member of the Board of Directors of SANE during the 1980s, Jackson reached out to the peace movement by inviting SANE and other national peace groups to join in his March on Washington for Jobs, Peace, and Justice in 1980. Jackson spoke at the Peace Sunday disarmament rally in California in June 1982, addressed nearly all of the major Central America solidarity rallies during the decade, and led the SANE/Freeze delegation to the Geneva Summit in November 1985 to meet with Soviet leader Mikhail Gorbachev. As a presidential candidate in 1984 and 1988, Jackson spoke out often for a more peaceful foreign policy and took a leadership position on such issues as reduced military spending and no-first-use of nuclear weapons. Jackson's leadership helped to articulate the message of peace nationally and internationally and provided important openings for the predominantly white peace movement within the African-American community.

In his University of South Carolina speech nearly seven years after release of the Catholic pastoral letter, Cardinal Joseph Bernardin reflected on the dramatic changes then occurring in world affairs: "In 1990 one has the sense of living on the other side of a fault line."[54] A principal characteristic of the period leading up to this change, said Bernardin, was "the degree of public engagement in the nuclear debate" and the fact that "the public wanted more attention paid to efforts for arms control." He continued:

> While it is always difficult to establish causality in large social movements, I believe this public pressure did influence the U.S. return to arms control negotiations, first through a series of proposals, then through the summits of 1985 to 1988 ... My own sense is that the public played a very useful role in pressing the policy process toward negotiations.[55]

What Bernardin did not say was that he and his colleagues in the religious community played a major role in generating that pressure and creating an important peace constituency in U.S. politics. The bishops did not elect senators or win votes in Congress, but their many actions for peace were a major factor in awakening public consciousness and encouraging citizen activism. The impact of this religious community involvement was decisive in shaping the political climate and building the movement for peace and nuclear disarmament.

5
Shaping Culture

"Who's the most popular person in North Carolina?"[1] asked Norris Frederick. Members of North Carolina SANE were meeting in Charlotte in the fall of 1982 to plan a peace advertising campaign. "We need someone who can appeal beyond the usual liberal audience," emphasized Jean Wood. Under the leadership of Frederick, a native North Carolinian and graduate of Davidson College, and Wood, a transplanted northerner who had moved with her family from New Jersey, the North Carolina SANE chapter had obtained a $25,000 grant from the Z. Smith Reynolds Foundation and was now in the rare and enviable position (for a peace group) of deciding how to spend a substantial budget for media advertising. Having determined that radio spots would be the medium and the nuclear freeze the message, the chapter was now trying to decide who would be the best spokesperson. "Think, people," implored Frederick, "who walks on water in this state?" Suddenly the light went on for everyone. Heads nodded and smiles broke out as the name was mentioned: Dean Smith, head basketball coach of the University of North Carolina Tar Heels.

In twenty years of coaching, Dean Smith had made the University of North Carolina a perennial national basketball powerhouse. The previous March, he had led the Tar Heels to a national collegiate championship—number one in the country. No doubt about it: Smith was an almost godlike figure in the state, the ideal person to narrate SANE's radio spots. But would he be willing to stick his neck out for the nuclear freeze? No one knew how Smith stood on the issue, but Frederick recalled that the coach had supported the desegregation struggles of the 1960s. While the Student Nonviolent Coordinating Committee and other groups were sitting in to challenge segregation in North Carolina and other states, Dean Smith was quietly encouraging racial integration and recruiting black athletes for the Tar Heels basketball squad. "That's the kind of person he is," observed Frederick, "a man of integrity. I bet he's for the freeze as well." Everyone agreed it was worth a try. I was asked as national director to write to Smith and request that he be our spokesperson. A few weeks later, a short note arrived at the SANE headquarters: "Coach Smith will be glad to participate in your campaign. Please call to arrange a time to visit." We were ecstatic. Recruiting Dean Smith to support the nuclear freeze movement was a major coup.

As we entered the Tar Heels athletic offices a few weeks later, the rich traditions of North Carolina basketball and Smith's illustrious career were plainly evident. Championship plaques and banners lined the walls, and photos of basketball legends were everywhere. After exchanging pleasantries with the coach's assistants and secretaries, we were quickly ushered into the inner sanctum, speechless and a bit awestruck in the presence of the great coach. Without pretense, Smith rose to welcome our group and in his direct and unassuming manner urged us to make ourselves at home. He then read over the scripts again, made a few last-minute changes, and sat down at the microphone to begin recording.

> Hello, this is coach Dean Smith. Winning the national championship was a great thrill. But there is one contest that nobody wins—the international arms race. We all lose in a nuclear war, and the risk grows greater every day unless we do something about it. A majority of Americans supports the bilateral nuclear freeze, but it won't happen unless you take action. Pick up the phone, add your voice to the growing demand for a nuclear freeze.[2]

After a couple of flawless takes, Smith then read the second script, this one focusing on children.

> Hello, this is coach Dean Smith. A child is one of life's greatest gifts. But today our children are an endangered species—because of the nuclear arms race. The United States and the Soviet Union together possess over 50,000 nuclear warheads. That's ten tons of explosives for every child on earth. It's insane.[3]

At the end of each spot, listeners were directed to call an 800 number and have a message in support of the freeze sent in their name to Ronald Reagan and Yuri Andropov.

After recording the scripts, Smith thanked us for coming and asked if we could stay and be his guests at the Tar Heels's game that night (unfortunately our plane reservations were for that afternoon). Before leaving, we were escorted on a tour of Carmichael Auditorium, the scene of so many of Smith's basketball heroics. As we gazed at the many championship banners hanging from the rafters, we exulted again at our good fortune in gaining the support of the legendary coach. We had scored a big win for the peace movement.

SANE's radio spots hit the airwaves on Monday, February 7. Nearly 300 sixty-second spots played that week on dozens of stations throughout the state. Seventeen outdoor billboards depicting the image of a child and calling for a nuclear freeze were also placed from Raleigh to Asheville. News of Coach Smith's participation in the SANE advertising campaign created a sensation. Articles on Smith and the media campaign appeared in every major newspaper in the state, making for more than thirty stories in all.[4] Television and radio stations reported widely on the ads. The combination of hundreds of advertising placements and extensive news coverage meant that SANE's media messages virtually saturated the North Carolina market. The news coverage was generally favorable, and the appeal to end the nuclear arms race reached millions of people.

The Dean Smith ads gave a powerful boost to North Carolina SANE. Not only did its message get wide exposure, but the group was now associated in the public mind with the popular basketball coach. Suddenly, the peace movement had credibility and access it had not known before. Freeze advocates were no longer on the fringes but were now part of the mainstream. Reflecting on the media campaign several years later, Norris Frederick summed up its importance:

> It had a fantastic impact on the issue and our organization. It boosted our confidence greatly. We were no longer outsiders but important players in the debate. People all over the state, even if they didn't know much about nuclear weapons, knew about SANE because of our association with Dean Smith. For years afterwards, we felt a sense of tangible achievement from that effort. If our goal is to change public opinion, this was a major success.[5]

Communications and Social Change

The North Carolina advertising campaign was one of many examples of the peace movement's using the media for education and outreach.

Throughout the 1980s, peace advocates maintained a constant effort to influence public opinion and shape popular culture. Although many activist groups lack media sophistication and often give insufficient attention to press relations, the freeze movement as a whole had an enormous impact on public consciousness. The most important breakthrough was the idea of the freeze itself. The concept shattered the previous framework of nuclear discourse and for the first time in the atomic age gave ordinary citizens a sense that they could have a say in this most important of issues. Peace groups seized upon this opening to build political support for an end to the arms race and improved U.S.-Soviet relations. A kind of "battle of the airwaves" ensued, with opponents of the Reagan administration struggling against the powerful White House communications apparatus to chip away at public support for the military buildup. Gradually, the political climate shifted and a desire for arms reduction began to permeate U.S. culture. This change in public mood was the result of conscious activity by concerned citizens—activists, artists, people in all walks of life—who became alarmed about the threat of nuclear war and made a commitment to work for peaceful alternatives. In the realm of public opinion, attitudes do not evolve simply on their own but are a response to "real world events." Many of these events and the accompanying press coverage were the result of peace activism. The accumulated impact of thousands of activities shaped public consciousness and, in the process, created a political climate conducive to arms reduction.

Challenging the White House for control of the airwaves was and is a daunting task. The White House communications apparatus has become one of the most powerful political forces on earth. No other political institution, certainly no social movement or public interest group, can match the capability of the federal government for shaping news coverage and public opinion. The Reagan administration devoted enormous attention to communications and public relations. Operating on the theory that control of the media is essential to political power, the administration enlarged an already vast White House communications apparatus, hiring legions of pollsters, press secretaries, and media specialists. Every issue was viewed through the prism of public relations, and events and programs were explicitly staged for the purpose of gaining favorable press coverage.

Mark Hertsgaard documented the administration's manipulation of press coverage in his book *On Bended Knee*. A "line of the day" was developed each morning in the White House and was systematically fed to the press and repeated throughout the federal government.[6] Media Counselor Michael Deaver meticulously planned presidential appearances to create attractive television images. Deputy Press Secretary for Foreign Affairs Les Janka described the Reagan administration this way: "This was totally a Hollywood production. There were two Reagan presidencies. There was the Reagan rhetorical/Deaver approach, which was about 80 percent of the presidency. The other 20 percent, the reality of having to manage and run the country, sort of went along."[7] Or, as Janka told Hertsgaard, "This was a PR outfit that became President and took over the country."[8]

Even with all of its media sophistication, however, the Reagan White House was not always able to control public opinion. There are limits to the government's propaganda powers. Throughout Reagan's Hollywood presidency, for example, the "great communicator" passionately argued the case for the Nicaraguan Contras but public opinion remained firmly opposed to military aid for the so-called freedom fighters. Similarly, despite the president's criticisms of the nuclear freeze and the huge public relations counteroffensive mounted by the White House, the American people continued to favor the call for a mutual halt to the arms race by margins of 70 percent or more. Through creative uses of the media and with the support of prominent cultural heroes and celebrities, the peace movement managed to hold its own against the communications power of the White House and on occasion even gained the upper hand.

Hollywood for SANE

One of the reasons Ronald Reagan was unable to win greater support for his nuclear policies was that many of his former colleagues in Hollywood went the other way and supported the peace movement. Like every other sector of society, the entertainment community was gripped by nuclear anxiety during the 1980s and responded with a surge of activism. Many of the biggest names in the television, film, and music recording industries supported the nuclear freeze and made a commitment to work for peace. The backing of media stars gave unprecedented legitimacy and recognition to the antinuclear movement and helped encourage millions of Americans to speak out.

The glamour life of Hollywood may have many attractions, but one of its drawbacks is the difficulty an artist may face in expressing his or her political commitments. It's hard to be just a normal concerned citizen when you're always the center of attention. Many stars were very committed to nuclear disarmament, but they were by no means experts on the subject and did not want to speak on it in public. They were not trained to deal with complicated questions of nuclear strategy. Their concern was more basic: Nuclear war must be prevented and the arms race stopped. Beyond that, the details didn't matter. Many artists felt passionately about these issues and as citizens wanted to make their voices heard, but how could they do so and retain credibility?

One easy but important way was to help with financial support. Hundreds of actors, producers, musicians, and industry executives contributed to antinuclear groups and raised money for the peace movement. The June 12, 1982, disarmament rally in New York's Central Park was funded in large part through benefit rock concerts held that week at the Nassau Coliseum on Long Island. In southern California, the Alliance for Survival, the largest antinuclear group in the region, received much of its financial support from "Survival Sunday" rock music festivals held each year at the Hollywood Bowl. In 1984, Freeze Voter, the electoral arm of the nuclear freeze campaign, raised more than $100,000 at a swank Hollywood reception organized by movie producer Lisa Weinstein at which Helen Caldicott and Ted Kennedy spoke. Among those attending were Sally Field, Lily Tomlin, Joanne Woodward, and Linda Gray.[9] Wealthy entertainers in Los Angeles, New York, and other major cities were constantly dunned for contributions to the peace movement, and many responded with extraordinary generosity.

One of the more visible expressions of celebrity involvement came with the revival of the old Hollywood for SANE committee in 1983. The original group, which had been formed by Steve Allen in the late 1950s and had played an important role in campaigns to end nuclear testing and prevent nuclear war, had enlisted many of the top entertainers in Hollywood—people like Robert Ryan, Harry Belafonte, Marlon Brando, Kirk Douglas, and Henry Fonda.[10] With the resurgence of SANE and the disarmament movement in the 1980s, it was only natural that the Hollywood committee be reborn. The task of organizing the group was assumed by Jimi Kaufer, a veteran writer and stage producer in her own right and a tennis partner of Norman Cousins, the original founder of SANE. Kaufer shared Cousins's deep concern about nuclear war, and when she was asked by Jim Shrider of the Greater Los Angeles SANE chapter to reactivate the Hollywood group, she readily agreed.

The first task, following the example of the earlier committee, was to release a statement of concern signed by prominent entertainers. It was decided to issue the public appeal in the trade magazine *Variety* immediately after the showing of the television film "The Day After." Kaufer and her team drafted a statement under the title "It's Still the Day Before" and began circulating it among Hollywood friends. As Kaufer recalled: "The response from the entertainers was overwhelming. I just called people on the phone and they immediately agreed to add their name and send money. There was no complaining or hesitation. People said yes right away. We raised more than $8,000 while hardly asking."[11] When the ad appeared in the December 16, 1983, issue, it contained the names of more than 250 actors, producers, writers, directors, and entertainment industry executives. Among those signing were Debra Winger, Anne Bancroft, Mel Brooks, James Earl Jones, Jack Lemmon, Dana Andrews, Ed Asner, Ralph Bellamy, Burt Lancaster, Patty Duke Astin, Tyne Daly, Shirley MacLaine, and Jean Stapleton.

Perhaps the most successful project for Hollywood SANE was the October 1984 theater production of *Handy Dandy,* a two-person, one-act play with ironic commentary on the nuclear dilemma written by William Gibson, author of *The Miracle Worker.* On the same evening in fourteen separate theaters throughout Los Angeles, twenty-eight of the leading stars of Hollywood appeared in benefit performances of *Handy Dandy* to raise money for the nuclear freeze movement. Among the performers, who also appeared at a press conference that day, were James Whitmore, Richard Dreyfuss, and Shelley Winters. The event was a media sensation in Los Angeles, and the newspapers and broadcast media were filled with stories about the Hollywood SANE production. As a result, the peace campaign received not only financial support but a great deal of favorable publicity.

Support for the antinuclear movement came not just from the older generation of stars but from younger celebrities as well. In 1987, SANE created a new program, the Filmmakers Exchange, specifically designed for the next generation of Hollywood stars. Conceived and directed by SANE Development Director Tom Seigel, the Filmmakers Exchange enlisted a dozen young actors and filmmakers to participate in a cultural exchange program with their counterparts in the Soviet Union. Among the stars involved in the project were Judd Nelson, Mary Stuart Masterson, Lisa Bonet, Esai Morales, and Helen Hunt. The October 1987 trip to Moscow and Leningrad helped educate the young entertainers on nuclear issues and U.S.-Soviet relations. The trip also generated favorable publicity for SANE and the peace movement. Articles on the project appeared in the *Los Angeles Times* and other newspapers and in such popular magazines as *People* and *Rolling Stone.* The filmmakers group was also interviewed live from Moscow for ABC's "Good Morning America" program.

Although these and other projects were successful in the short run, the hope for an enduring relationship with Hollywood stars that many in the peace movement sought never materialized. Entertainers and artists are not normally peace activists, and they usually become involved only in extreme situations. When the crisis passes, as it did for many people in the late 1980s, other issues and concerns take priority. When the threat of nuclear war diminished, celebrity involvement in peace activism declined (although many artists went on to address other issues such as hunger, human rights, AIDS, and the environment). Nonetheless, Hollywood stars were an important ally of the peace movement. The involvement of celebrities created an image of acceptability for the antinuclear cause just as the engagement of religious leaders cast a mantle of respectability. Peace was "in" during the 1980s, and it became relatively easy and even hip to support the movement. This phenomenon had its drawbacks, such as fostering a superficial or faddish involvement by some, but on balance the endorsement of stars was beneficial in building public acceptance for the peace movement.

Music and Pop Culture

Nuclear anxiety reverberated everywhere in society, including the world of rock music. Some popular musicians even became political activists. This was the case in 1982 when singer James Taylor came to the aid of the June 12 rally committee in New York. Taylor gave of his time selflessly that spring, contacting fellow musicians and arranging the performances that made the huge demonstration and its fundraising concerts a success. Many other musicians gave of their time, talent, and money during the decade as well—including Paul Simon, Bob Dylan, Gil Scott Heron, Bonnie Raitt, The Whalers, Tracy Chapman, Bruce Cockburn, Pete Seeger, and so on. In dozens of ways large and small, these artists supported the movement to end the arms race.

Musicians made perhaps their most significant contribution to peace with antinuclear lyrics. Some of the most popular groups in Europe and the United States sensitized a generation of music listeners to the threat of nuclear war. Sting, in his 1987 hit "Russians," contested Reagan's assertion that a nuclear war was winnable and challenged listeners to rethink their perceptions (or misperceptions) of Soviet people. He wrote,

There is no historical precedent
To put the words in the mouth of the president
There's no such thing as a winnable war
It's a lie we don't believe anymore
Mr. Reagan says we will protect you
I don't subscribe to that point of view
Believe me when I say to you
I hope the Russians love their children too.[12]

Sting evoked an image of Soviet culture with a human face. As he says at the end of the song,

We share the same biology
Regardless of ideology
What might save us me and you
Is that the Russians love their children too.[13]

Sting not only challenged Reagan's rhetoric but also questioned the underlying attitudes responsible for mistrust between East and West.

A number of groups joined Sting on the peace bandwagon. The 10,000 Maniacs was responsible for reviving Cat Stevens's 1960s hit "Peace Train" on their antiwar album *The Wishing Chair*. R.E.M. challenged listeners with haunting lyrics generated by their fear of nuclear and environmental threats. The song "Hyena," from their 1986 album *Life's Rich Pageant,* states ominously, "The only thing to fear is fearlessness,/the bigger the weapon, the greater the fear."[14] Midnight Oil performed at the June 11, 1988, disarmament rally in New York (a little-noticed but important event that drew more than 100,000 people on the sixth anniversary of the earlier Central Park rally). Many other examples could be cited. The point is not to suggest that rock music is politically consistent or profound but rather to show that the involvement of popular musicians reflected a general social trend, one with broad impact on culture and public attitudes.

By the end of the 1980s, antinuclear images and the message of peace had permeated American popular culture. The initiatives of peace groups and the contributions of individual artists and entertainers had made the cause of peace and U.S.-Soviet detente increasingly popular. Cold War images were beginning to ebb, and favorable perceptions of the Soviet Union, greatly aided by the rise of Gorbachev, were spreading. These changes even began to show up in television advertising. To a substantial extent, commercial advertising in U.S. culture both reflects and shapes social values. As attitudes changed during the 1980s, so did advertising images. In the early part of the decade, Soviets were depicted as KGB police thugs or fat babushkas. An early commercial for Wendy's shows a "Russian fashion show" with a rotund peasant woman wearing a potato-sack dress. She emerges in this dowdy garb first with a beach ball to model "swim-wear" and appears next in the same sack but carrying a flashlight to display "evening-wear." Such stereotypes ended with glasnost.[15] In the latter half of the 1980s, the images were very different. A Pepsi commercial in 1987 featured a Russian teenager in blue jeans—cool, friendly, and maybe even a bit hip.[16] A 1991 billboard for Pabst Blue Ribbon beer shows a picture of Gorbachev and the words: "PBR me ASAP." The use of a leader of the Soviet Union to sell beer in the United States was surely proof of a fundamental shift in popular culture. Enemy images faded, and friendship toward the Soviet Union became acceptable and even desirable. These transformations in popular culture preceded, and made possible, the policy changes later adopted in the boardrooms of Washington.

Nuclear War Comes to Television

For David Gergen and the White House communications office, the greatest challenge on nuclear policy came not from freeze rallies but from a television show. No cultural event of the 1980s had greater impact than the "The Day After." With an audience of more than 100 million viewers, the film was one of the most widely viewed programs in history.[17] Among nonsports broadcasts, it was the sixth top-rated television show of all time.[18] The impact of the show came in part because of timing. When ABC broadcasted the program on November 20, 1983, INF missiles were about to be deployed in Europe and the United States and the Soviet Union were trading bitter recriminations and military threats. The *Bulletin of Atomic Scientists* was about to move its famous doomsday clock closer to midnight, signifying one of the most frightening moments of the entire nuclear age. For many people, witnessing nuclear war on the television screen was extremely traumatic—for some, caught up in the world of the tube, perhaps more real than life itself. On that Sunday evening in November, nearly half the population of the United States sat transfixed, bound together in a communal media experience and gripped by the horror of nuclear war.

The press debate over the "The Day After" was intense. The show became a media event of historic proportions. The broadcast was preceded and followed by months of public controversy. Hundreds of press stories and talk show discussions addressed the show and its subject. For at least one of the national television networks, CBS, the film and the controversy surrounding it received more coverage than any other aspect of the nuclear debate.[19] By its very nature, this discussion benefited the peace movement because it focused attention on the number one issue—the threat of nuclear war. Many activist groups took advantage of the occasion to increase their visibility, while the Reagan administration tried to downplay the event.

Many in the White House saw the film as a genuine threat. As White House Communications Director David Gergen related: "This was one instance in which we were worried. The film gave us a lot of pause. There was a lot of feeling that it could be somehow one of those hinge events which changes a nation's mind about itself."[20] Although some in the White House criticized the communications office for overreacting ("We allowed ourselves to be panicked," said former Deputy Press Secretary Robert Sims),[21] the concern of Gergen and others was perhaps well placed. The film's graphic depictions of nuclear war certainly made it more difficult for the White House to promote the nuclear buildup or to justify concepts of limited war.[22] Gergen was sufficiently alarmed to arrange for a prebroadcast screening of the film in the White House. The audience's reaction only deepened his concern:

> I decided we ought to take a look at it with a group, to gauge how people are going to respond. We showed it over at the Old Executive Office Building one afternoon. We brought in people from State, Defense, and elsewhere and secretaries from the White House. Some of the women were crying and that sort of thing. It seemed to have a real impact on the people who would be closer to the man on the street.[23]

A special screening of the film also took place at the Pentagon, where the Joint Chiefs of Staff watched the film in stony silence. According to a psychologist who was invited to participate, the generals came away very depressed.[24] That senior government officials could become so concerned about a television show says a great deal both about the sensitivity of the nuclear issue at the time and the power of the media to influence social reality.

The Days Before and After

The making of "The Day After" was not a serendipitous event but the result of conscious decisions by writers, producers, directors, and actors who wanted to make a statement on the prevention of nuclear war. The fact that ABC also saw it as an occasion to turn a commercial profit merely reflected the widespread and intense interest in the subject. That the film survived the political buffeting to which it was subjected and actually made it on the air (after two years and the expenditure of $7 million) was a minor miracle and a tribute to the dedication and determination of those who labored to make it a reality.

One of the those who sacrificed most to bring the film to life was its director, Nicholas Meyer. As Meyer recounted in an interview, it was an experience that defined his very being:

> I was the fourth director invited to tackle this project. When I told a friend, he said now we're really going to find out who you are. I wished he hadn't said that. I realized this was now a question of whether I would simply sit at dinner parties and bitch about something or, when presented with an opportunity on a silver platter, would I push this cup away. I knew I had to do it, to define who I was. I used the same logic to convince others. How often does Hollywood allow you to put your abilities in the service of your beliefs? The answer is rarely if ever. [25]

Working on the film forced Meyer and others to confront painful political realities:

> My first impulse, which I think not only echoed the other three directors but was a microcosm of American opinion, was I don't want to poke my nose into this. It's too upsetting. That's when I became aware of the central paradox regarding the nuclear issue. Here is the most important issue that mankind has ever faced and we can't bear to think about it.[26]

The project was a grueling emotional experience as well. Meyer reported that the cast was prone to having nightmares, which they dubbed "nukemares." A kind of gallows humor developed to ease the tension: "We would make jokes like, wouldn't it be great if there was a nuclear holocaust now—so we could get some great stock footage. It was the only way to keep sane."[27]

To help the filmmakers understand nuclear issues, ABC hired Los Angeles physician Timothy Hayes as a special consultant. A leader of Physicians for Social Responsibility in California, Hayes was an acknowledged expert on the medical and psychological impact of nuclear war. He had also been a principal organizer of the PSR nuclear war conference held at UCLA in October 1981 and was producer of a documentary film from the conference, *The Race to Oblivion: The Medical Consequences of Nuclear Weapons and Nuclear War.* Hayes was called in during the early stages of the project and worked with the producers through seven rewrites of the script. He recalled: "From the outset I was very clear with them. I said I will not be part of anything that tries to fictionalize the prospects of nuclear war by suggesting that society could bounce back quickly. We talked about the problem of illusions, and they agreed that we do not wish to promote illusions."[28]

Fulfilling these intentions was not easy, however. From the earliest drafts of the script right up to the last-minute editing before broadcast, the producers were subjected to powerful political pressures from the network, the military, and the White House. An example is the struggle over the reference to electromagnetic pulse (EMP). EMP is the powerful electromagnetic wave arising from a nuclear detonation that would knock out all solid-state electronics and therefore incapacitate communications. Hayes insisted it was necessary to depict the phenomenon and the chaos it would induce, while network officials claimed that the concept was not scientifically proven. Hayes said, "I would call scientists like Kosta Tsipis, and he would say, yes we're sure EMP will happen. Then ABC would produce a physicist who would say, no it won't. We went back and forth like this for weeks."[29] In the end, the reference to EMP remained in the show.

Pentagon officials had initially agreed to cooperate with ABC on the project, but they changed their minds when they saw the script. The original agreement, according to Hayes, was for ABC to film the scenes of a missile silo at a U.S. Air Force base. After reviewing the script, however, the Pentagon wrote to ABC expressing displeasure with the network's approach. Civil defense should be portrayed in a better light, the Pentagon suggested. The producers refused to sanitize the script, though, agreeing with Hayes that civil defense is an illusion. This was not just a matter of artistic purity, for the cost to ABC of constructing a silo mock-up if the Air Force backed out would be $100,000. When the producers refused to give in, the Pentagon withdrew its offer. As Hayes put it, "They took their silo and went home."[30] ABC had to shell out the extra $100,000.

The White House also went into what David Gergen described as "a defensive reaction." Gergen's office made calls to ABC with suggestions for cuts and script changes. These were echoed by *National Review* editor William F. Buckley, who editorialized against the film in his weekly column. Of particular concern was a passage in the script in which a Pershing II missile is being moved forward in Europe in the political crisis that leads to war. With public anxiety about the deployment of INF missiles already at fever pitch, administration officials labeled the passage provocative and insisted that it be dropped. In the end the offending line about the Pershing II missiles was deleted.[31] Director Meyer confirmed that last-minute changes were made: "They censored it. Changes were made in the final editing phase, although I don't know for sure if they were in reaction to the calls of Gergen. The movie barely made it on the air."[32]

Reagan administration officials not only tried to edit the film, they demanded the opportunity to respond on the air. As Gergen noted, "We went to the networks and sought a chance to put a spokesman on."[33] The person selected by the administration was Secretary of State George Shultz, who appeared immediately after the show's conclusion. As Gergen observed, "Many people thought Shultz was terribly soporific, but I think he was reassuring."[34] Also beneficial to administration policy was a Ted Koppel roundtable discussion that ABC aired after Shultz's appearance. The Koppel roundtable was ABC's own form of "spin control" to dampen the concerns about nuclear war raised by the film.[35] The all-male panel consisted of former national security officials Henry Kissinger, Robert McNamara, and Brent Scowcroft, along with William F. Buckley, Elie Wiesel, and Carl Sagan. Kissinger set the tone for the discussion when he labeled the film "simpleminded," and others joined him in downplaying the threat of nuclear war. Sagan gamely tried to point out that the film's depictions were actually understated, since the prospects of nuclear winter, just then being discovered in scientific research, were not even mentioned, but he was overshadowed by the others. When a member of the invited audience (Charlie Kraybill of the national SANE staff) finally brought up the issue of the nuclear freeze forty-five minutes into the discussion, Kissinger dismissed it out of hand. No wonder that David Gergen later described the Koppel roundtable as "very helpful."[36]

While the Reagan administration tried to quiet the storm raised by "The Day After," peace groups sought to fan the flames of controversy and took advantage of the opportunity to urge greater public involvement in the fight for disarmament. In dozens of communities around the country, local groups placed spokespersons on talk shows and arranged panel discussions about the film. In some places, vigils and demonstrations were held. In Lawrence, Kansas, where the film was set and much of the filming took place, the local peace coalition held a candlelight vigil attended by more than 1,000 people. On the national level, philanthropist and political maverick Stewart Mott created a special organization that gave concerned viewers an opportunity to call a toll-free number and receive a packet of information on what to do to help prevent nuclear war. Mott's 800 number received more than 75,000 calls.

In the days immediately following the broadcast, pollsters questioned viewers to see if their opinions were altered as a result of the film. The initial findings suggested that little had changed. But these quick response surveys tended to miss the deeper impact of the film. By evoking and visualizing the reality of nuclear war more graphically than it had ever been done before, "The Day After" made the nuclear threat dramatically concrete. This heightened awareness did not translate into immediate political results, but over the long run the film turned out to be an important event in awakening public consciousness. Nicholas Meyer's appreciation of his work's impact crystallized only several years later:

> During Ronald Reagan's meeting with Mikhail Gorbachev to sign the INF Treaty, someone wrote to me saying, don't think your movie didn't have something to do with that, because it did. I realized the person was right. The film didn't change things immediately, but it did gradually alter the climate. Whether Ronald Reagan was affected personally or was just reacting as a politician to a change in the political climate, I don't know. "The Day After" was a catalyst. It broke the ice. This was the most worthwhile thing I did with my life.[37]

6
Peace Opinion

Democracy and Public Opinion

Does public opinion shape government policy, or do political leaders manipulate public attitudes? Did public opposition to nuclear arms during the 1980s influence the direction of White House policy, or was the administration able to parry these concerns and win support for its agenda? In this chapter, I examine the relationship between public opinion and nuclear policy and how this was affected by citizen activism.

The classic democratic model assumes that elected representatives reflect the views of their constituents and that when public views change, as reflected in opinion polls, the representative adapts policy accordingly. The entrepreneurial model, associated with economist Joseph Schumpeter, asserts that the public does not have definitive opinions but instead chooses among policies or perspectives offered by competing "entrepreneur" politicians. This view is similar to that of Walter Lippman, who saw public opinion as the approval or rejection of already formulated options. The entrepreneurial model suggests that politicians lead public opinion, while the democratic model implies that they follow. In fact, both processes occur. Politicians do indeed formulate options for voter opinion (social movements can also serve this function), but the public can accept or reject these plans and can occasionally develop independent ideas. Public opinion can be considered both input and output to the policy process.[1]

Some analysts argue that ruling elites create and dominate public opinion to suit their purposes. C. Wright Mills wrote that the state apparatus makes decisions and then uses the media to legitimate them.[2] Noam Chomsky and Edward Hermann asserted that governments "manufacture consent" and manipulate public opinion to win approval of their policies.[3] These studies provide important insights into the degree of elite control over news coverage and public opinion, but, as Charlotte Ryan observed in *Prime Time Activism*,[4] they are overly pessimistic. Despite the attempts of governments and corporations to dictate public thinking, pressures from below can sometimes break through the dominant frame and play an important role in political decision making.

In fact, although political leaders do indeed try to control public opinion, scholarly evidence suggests that public opinion more often influences policy than the other way around. The pioneering studies of Benjamin Page and Robert Shapiro, for example, show that public opinion frequently influences the development of public policy. Their examination of hundreds of polls dating back to 1935 shows a marked pattern of changes in public opinion reflected in subsequent policy shifts.[5] As the scholars concluded in an important article on the subject, "Public opinion does in fact have substantial proximate effects on policy-making in the United States."[6] Page and Shapiro noted that "policy tends to move in the same direction as public opinion most often when the opinion change is large and when it is stable—that is, not reversed by fluctuations. Similarly, policy congruence is higher on salient issues than non-salient issues."[7]

Public opinion may shape policy generally, but does it influence the determination of foreign policy specifically? Some contend that the American people are not well informed on foreign policy issues and thus cannot make knowledgeable judgments.[8] James Rosenau suggested that the "mass public" is ill-informed and lacks a consistent opinion on foreign policy matters.[9] Yet Page and Shapiro argued that Americans have developed their foreign policy beliefs "in a rational fashion" and that these beliefs deserve "serious consideration in deliberation about the direction and content of U.S. foreign policy."[10] In their major study of public opinion and national security policy, Bruce Russett and Thomas Graham likewise concluded that public beliefs can indeed influence decision making on foreign and military policy. As Russett and Graham stated, "Any interpretation holding that public opinion does not affect policy is clearly and seriously an exaggeration."[11]

Political leaders act as if they believe that public opinion is essential. In recent decades, the White House has hired increasing legions of pollsters and media specialists to interpret and control public attitudes. The Reagan administration was particularly obsessed with these matters, and the actor-president and his handlers approached nearly every issue from the perspective of how it would affect public opinion. Richard Beal, the first director of the White House Office of Planning and Evaluation, an agency created to track and analyze public opinion, succinctly captured the Reagan administration's philosophy of governance in a 1984 presentation before the American Academy of Political and Social Science: "Opinion polls are at the core of presidential decision-making."[12] Beal's White House assistant, Ronald Hinckley, confirmed that popular attitudes affect foreign policy: "Public opinion does … influence national security policy decisions. … Foreign policy and political rhetoric are adjusted and even made on the basis of what the polls say."[13] According to Beal and Hinckley, information from opinion polls was discussed in more than half the senior staff meetings in the Reagan White House.[14] The president's top pollster, Richard Wirthlin, met with Reagan more than twenty-five times during the first year and a half of his presidency and delivered more than forty reports on public opinion trends and how to address them. A "public opinion digest" was regularly circulated to senior White House staff, and summaries of major news media stories and polls were constantly made available to the president and his top advisers. As Beal and Hinckley have noted, public opinion was extremely influential within the Reagan administration, far more so than conventionally assumed.[15] The president and his advisers were closely attuned to the shifting winds of public opinion.

A "Sea Change" in Public Thinking

What did Reagan administration officials see as they peered out over the U.S. political landscape in the 1980s? Unfortunately for the White House, the tide of support for arms expansion that helped carry Reagan into office quickly dissipated. By the end of the president's first year in office, public attitudes were shifting against White House policy. According to White House Counselor Michael Deaver, "When Reagan came into office there was an overwhelming majority of Americans that supported his strong defense policies. That changed in about a year and a half."[16] Deputy Press Secretary for Foreign Affairs Robert Sims offered a similar assessment: "There was a lot of momentum at the beginning. But public opinion turned around in '82 and '83 on arms control issues, and it turned around in '84 on defense budget issues."[17]

A sharp rise in concern about nuclear war was creating political opposition to the administration's military policies. Surveys found a huge jump in the percentage of people fearing nuclear war.[18] According to a Gallup poll of September 1981, 70 percent of those surveyed felt that nuclear war was a real possibility and 30 percent felt that the chances of such a conflict were "good" or "certain."[19] The shift in public opinion on military spending issues was also quite dramatic. According to a CBS/*New York Times* poll, the percentage of people supporting an increase in military spending dropped from 61 percent in January 1981 to 16 percent in February 1985. During the same period, the percentage favoring a cut in military spending rose from 7 percent to 30 percent.[20]

Perhaps the most extensive study of voter opinion on nuclear policy during the 1980s was conducted by Daniel Yankelovich for the Public Agenda Foundation.[21] According to the Yankelovich analysis, "A great change ... has transformed the outlook of the American electorate." Yankelovich found the public "determined to stop what they see as the drift toward nuclear confrontation" and eager for "more dramatic and far-reaching arms control policies."[22] This change was marked most significantly by a widespread public recognition that the chances of surviving a nuclear war are extremely low. Whereas in 1955, only 27 percent of the public thought humankind would be destroyed in an all-out nuclear war, in 1984 those agreeing that both the United States and the Soviet Union would be completely destroyed stood at 89 percent.[23] Other studies found similar results: In 1961, 43 percent of the population thought the chances of surviving a nuclear war were "poor," but by 1984 this percentage had risen to 77 percent.[24] As Yankelovich concluded, "Americans have experienced a serious change of heart about the impact of nuclear weapons on national security."[25]

The Yankelovich study found the public specifically rejecting the Reagan administration policy of applying military pressure to force political concessions from the Soviets. Whereas 50 percent of the public agreed that the United States would be safer if it spent more time negotiating with the Soviet Union and less time building up military forces, only 22 percent did not agree, and 62 percent rejected the idea of building more dangerous nuclear weapons to get the Soviet Union to make concessions.[26] Other polls showed a similar rejection of the Reagan administration philosophy. The Gallup poll of December 1983, for example, found 47 percent of the public agreeing that the Reagan military buildup had brought the United States "closer to war" rather than "closer to peace," with only 28 percent disagreeing.[27]

While the Yankelovich study found strong public opposition to the Reagan administration's arms policies, it also found the public deeply suspicious of the Soviet Union. For example, 61 percent of those questioned in the 1984 survey agreed that the Soviets "lie, cheat, and steal." However, the desire for arms limitation overrode these concerns. The ABC/*Washington Post* poll of January 1985 found 76 percent of the public agreeing that the United States should negotiate an arms agreement even if there is risk that the Soviets will cheat. Former White House Communications Chief David Gergen, among others, found this result startling.[28] It is noteworthy that this preference for arms limitation agreements with Moscow was measured prior to the rise of Mikhail Gorbachev.

Perhaps most troubling for the Reagan administration was the overwhelming public support for the nuclear freeze. Throughout the 1980s, public opinion surveys consistently found Americans strongly endorsing the freeze. From the first moment pollsters began asking about the proposal, popular support stood at 70 percent or more. According to Yankelovich, the idea of a nuclear freeze "has been supported by upwards of 75 percent of the public for several years."[29] One survey from the National Opinion Research Center put the figure at 86 percent.[30] Richard Wirthlin confirmed that "support for an agreement to freeze testing, production, and deployment looked very strong." When White House pollsters asked people if they supported the proposal "despite the problem we may have in verifying such actions," 74 percent said yes.[31] This support for the freeze cut across all classes and political philosophies. Even those who had voted for Ronald Reagan favored the freeze by a wide margin.[32]

Freeze Support: Shallow and Deep

It was sometimes said about the nuclear freeze that support was "a mile wide but an inch deep."[33] Large majorities claimed to support the freeze, but few people had a clear understanding of the complexities of the arms race or the implications of attempting to end it. Pollsters confirmed that support for the specific details of the freeze was soft and that opinions varied greatly as qualifications or conditions were added. The Lou Harris organization found as much as a 69 percent variance in public opinion toward the freeze when other considerations were mentioned. Analyses by Mark Melman and Ed Lazarus of Information Associates found similar results. When issues of verifiability or possible Soviet cheating were raised, support for the freeze tended to decline. Some voters even mistakenly believed that Ronald Reagan was in favor of the freeze.[34]

What the freeze lacked in specificity, though, it more than made up in intensity. Although much of the public backing for the freeze was soft, the peace movement in the 1980s also enjoyed an important reservoir of hardcore support. In 1984, Stan Greenberg of The Analysis Group conducted a study of nuclear freeze sentiment to determine the depth of peace support.[35] By examining how freeze supporters felt about such issues as military spending and the war in Central America, Greenberg attempted to define the degree of "intense support"—that is, the percentage of people who understood and supported the full range of peace movement positions. Greenberg estimated this hardcore peace support at about 20 percent of the public. These were the people, Greenberg estimated, who might be willing to join and support a peace organization.

Greenberg's findings were extremely important from an organizational development and fundraising perspective. They showed that one in five Americans was a strong freeze supporter and might be willing to join or contribute to a peace movement organization. This meant that the peace movement had a strong popular base within U.S. society during the 1980s and that the potential for recruiting members and raising money was significant. In the context of classic resource mobilization theory, the peace movement enjoyed fertile ground for planting the seeds of organizational growth. It was precisely this realization that prompted SANE and other groups to set up canvasing programs and intensify fundraising and membership development efforts (although this was done more on the basis of intuition than the kind of scholarly analysis offered by Greenberg). As a result of these efforts, at least some of the public's support for ending the arms race was translated into organized political pressure and institutional clout. It was this organized peace constituency that came to play a key role in mobilizing political opposition to the MX, SDI, and other Reagan administration policies.

The Democrats Blow the Issue

Former Reagan administration officials have contended that, because the nuclear freeze had little impact on national elections, it had no influence on policy. Michael Deaver observed that "the freeze was never a big issue" politically.[36] Deputy Press Secretary Les Janka said, "On the level of popular politics there was some influence from the freeze, but on the level of electoral politics there was very little."[37] It is true that despite the popularity of the freeze and the widespread public doubt about White House nuclear policies, the peace movement was unable to challenge Reagan electorally. In part, this is because national elections are usually determined by domestic economic concerns, not peace issues.[38] Pocketbook issues are usually more immediate to voters than nuclear policy or the threat of war.

Nonetheless, the 1984 presidential election might have been one of those occasions when nuclear policy could have significantly influenced the political outcome. As the electoral season approached, Peter Hart, pollster for Democratic contender Walter Mondale, conducted a survey of nuclear issues among voters in Illinois.[39] The results confirmed the deepening public unease over the administration's nuclear policies and revealed a striking vulnerability in Reagan's re-election drive. Fifty percent of the voters agreed that White House policy had brought the country closer to war than to peace whereas 29 percent disagreed. By a 2-1 margin, voters felt that Reagan had not done enough to pursue peace and arms control. Fifty percent felt that the world was less safe in 1984 than it had been in 1980, with 22 percent disagreeing.[40] Herein lay an important avenue of challenge for the Democratic candidate. Just as Reagan had asked voters in 1980 whether they were better off then than they were four years ago, Mondale could ask, Are you safer now than you were four years ago? If the Democrats exploited the public concern about nuclear war, perhaps they could defeat the incumbent president and regain the White House.

Administration officials worried about the nuclear issue. As Michael Deaver recounted, this was a "big negative" going into the 1984 campaign:

> There were some polls showing the president vulnerable on war and peace issues. This was in relation to Walter Mondale. So in planning our television for the campaign, we had a two-track system. In the spring we started off with feel-good stuff, "It's morning again in America." Then we

had back-ups, including the bear-in-the-woods commercial, to use if Mondale pressed. After the first debate, we saw some slippage on the defense issue, and after much debate within the campaign we aired the bear ad.[41]

The Democrats failed to capitalize on the issue, however, and let the president's vulnerability pass unchallenged. Deaver continued: "The Mondale people didn't understand that they had to ride an issue for several weeks in order for it to damage somebody. They spent three or four days on the defense issue and then went on to something else. So we took the bear ad off the air and went back to morning in America."[42]

Many activists in the freeze movement hoped that the Democrats would offer a genuine alternative to Reagan administration policy. In January 1984, candidate Mondale had met with leaders of the Freeze Campaign, SANE, and other peace groups and made fulsome promises of his devotion to the freeze.[43] Not only Mondale but Senator Gary Hart, the Reverend Jesse Jackson, and other Democratic contenders pledged their support for the freeze and a variety of peace movement proposals, including a moratorium on nuclear testing. Mondale was the front-runner, though, and his campaign received the greatest support. Many freeze activists believed the candidate's promises and worked for his campaign.

Once the primaries were over, however, the promises of the spring were forgotten. Peace positions were jettisoned, and the campaign began to backpedal on the freeze. Instead of urging a halt to the arms race, Mondale proposed a 3 percent a year increase in the rate of military spending. At the 1984 Democratic Convention in San Francisco, the Mondale campaign mobilized to defeat an amendment introduced by Jesse Jackson in favor of no-first-use of nuclear weapons. SANE and other peace groups worked with the Jackson campaign to support this proposal, but the official representatives of the Freeze Campaign in San Francisco initially were unwilling to buck the Mondale organization. Mondale and the Democratic leaders also rejected a Jackson campaign amendment urging a cut in the military budget. It became apparent that Mondale had used the freeze movement and thousands of its volunteers to win the nomination, but that his campaign had no intention of actually adopting the freeze message.

One of those disappointed by the Mondale campaign's performance was David Johnson, a vice president for the New York advertising firm

BBD&O and an occasional volunteer for the Nuclear Weapons Freeze Campaign. Johnson said, "I did a poster on the freeze for the Mondale/Ferraro campaign. At the top was a great big headline saying 'They Invented a Machine That Can End the Nuclear Arms Race.' In the middle was a photo of a voting machine, and at the bottom it read, 'Pull for the Freeze. Vote Mondale/Ferraro.'"[44] Johnson's ad ran for a while in Maryland and won acclaim within the advertising industry. It received the Clio award that year as the top print ad for a political candidate. The Mondale campaign was unimpressed, though, and failed to pick up on the theme, much to Johnson's dismay: "It was such an obvious connection to make. People supported the freeze, so just connect that with your candidate. I thought the Democrats totally blew the issue."[45]

The Reagan administration, meanwhile, toned down its bellicose rhetoric and portrayed itself as the guardian of peace. The president repeatedly pledged during the campaign to secure arms reduction and talked of his commitment to serious bargaining with the Soviets. Just a few weeks before the election, the White House convened a highly visible meeting between the president and Soviet Foreign Minister Andrei Gromyko. Promising summit meetings and arms negotiations with the Soviets, Reagan swept to a landslide victory.

A similar drama was played out by the Democratic party in 1988. Once again, the Democratic front-runner, Governor Michael Dukakis, pledged his support for the freeze and attracted the support of many peace activists. This time, however, the Jackson campaign attracted an equal or greater number of peace activists—in part because of Jackson's consistent support for the peace movement over the years. Once again, the Democratic nominee began backpedaling on earlier peace commitments as soon as the primaries were over. Once again, at the Democratic Convention the candidate and the party leadership campaigned against no-first-use and reduced military spending proposals. Perhaps the low point of the Atlanta Convention in 1988 came when Representative Ed Markey, the earliest congressional sponsor of the freeze, gave a speech urging delegates to vote against an amendment calling for no-first-use of nuclear weapons. When Dukakis was challenged during the general campaign for having once supported the freeze (Bush called it "unilateral"), the candidate made no attempt to respond or correct the vice president's distortions. In the face of the Dukakis campaign's eerie silence, SANE/Freeze acted on its own to place an ad in the

New York Times setting the record straight. The October 25 ad bore the headline, "Mr. Bush, Read Our Lips: The Freeze Means Both Sides."

Perhaps the Democrats couldn't have defeated Reagan in 1984 or Bush in 1988 under any circumstances, but they failed to exploit one of the main weaknesses of Reagan/Bush policy and thereby lost an opportunity to gain an advantage. No wonder that David Gergen and other White House officials were comforted by the lack of Democratic party support for the freeze: "You had the Nunns and Aspins and others who simply weren't going to join up. That made it a hell of a lot easier for the administration."[46] Contrary to what some have suggested, Mondale's rout in 1984 was not a defeat for the peace movement or a popular rejection of the nuclear freeze. A genuine peace alternative was never presented to the voters. The Democrats let the nuclear issue slip away.

Making News and Shaping Opinion

Scholarly studies confirm that public opinion is greatly influenced by news media coverage. This seems only logical, since people receive most of their information about political issues from the media and form their opinions based on this knowledge. In their 1987 study for the American Political Science Association, Benjamin Page and Robert Shapiro reported that "news variables alone account for nearly half the variance in opinion change."[47] By applying statistical analyses to the various influences on public opinion, Page and Shapiro were able to isolate news media coverage as the dominant factor influencing subsequent changes in public opinion. They stated: "We have had striking success at finding out what moves public opinion," that is, media coverage.[48] These findings confirmed a 1985 study by Roy Behr and Shanto Iyengar that also found news media coverage to be the major determinant of public opinion. As Behr and Iyengar concluded, "Longitudinal studies of agenda-setting ... find that changes in the level of media attention do indeed produce changes in public concern for national issues."[49]

If news media coverage accounts for change in public opinion, what factors determine news media coverage? Do reporters and media executives make up stories on their own, or are they in turn responding to what Behr and Iyengar called "real world events"? Although some critics believe that reporters and media executives do indeed fabricate the news and distort reality (some right wingers still argue that Walter

Cronkite caused the United States to lose the war in Vietnam through his biased news coverage), others believe that in most cases reporters merely respond to the world around them. Certainly news professionals have political opinions, and their biases inevitably shape how stories are presented. However biased reporters may be, though, they cannot simply make up reports when there are no corresponding real-world events. Behr and Iyengar concluded that news coverage is affected not by changes in public opinion but by actual events and conditions.[50] The analyses of Page and Shapiro likewise confirm that objective events determine news coverage and public opinion.[51] Real-world events are the essential first link in the chain of causation.

During the 1980s, the peace movement was responsible for creating many of the events that prompted news media coverage. A review of newspaper and television news coverage by Tufts University professor David Meyer shows a dramatic increase in the number of stories on nuclear war protest in the early years of the decade.[52] The *New York Times* Index showed a sharp rise in press coverage of the freeze in early 1982, with coverage peaking in June 1982 at the time of the Central Park rally. Listings on peace activity in the *Readers Guide to Periodical Literature* reached a peak in November of 1982, and coverage on network television peaked at the end of 1983. An illustration of these trends, drawn from Meyer's work, is presented in Figure 6.1.

The reports about the freeze and antinuclear protest that dominated news coverage in 1982 and 1983 often took precedence over other important issues. One study shows that in 1982, a year of severe economic recession in the United States, network television reported more studies on nuclear war issues than on unemployment.[53] This trend did not just occur in major newspapers and network television. At every level of society, from popular magazines to scholarly journals and even local broadcasts, reports and articles about nuclear war issues and the freeze movement were pervasive. Wherever one looked, the debate over nuclear policy dominated public discourse.

What caused this sudden and dramatic public preoccupation with peace and nuclear war issues? What real-world events sparked the avalanche of news stories and reports about the nuclear threat? Some have argued that the major factor was the Reagan military buildup and the administration's alarming rhetoric about winnable nuclear war and confrontation with the Soviets. Certainly the statements of the new administration played a role in intensifying the public debate. But the

FIGURE 6.1   News Coverage of Nuclear Weapons Protest, 1979–1985

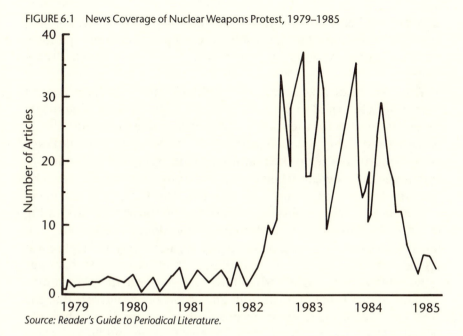

Source: *Reader's Guide to Periodical Literature.*

majority of stories were not on the administration's policies but on the political opposition to them. It was not the military buildup itself, but the sharp public reaction to it that generated most of the news coverage. The intensive public debate resulted primarily from the unprecedented wave of public opposition.

A closer look at specific news stories confirms this. The Catholic bishops' pastoral letter drew thirty-two *New York Times* stories between October 1982 and May 1983, nine of them on the front page.[54] There were many articles about the NATO decision to deploy missiles in Europe, for example, but there were many more stories about the political opposition to that policy and the massive public protests it sparked. A few stories appeared about the MX missile itself, but the vast majority of articles focused on resistance to the missile in Congress and local communities. An analysis of 120 MX articles that appeared in the *New York Times* in 1982 confirms this pattern: Fifty-three were prompted by the MX opposition and the debate in Congress, twenty-eight reported on the administration's response to the opposition, and twenty-one were editorials or commentaries on the political debate. Only eighteen stories were on the missile itself. Without the political opposition generated by the peace movement, the deployment of INF or MX missiles, or even the military buildup itself, would have occasioned periodic news stories but nothing like the massive coverage that actually resulted.

This pattern of peace movement–initiated press coverage is most pronounced in regard to the nuclear freeze itself. The idea of a nuclear freeze, the very words themselves, were entirely due to the initiative of peace activists. They did not exist outside the peace movement. Peace groups put the freeze on the political agenda and made it a subject of extensive public debate. Their activities inspired thousands of articles and broadcasts. Prior to the Call to Halt the Arms Race, there had never been a news story or a public opinion survey on the freeze.[55] Beginning in 1981, the nuclear freeze was suddenly mentioned everywhere, millions of people were voting on the proposal, and the White House was actively campaigning against it. All of this attention and news coverage came in response to the initiative of the peace movement, to the simple but radical idea brought forth from grass-roots peace activists that the arms race should be stopped on both sides. As Pam Solo rightly observed, "The freeze was a dazzling success at raising public awareness and at setting the terms of the debate."[56]

A comparison of the 1980s with earlier periods in the arms race makes the agenda-setting power of the freeze movement all the more striking. Previous missile buildups had occurred in Europe and the United States without generating either protests or major news coverage. The deployment of 1,000 Minuteman missiles by the Kennedy and Johnson administrations in the 1960s, for example, was much larger than anything proposed during the 1980s, and yet little protest or news coverage resulted. The only comparable stories to generate news interest of such magnitude were the 1961–1962 Berlin and Cuban missile crises, when the world seemed on the brink of nuclear war, and the Soviets' explosion of the H-bomb in the early 1950s. In these cases, though, world events caused the rise in news interest. In the 1980s, it was the peace movement itself that generated interest.

The pattern of opinion polling during the 1980s confirms the intensity of public interest. The *Journal of Social Issues* published an important study of opinion polls in 1983 that showed an unprecedented increase in the number of survey items on nuclear issues. The number of such surveys in 1982 greatly surpassed that in any previous year.[57] What accounted for this increased attention to nuclear issues? Accord-

FIGURE 6.2   The Pattern of Influence

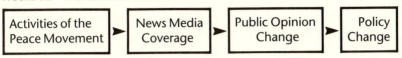

| Activities of the Peace Movement | ➤ | News Media Coverage | ➤ | Public Opinion Change | ➤ | Policy Change |

ing to the study, it "coincides with an upsurge in nuclear-related political activity in the West: a nuclear freeze movement together with various anti-nuclear demonstrations."[58] The authors of the study attempted to correlate this increase with changed world conditions, as they had been able to do with previous surges in polling activity, but found that "no single current nuclear-related event appears to account for this increase."[59] The cause for the increase in public attention was not policy but the massive political opposition it generated.

The peace movement did indeed have a major impact on public opinion. Strong political opposition to the nuclear buildup created significant news coverage, which led to greater public awareness and a shift in public opinion. Public opinion, in turn, created pressure on the Reagan administration to moderate its policies. The pattern of influence is depicted in Figure 6.2. Of course, the flow was not always in one direction. There were feedback loops, and major changes in government policy (such as the announcement of the SDI program) could reverse the sequence. Nonetheless, for much of the 1980s the initiatives of the peace movement set the pattern for and significantly influenced news media coverage, public opinion, and ultimately government policy.

7

Accommodation: The Reagan Administration's Response to the Freeze

In reaction to the June 12 disarmament rally in New York's Central Park in 1982, Defense Secretary Caspar Weinberger said that the rally would have no effect on administration policy.[1] Weinberger's reaction was similar to that of Richard Nixon thirteen years earlier during the Vietnam War. When demonstrators amassed near the White House in November 1969, the president claimed to be unfazed and said he had watched football on television throughout the protest. In his 1978 memoirs, however, Nixon admitted that the Vietnam antiwar movement, particularly the moratorium rallies in the fall of 1969, had an important impact on military policy.[2] The presence of millions of people in the streets that fall prevented Nixon from carrying out his plan for further military escalation in Vietnam.[3] Historian Mel Small has shown in his important study, *Johnson, Nixon and the Doves,* that the peace movement "had significant impact on the Vietnam policies of Johnson and Nixon."[4]

Was the same thing true in the 1980s? Did the peace movement influence the direction of White House policy, or were the president and his advisers unaffected by public pressure? Certainly the Reagan administration was acutely aware of the freeze movement. The president's pollsters and political analysts closely tracked the growing antinuclear ferment. "There was a growing awareness in the White House of the nuclear issue, particularly the nuclear freeze question,"[5] according to former Director of Public Affairs Michael Baroody. Richard Wirthlin, chief White House pollster and strategist, added questions about nuclear policy to his frequent polls and included analyses about how to handle the issue in his regular meetings with the president. The administration was paying attention to the freeze movement, according to Wirthlin: "We were measuring it. It was a consideration. It did assist in determining the basic paradigm that Americans really did seek a way to reduce tensions."[6]

In the National Security Council, the State Department, and elsewhere in the administration, pressures from the burgeoning peace movement became a mounting concern. While some in the White House discounted the freeze, arguing that peace activists had already voted against the president and would be unlikely to support him in the future, others worried that freeze support might reach into the mainstream.[7] Eventually, it was agreed that a counteroffensive was necessary. As chief speech writer Aram Bakshian put it, "There was a highly active, highly organized campaign on the left that was being waged and you couldn't just sit back and let them have the initiative."[8]

Attacking the Freeze

By early 1982, the White House was moving toward a multifaceted effort to contain nuclear freeze sentiment and preserve support for the president's military buildup.[9] The administration's response came at several levels—communications strategy, presidential rhetoric, and ultimately, in the substance of arms control policy.

The initial public relations campaign against the freeze was coordinated through the offices of Deputy Assistant for National Security Affairs Robert McFarlane. McFarlane described this effort in an interview with author Mark Hertsgaard:

> I got communications and policy people from State, Defense, and the White House in a room. ... I said every deputy assistant secretary and above had to spend four days in one of these 14 media markets in the next 60 days or report to me why not. And at each stop, if you're in Atlanta, in these four days, you had to do a *minimum* of [a] meeting with a [newspaper] editorial board, a drive-time talk show, a meeting with a civic club and a speech in a campus setting. ... By late 82 we ended up with about 600 appearances by somebody at the DAS [deputy assistant secretary] level or above.[10]

This White House communications blitz was a massive effort. An organization seeking to replicate such a campaign would have to spend hundreds of thousands of dollars for travel and publicity services. Most of the White House public relations visits were targeted to states with freeze referenda. A report from the *St. Louis Post-Dispatch* found that nearly three-quarters of the speaking trips and associated events by State Department personnel took place in states or cities where the nuclear freeze was on the ballot.[11]

The administration's campaign completely overmatched the meager efforts of the freeze movement. The Nuclear Freeze Clearing House in St. Louis had no full-time press officer, and few of the state and local campaigns had media budgets. Only in California, thanks to the fundraising efforts of Harold Willens and the campaign management of Bill Zimmerman, did freeze forces mount a modest media campaign, but even here the counteroffensive of the White House far surpassed the efforts of the peace movement. In view of the intensity of the administration's public relations effort, it is remarkable that freeze referenda nonetheless won in so many states and cities. The fact that they did is testimony both to the appeal of the idea itself and to the widespread public concern about the threat of nuclear war.

Some of the administration's critique of the freeze was substantive— for example, questioning whether such an agreement could be verified—but much of it was based on distortion and lies. Administration spokespersons repeatedly claimed that activists wanted a unilateral freeze aimed only at U.S. weapons—this despite constant reminders by peace leaders that the proposal required a halt to both U.S. and Soviet nuclear weapons. Right-wing groups and administration officials also charged that the freeze movement was Soviet-controlled and even Soviet-funded.[12] These charges were first raised by organizations like the Heritage Foundation and Jerry Falwell's so-called Moral Majority. *Reader's Digest* ran a series of anti-freeze articles in 1982, claiming, among other things, that "the KGB has induced millions upon millions of honorable, patriotic, and sensible people who detest communist tyranny to make common cause with the Soviet Union."[13] President Reagan himself joined the red-baiting campaign. Citing *Reader's Digest* as his source, the president asserted in an October 4, 1982, speech before an Ohio veterans' group, and in comments with reporters afterward, that the freeze was "inspired not by the sincere honest people who want peace, but by some who want the weakening of America and so are manipulating honest people and sincere people."[14]

For the record, it is important to emphasize that the nuclear freeze movement was made in America, not Moscow. The administration claimed that the Soviet Union was manipulating the U.S. peace movement, but in fact the influence was often in the other direction. The peace movement brought forth a number of proposals during the 1980s that the Soviet Union eventually adopted (see Chapter 12). The administration's attempts to red-bait the peace movement didn't stick. Millions of Americans were themselves active in the new freeze movement, and they knew from personal experience that this was an authentic expression of grass-roots populism deeply rooted in American culture and politics. No one could believe, for example, that the U.S. Catholic bishops, or more than 200 members of Congress, or dozens of former government officials like CIA Director William Colby were dupes of the Soviet Union. The movement had too broad a base of support to be so easily discredited.

"Angling" the Rhetoric

Although the Reagan administration tried to club the nuclear freeze movement, it also employed the velvet approach. In addition to attacking and discrediting the peace movement, the White House sought to co-opt and appropriate part of its message. The result was a conscious effort within the administration to tone down the belligerent rhetoric emanating from Washington and offer soothing reassurances for a public increasingly worried about nuclear war. Beginning in 1982 and continuing throughout its remaining years in office, the Reagan administration downplayed its radical right-wing philosophy and emphasized instead the traditional policies of arms control and U.S.-Soviet negotiation. This policy proved to be more successful than the "big stick" strategy and enabled the White House to keep its opponents off balance.

Senior Reagan officials confirmed in personal interviews that White House communications strategy and rhetoric were altered in response to nuclear freeze pressures. According to Michael Deaver, Ronald Reagan had two big public opinion "negatives"—people felt that he was unfair to ordinary people and that he was "likely to get us into a war."[15] In his capacity as White House counselor and master of television imagery, Deaver tried "to keep Ronald Reagan away from any event, any photo, any visual that had to do with defense. And I was successful most of the time."[16] Deaver also tried to keep Reagan away from the MX controversy. On this issue he was less successful because, as he phrased it, "Ronald Reagan wouldn't let it be successful. He wanted to be in on that issue with both feet."[17]

The chief White House speech writer in the early years of the Reagan presidency, Aram Bakshian, explained the process of adjusting the president's rhetoric and declaratory statements in this way:

> Beginning in 1982 there were efforts made to address the growing freeze issue. … We tried to portray Reagan not as the crazy cowboy that the press was always thinking about but as having a more thoughtful position. … He was constantly concerned that the press was depicting him as this merchant of death not really interested in arms reduction.[18]

As Michael Baroody described it, "A decent respect for the opinions of mankind … dictated an impact on policy articulation, on communication efforts—to deal with the fact that there was the reality of a nuclear freeze strain within American public thought, indeed elsewhere in Europe. So we had to recognize that reality in terms of the public opinion landscape."[19] Communications Director David Gergen was particularly concerned about the impact of administration rhetoric in Europe: "We were intentionally very tough early on, but we also realized that bellicose remarks had a negative impact in Europe. So we had to start to find ways to do things to keep the Soviets at bay while also persuading the Europeans that we were reasonable."[20]

White House communications officials thus made a conscious effort to tone down the president's message. Although the "real" Reagan would occasionally slip through in offhand remarks or statements to special audiences, as in his infamous "evil empire" speech to right-wing religious broadcasters, the language of major presidential declarations was carefully controlled. Bakshian said, "You will find that generally where the rhetoric was angled that way, it was in a major foreign policy or arms speech. That was where the policy people dealing with that issue had firm control of the speech vehicle."[21]

Promising Peace

A careful look at presidential statements during these years shows that their political content did indeed begin to change. Peaceful rhetoric

steadily increased, and Soviet bashing declined. The zero option statement that was broadcasted live to 200 million Europeans in November
1981 was perhaps the president's first "peace speech." This speech, and
the negotiating proposal accompanying it, was a direct response to the
European peace movement and the growing pressure within NATO
countries for progress at the bargaining table. Since peace movement
pressure emerged later in the United States than it did in Europe, the
White House did not begin to respond to domestic pressures until
1982. One of the first occasions came in a nationally televised news
conference on March 31, when the president declared, "I invite the Soviet Union to join with us to substantially reduce nuclear weapons and
make an important breakthrough for lasting peace on earth."[22] During
the same news conference, when asked if he thought a nuclear war was
winnable, Reagan responded, "I just have to say I don't believe there
could be any winners."[23] This was a significant shift from his earlier,
highly controversial statement of October 1981, in which he had pro-
fessed the belief that nuclear war could be kept limited.

As the tempo of peace movement activity accelerated in the spring
of 1982, White House peace rhetoric quickened apace. In mid-April,
Reagan called twice in three days for informal talks with the Soviets. In
his April 17 radio speech, he spoke directly to the nuclear freeze movement and tried to address the concerns of peace activists: "I know there
are a great many people who are pointing to the unimaginable horror
of nuclear war. ... I welcome that concern. No one feels more than I the
need for peace. To those who protest against nuclear war, I can only say
I'm with you ... heart and soul in sympathy."[24] The president went on
to make the famous statement that he would subsequently repeat
many times: "A nuclear war cannot be won and must never be fought."
The president was beginning to sound like a freeze activist himself. As
his audience changed, the actor/president began to alter his lines.

On May 9, Reagan delivered his most important and most conciliatory speech on arms control since taking office. The occasion was the
commencement ceremony for the president's alma mater, Eureka College in Illinois. Ever eager for the dramatic touch, the president used
the occasion to unveil the administration's negotiating proposal for
the Strategic Arms Reduction Talks (START). The acronym "START" was
itself a brilliant public relations stroke, suggesting that the White
House wanted a new beginning in U.S.-Soviet relations and would go
beyond a nuclear freeze to actual reductions. The speech outlined the

terms of the administration's proposal and proposed direct talks with the Soviet Union without preconditions (which meant without linkage to then heavy-handed Soviet pressure on Poland). The president said, "I do not doubt that ... the Soviet leaders have an overriding interest in preventing the use of nuclear weapons."[25]

A few days later, columnist Anthony Lewis wrote an editorial in the *New York Times* entitled "The Reality Principle." Describing the president's Eureka speech and the rhetorical change it signified as an important breakthrough, Lewis said that he saw it as a positive response to rising calls for restraint: "Mr. Reagan might instead have ... dug himself in as Lyndon Johnson did on the Vietnam War. Adjusting to reality, even if it begins only with political rhetoric, may have substantive consequences."[26]

Reagan for SANE?

As pressure from the peace movement intensified, so did the stream of reassuring statements from the White House. In a Memorial Day speech at Arlington National Cemetery, the president set a date for the beginning of arms negotiations with the Soviets.[27] During his trip to Europe in early June, he told a gathering in Bonn: "To those who search for peace, my heart is with you. I would be at the head of the parade if I believed marching alone could bring about a more secure world."[28] The week after the June 12 disarmament rally in Central Park, the president declared to the United Nations that the United States was ready to "take the next steps towards arms reduction." The president ended the speech as if he were addressing the nearly 1 million people who had gathered the week before in Central Park: "We must serve mankind through genuine disarmament. With God's help, we can secure life and freedom for generations to come."[29]

Despite these and other paeans to peace, however, Reagan retained many of his previous anti-Soviet attitudes and misunderstandings about the arms race. In the March 31 press conference, for example, the president blurted out his egregious claim that the Soviets "have a definite margin of [military] superiority."[30] In his address to the United Nations, he upbraided the Soviets for promoting tyranny and oppression throughout the world. The administration was beginning to soften its rhetoric, but this was still the most right-wing presidency in modern U.S. history.

The change in rhetorical posturing continued into 1983 and beyond. At the beginning of 1983, Reagan asserted his belief that an arms reduction agreement could be reached soon and even put a time frame on it—within one year. A month later, Vice President George Bush said after a meeting with Soviet negotiators in Geneva that the United States was "deadly serious" about reaching an arms agreement.[31] In September 1983, after the shooting down of the Korean Air Lines passenger jet, the president declined to retaliate diplomatically against the Soviets, declaring that he was still committed to arms reduction talks. (Here was another retreat from the principle of "linkage" that Reagan had long espoused.) A month later, still claiming that an arms agreement was likely, he shifted the timetable to 1984. On October 31, Reagan addressed the Japanese Parliament and repeated his belief that a nuclear war could never be won and must never be fought.[32]

As the 1984 elections approached, the president went even further in declaring his support for negotiated arms limitations. In a statement prepared for the January opening of the Conference on Disarmament in Europe in Stockholm, Reagan declared, "It makes sense to compromise." Abandoning earlier statements (and perhaps his real feelings), the president asserted, "We're prepared to discuss the problems that divide us and to work for practical, fair solutions on the basis of mutual compromise."[33] According to historian John Newhouse, diplomats and White House officials viewed this speech as the most significant of Reagan's presidency up to that point.[34] It was a "curtain raiser" on the 1984 presidential political campaign and set the tone for Reagan's appeal to the voters. David Gergen agreed: "The turning point in Reagan's whole handling of the Soviet Union came in a speech in January 1984 at the Conference on Disarmament in Europe. He gave a speech that was a McFarlane special that was intended to soften the rhetoric and now begin to negotiate seriously."[35] The message of reassurance was repeated frequently that year before domestic audiences and was also the theme of an address in June to the Irish Parliament. By the final weeks of the presidential campaign, Reagan was making frequent promises of progress toward peace (although continuing to evoke the image of the Russian bear) and pledging to achieve substantial arms reduction.[36] The day after the election, Reagan declared his overwhelming victory a mandate for arms control.[37]

The peaceful tone of White House rhetoric continued and accelerated into the second term of the Reagan administration. Around the time of the first Reagan-Gorbachev summit meetings in 1985, declarations for disarmament were becoming more and more frequent and a kind of frenzied rhetorical escalation was taking place. The president and the Soviet leader sought to outbid one another in their devotion to disarmament and their appeals to the public desire for peace. This process reached a culmination at the hastily convened summit in Reykjavik in October 1986, when the two leaders came breathlessly close to agreeing on the elimination of all nuclear weapons, or at least the elimination of all ballistic missiles. For many of the remaining true believers in the Reagan administration, the president's rhetorical flights of fancy were downright alarming. As Arms Control and Disarmament Agency Director Kenneth Adelman described it, Reagan's nuclear policy "metamorphosed ... into extreme anti-nuclear talk that resembled the nuclear bashers of SANE."[38]

Rhetoric or Reality?

Former Reagan administration officials such as Aram Bakshian and Michael Baroody claim that, although presidential rhetoric changed during the 1980s in response to domestic pressures, the substance of military and nuclear policy remained the same. Even observers sympathetic to the peace movement tend to agree. In their *Turnabout* study (commissioned by Women's Action for Nuclear Disarmament), pollsters John Martilla and Tom Kiley interpreted the president's rhetorical moderation as "coopting the language of legitimate arms control to justify new steps in the arms race."[39] John Newhouse likewise saw a "course direction" in rhetoric but no substantive change in actual policy.[40] Many peace movement activists felt the same way at the time. For those of us who were campaigning to bring an end to the arms race, the president's rhetorical compromises offered little comfort. The prospects for a genuine change in policy still seemed remote.

These judgments may be too limited and miss the significance of Reagan's rhetorical shift. What a president says about an issue—especially in the sensitive area of nuclear arms control—is itself a form of policy. When an administration abandons assertions of surviving and fighting a nuclear war and overcomes its objections to negotiations with the Soviet Union, when it comes forward with an arms reduction proposal and declares its sincerity in reaching agreement—these are important steps toward moderation. They mark a partial victory for the peace movement and an abandonment of the radical right-wing philosophy of the Reagan "revolution."

Administration officials may have hoped that they could alter rhetoric without changing policy, but their words inevitably led to actions. There are limits to how far rhetoric can diverge from substantive policy. When asked about the relationship between the two, Director of Public Affairs Michael Baroody admitted, "At the level of the presidency, rhetoric and policy are to a certain degree the same thing."[41] In the arena of nuclear diplomacy, where presidential authority and declarations of intent are critical to policy, words and actions are inextricably intertwined. The pattern within the Reagan White House was not always consistent, and the administration drifted back at times to earlier confrontational themes. But overall, the tone of presidential declarations steadily became more conciliatory. The transformation of rhetoric gradually led to a change of substance as well.

These changes began well before the rise of Mikhail Gorbachev as leader of the Soviet Union. Some analysts have mistakenly ascribed the shifts in U.S. policy during the decade to Gorbachev's arrival on the political scene in 1985. Although the influence of the Soviet leader was indeed profound, the United States was already beginning to adjust its approach in 1982 and 1983. The changes in rhetoric, the decision to begin negotiations, the rejection of certain hardline policies—all these occurred prior to Gorbachev's rise to power.

The Role of Domestic Pressure

The Reagan White House was not a single administration but a coalition government torn by ideological divisions. Alexander Haig called it "a cacophony of vested interests."[42] On one side were right-wing hardliners who gave top priority to the military buildup and believed that the Soviets were implacably evil. Left to their own devices, these officials might have avoided arms control negotiations altogether. On the other side were more traditional conservatives, less wedded to the military buildup, who were committed to at least some semblance of arms control. The struggle was to an extent between the Defense Department and the State Department. The arms builders included Secretary of Defense Caspar Weinberger, National Security Adviser William Clark, Assistant Secretary of Defense for International Security Policy Richard Perle, START negotiator Edward Rowny, and Arms Control and

Disarmament Agency Director Kenneth Adelman. Those supporting arms control included Secretaries of State Alexander Haig and George Shultz, Assistant Secretary of State for European Affairs Richard Burt, Deputy Assistant for National Security Affairs Robert McFarlane, and Chief of Staff James Baker. Ronald Reagan leaned toward the hardline faction, as did White House Counselor Edwin Meese, which gave this group a major advantage in White House deliberations.

Perhaps the dominant figure in this internecine battle was Richard Perle. A former aide to the late Senator Henry Jackson (D-WA), skilled and assertive in the ways of political infighting, Perle became a central force in obstructing progress toward arms control. Dubbed by his enemies "the Prince of Darkness," Perle was determined, as Strobe Talbott phrased it, to "separate arms control from the vicissitudes of American domestic politics." Perle's mission was to block arms negotiations until the military buildup could be completed. His role was "to stop things from happening."[43]

Thanks in part to Perle's effectiveness, and to the political sympathy he enjoyed at higher levels, the administration's decision-making process became a shambles. The constant bureaucratic squabbling created chaos and near gridlock in the normal process of nuclear policy making.[44] The warring factions of the divided coalition would churn out proposals and engage in bureaucratic battle to win approval for their recommendations. In Talbott's words, "It was a process that produced constant squabbles ... and permanent, institutionalized acrimony."[45] The various disagreements would be bucked upward toward the Oval Office where the president and the National Security Council staff would attempt to make decisions.

The president himself, according to Talbott, was a "reluctant and uninformed arbiter."[46] His philosophy and political instincts put him on the side of the hardliners, but he was often so abysmally ignorant of the details of policy that the shaping of decisions fell to lower-level officials. Reagan maintained his simplistic belief in the military buildup, but political pressures forced the administration to accommodate the growing demand for negotiated arms control.

The moderates within the White House and at the State Department were at a distinct disadvantage in terms of the balance of political power within the administration. In the political arena beyond the White House, however, they had a major advantage. As Deputy Press Secretary Les Janka observed, public support for the freeze and the change in the political climate helped to tip the balance within the White House: "I think in the broader sense public concern about arms control and then especially pressure from Congress ... forced them to pay more attention to it than their instincts would have led them to do."[47] Rising citizen activism and public demands for peace were closing in on the White House, and these pressures became part of the calculus of administration decision making. Domestic political factors became a kind of third force in the internal White House coalition, lending weight to the moderates. The peace movements of Europe and the United States were like silent partners in the White House deliberations, standing over the shoulders of the president and his advisers and constantly pushing them toward the bargaining table. Richard Burt and James Baker were no friends of the peace movement or of their legislative allies, but they were perhaps grateful for the political pressures that gave weight to their arguments and reinforced their pleas for moderation.

The Visionary?

It may be helpful to reflect for a moment on Ronald Reagan's befuddlement over the details of nuclear policy. The matter bears directly on the determination of administration policy and the attempts of former White House officials to rebut the image of Ronald Reagan as "an amiable bumbler." Martin Anderson, a longtime Reagan loyalist, has claimed that the president had a vision and a plan for peace and that he succeeded by sticking to it.[48] This is a variant of the argument that "hanging tough" diplomatically was successful and resulted in improved U.S.-Soviet relations and the INF Treaty.[49]

Although Anderson and others may want to portray Reagan as a clever and farsighted leader, the fact remains that the president did not grasp even the simplest truths of the atomic age. He knew very little about basic aspects of nuclear weaponry and was ignorant of the very issues upon which negotiations are based. A few examples will illustrate the point. In a May 13, 1982, press conference, Reagan extemporaneously attempted to explain why the administration's START proposal focused almost exclusively on land-based missiles and put little emphasis on submarine-launched weapons. He stated that submarine-launched weapons are less threatening because, like bombers, they can be recalled after being launched.[50] Amazingly, when Reagan committed this gaffe, the press and members of Congress failed to challenge him and let the matter quietly drop. Reagan returned to the subject of submarine missiles in off-the-cuff remarks to a group of congressmen in October 1983. Again he attempted to explain why submarine-based weapons are less threatening. Strobe Talbott picked up the story:

> Reagan noted that the most destabilizing weapons were land-based weapons because they were "the biggest and most accurate." So far so good. But he continued: "Also land-based missiles have nuclear warheads, while bombers and submarines don't." Even as he said these words his voice dropped and wavered, as though he had forgotten his lines and knew there was something not quite right about his attempt to improvise. [51]

Reagan was obviously a master at delivering lines in set speeches, but at important government meetings on nuclear policy he could become hopelessly confused. The following is an exchange between the president and Deputy CIA Director Admiral Bobby Inman at a National Security Council meeting on May 21, 1982:

Reagan: Isn't the SS-19 their biggest missile?

Inman: No that's the SS-18.

Reagan: So they've even switched the numbers of their missiles in order to confuse us!

Inman, smiling: No, it's we who assign those numbers to the weapons in the sequence that we observe them, Mr. President.[52]

Starting START

The turning point for administration policy on arms control came in 1982. With political pressures on the White House mounting rapidly, it was incumbent upon the administration to take action. As an administration official told Leslie Gelb of the *New York Times,* "Our main concern ... is to go on the record quickly with a simple and comprehensible plan to show that the Reagan team is for peace, thus taking some of the steam out of the nuclear freeze movements in Europe and the United States."[53] In effect, as Talbott observed, the White House was "pushed to the bargaining table by political forces."[54]

Les Janka traced these political pressures to the freeze movement and its allies on Capitol Hill:

> The Freeze had an impact in Congress where it really did catch fire ... and that obviously put some pressure on the administration ... with the White House reacting and saying, if we don't do something, Congress will. Congressional pressure on issues like arms control does put pressure on the administration to show progress.[55]

Talbott directly credited the peace movement as well (although he did not name it specifically):

> Congress was getting impatient. A number of trends in public opinion were beginning to coalesce. A wide variety of religious and academic leaders were questioning the administration's policies. ... There was rising sentiment in favor of a negotiated agreement with the Soviet Union to stop all further testing, production and deployment of nuclear weapons. ... The administration had to overcome its own inertia ... to avoid seeing its own defense policies swept aside by a potent new movement.[56]

Kenneth Adelman described these events in this way: "Congressional obsession with arms control feeds the press, who ask about it at the daily White House and State Department briefings. This feeds the White House staff and the President."[57] Adelman might have added that this congressional "obsession" was largely the result of constituent pressure in home districts, which in turn had resulted from citizen activism and organized campaigns from the peace movement.

Further evidence that peace pressures helped to push the administration to the bargaining table can be found in an internal memorandum that Eugene Rostow, the administration's first Arms Control and Disarmament Agency director, sent to National Security Adviser William Clark in early 1982. The memo urged that the White House "combine the decision about starting START with the problem of the freeze resolutions."[58] Although a hardliner and one of the founders of the Committee on the Present Danger, Rostow was increasingly concerned about what he termed "an isolationist movement" and the rising tide of antinuclear sentiment. Moving ahead with strategic arms negotiations, Rostow felt, would be a means of deflecting these political criticisms.

Robert McFarlane and others in the White House agreed, but they were frustrated by the continued foot-dragging of arms control opponents. By February 1982, it was clear to McFarlane that there had to be what he termed a "management impulse" from the White House, "an explosive charge to blast apart the log jam in the bureaucracy."[59] The political costs of continuing to stonewall on arms control were too great, McFarlane and others believed. In late February, McFarlane and William Clark decided to issue a National Security Council Directive ordering the executive branch to develop a START proposal within two months.[60] The directive set a series of deadlines for the various levels of the bureaucracy to come forward with positions and mandated that the final proposal be on the president's desk by May 1. It is a remarkable commentary on the depth of opposition to arms control within the Reagan administration that McFarlane and Clark had to resort to such heavy-handed means just to develop a negotiating proposal.

The timing of the White House "management impulse" was dictated in large part by the beginnings of the freeze debate in Congress. The Markey resolution had already been introduced in the House of Representatives, and the more serious challenge by Edward Kennedy in the Senate was about to emerge. On March 10, the Kennedy-Hatfield freeze resolution was introduced in the Senate, a story that received front-page coverage in the *New York Times*. Two days later, Lawrence Eagleburger, undersecretary of state for political affairs, announced that the administration would soon introduce its START proposal. The announcement, which also received front-page coverage in the *Times*, could hardly have been a coincidence.

Richard Wirthlin admitted that the pressure of public opinion "might have influenced the timing" of the decisions to begin negotiations.[61] In an interview, Wirthlin at first denied the influence of public pressure on policy formulation but admitted that public opinion was vital in "determining some of the timing of his policies as well as some of the tactical positioning." When asked whether this meant that policies were adjusted according to what the polls said, he said, "Tactically there were some adjustments."[62] Caspar Weinberger agreed that peace pressures had an impact. While insisting that "you can't bend policy every time a few thousand people wander around in the streets," the former secretary acknowledged that the timing of the START negotiations was influenced by domestic politics:

Q. Did pressures in Congress and in public opinion have anything to do with the timing of the decision to begin the START talks?

A. Well, I suppose something, surely. In a democratic society you've got to respond to what the people want in one way or another.[63]

On the day of the historic June 12 rally in Central Park, the *New York Times* ran an editorial under the title "Leadership on the Lawn." Paying tribute to "the multitudes that will stretch out across the Great Lawn this afternoon," the *Times* gave credit for the beginning of arms talks to the demonstrators: "In 17 days American and Soviet officials will at long last sit down in Geneva to renew negotiations. ... It's a stirring accomplishment, and Americans at the grass roots deserve the credit."[64]

Pressure for Plausibility

The National Security Council Directive to develop a negotiating proposal did not end the internal feuding within the administration. The battleground now shifted to the question of plausibility, or negotiability. Would the White House proposal be politically realistic? Would it have any chance of producing a successful negotiation? Richard Perle and the hardliners fought for a proposal that would be as one-sided as possible. The moderates, in contrast, wanted a START proposal that at least appeared to be reasonable in order to achieve the desired political effect of showing White House sincerity in arms control. A furious bureaucratic battle ensued as the administration lurched hesitantly toward the May 1 deadline. Once again, outside political pressure from peace forces played an important role in tilting White House deliberations toward a slightly more reasonable—or at least less unreasonable—START proposal. James Baker and the moderates were especially concerned to make the START plan as politically plausible as possible.[65] As Strobe Talbott explained, "Baker was particularly worried in the face of the pro-freeze movement. Reagan shared these concerns. In talking with Baker and other close aides, Reagan had commented a number of times that he could not afford to subject himself to the accusation that 'we aren't serious about wanting an agreement.'"[66]

Alexander Haig shared Baker's political worries and raised the additional concern of the European allies. The NATO countries were being pressured by domestic peace movements as well and were urging Washington to get moving on strategic arms negotiations. At an April 1982 meeting of the National Security Council, Haig warned the president and his advisers that a START proposal seen as implausible would be a "political catastrophe" and would create a backlash against the administration both at home and abroad.[67] His steely gaze fixed on Reagan, Haig told the president that the decision on shaping the START proposal would be "the most important of your administration."[68]

The hardline faction fought tenaciously against the pressures for moderation, but they were unable to prevent the adoption of a compromise position. As the May deadline approached, a so-called "consensus" proposal emerged under the authorship of Richard Burt. Burt told Chief of Staff Baker that his proposal "was designed with the President's political interests in mind ... and would meet the criterion of plausibility."[69] Baker agreed, and the White House approved the plan. The actual negotiating position that emerged from the bureaucracy, however, was still grossly one-sided and unrealistic. It asked the Soviets to make deep cuts without offering countervailing U.S. reductions. It was only in comparison with the original extremist position of Perle that the START proposal seemed in any way reasonable. By any objective standard, it was completely unrealistic.

The results of the administration's convoluted moves toward strategic arms negotiation were highly ambiguous. On the one hand, political pressures from the peace movement and its allies in Congress were successful in forcing the White House to the bargaining table and steering it toward a slightly more plausible proposal. On the other hand, hardliners within the administration succeeded in obstructing the process and blocking realistic negotiations. The peace movement exerted pressure and had a real if indirect impact on the policy process, but it did not produce a negotiated agreement or improved U.S.-Soviet relations, at least not immediately.

Starting Again

The decision to begin strategic arms talks in Geneva initially allowed the Reagan administration to beat back the challenges of the nuclear freeze movement and maintain political support for its arms buildup. When the House of Representatives initially voted down Markey's nuclear freeze resolution on August 4, 1982, administration officials congratulated themselves for outflanking their opponents. The president had been able to prevent an embarrassing defeat on the freeze resolution by pointing to the arms talks that were just getting under way and by urging that the negotiations be given a chance to succeed. The same tactic worked in securing congressional support for the record military spending increases approved that year. Secretary of State Haig and other officials told Congress that failure to fund the strategic buildup would hinder the chances of success in the START negotiations.

This gambit worked for a while, but the administration soon found itself caught in its own web. The tactic of pointing to START could work only so long as there was a plausible case that an agreement might be forthcoming. As the talks in Geneva lagged, however, and as political pressure in the United States intensified (in part because of the success of city and state freeze resolutions and the Republican party's poor showing in the November 1982 mid-term elections), the White House found itself painted into a corner. The tables began to turn. Where the administration had previously urged support for the arms buildup to achieve arms control, congressional critics now demanded progress toward arms control as the price for their support of the arms buildup. Once again, moderates raised the issue of plausibility and demanded greater flexibility in the U.S. negotiating position.

A critical factor here was continuing pressure from the grass-roots peace movement around the country. Freeze activists were unimpressed by the beginning of START and saw no evidence that the danger of nuclear war had eased. The number of local and national peace groups continued to grow, and demands for an end to the arms race steadily mounted. These pressures were directed mainly at members of Congress, who responded by turning up the heat on the White House.

The principal instrument that pro–arms control members of Congress used to prod the Reagan administration toward a more serious bargaining posture was the MX missile. This homeless missile, the centerpiece of the administration's strategic nuclear buildup, was subjected to a furious, unrelenting campaign of opposition (see Chapter 9). When the much-coveted missile ran into political difficulty, the White House had to expend enormous amounts of political capital trying to rescue it. Congress reacted to these White House entreaties by holding the MX hostage to progress in strategic arms negotiations. The struggle to save the MX thus became linked to congressional demands for a new START proposal and for greater flexibility at the bargaining table.

The White House was plunged into internal deliberations to devise a more coherent arms control policy. Kenneth Adelman reported that during 1983 the president met with the National Security Council and his senior advisers to develop arms control policy fourteen times and that the Senior Arms Control Policy Group met without the president another eighteen times.[70] Under the heat of mounting political criticism, proposals and counterproposals once again churned through the divided administration.

Recognizing the administration's worsening political difficulties, Robert McFarlane and others in the White House decided that another "management impulse" was necessary. The vehicle they chose was the Scowcroft Commission, a group of so-called "wise men" from outside the bureaucracy headed by Brent Scowcroft, former general and deputy to Henry Kissinger. One of the commission's principal purposes was, in Strobe Talbott's words, to "ram policies through an impacted, fractious bureaucracy."[71] The commission report, released in April 1983, signaled a break with the extremist positions of the early Reagan administration and marked a return to a more conventional arms control policy. Among the commission's recommendations was a call for a more plausible START negotiating proposal. The commission used diplomatic language, but its emphasis on the need for a more realistic approach was unmistakable.[72]

Moderate members of Congress worked closely with the Scowcroft Commission and strongly supported its recommendations for negotiating flexibility. At a crucial White House meeting in May 1983, Representative Al Gore (D-TN), one of the key "swing" votes on the MX, presented McFarlane and Adelman with a kind of ultimatum: Overhaul the START proposal if you want my vote. A crucial MX vote was coming up, and Gore's support was essential if the administration was to have any hope of resuscitating the beleaguered missile. As their price for supporting the MX, Gore and his congressional colleagues were demanding the abandonment of the Perle-Weinberger hardline position.[73] Faced with these political pressures, the administration relented. At a National Security Council meeting in June, the White House agreed to change the START proposal and accepted the recommendations of the Scowcroft Commission.[74]

These conciliatory gestures calmed the political storm for a while, but freeze activists and their allies on Capitol Hill continued to stir the waters, and congressional moderates were soon back demanding additional concessions. In the fall of 1983, these pressures came to a head as another major vote on the MX approached. In late September, Senator William Cohen (R-ME), a leader of the centrist group, challenged administration policy at a White House meeting and demanded further changes in the U.S. bargaining position.[75] A breakthrough of sorts finally came in early October 1983 when the White House and its congressional critics came to a compromise agreement, the so-called "Magna Carta." Under this agreement, the administration again formally changed its negotiating position and pledged to incorporate the congressional "build-down" proposal, a formula calling for the retirement of two older weapons for every new one deployed, into the START negotiations. Once again, political pressure entered into the making of arms control policy. Despite the administration's new position at the Geneva talks, however, the deadlock in Geneva remained. A month later, the Soviets walked out of the negotiations in response to the NATO INF deployments and the talks were suspended altogether.

A Learning Experience

The White House's October 1983 agreement with Congress marked a watershed in the evolution of Reagan's thinking on arms control. For the first time, Reagan and his senior advisers accepted the concept of offsetting asymmetries, the idea that limits in one category of weapons would need to be offset by limits in another. In place of the previous attempt to force massive Soviet reductions without countervailing U.S. constraints, the administration now recognized that U.S. forces would also have to be reduced and that U.S. submarine- and air-launched weapons would have to be limited in exchange for Soviet concessions on heavy missiles. Reagan admitted in discussions with members of Congress at the time that he had not previously understood that Soviet weapons were concentrated in their land-based missiles. He apparently hadn't realized that his original START proposals were so one-sided.[76] Brent Scowcroft and Secretary of State George Shultz had been attempting for some months to brief the president on these matters, and they considered his concessions in October 1983 to be "potentially a major turning point in the education of Ronald Reagan."[77]

Thus did the Reagan administration finally come to accept the realities of the nuclear age. Nearly three years after taking office, under political pressure from the peace movement, Congress, and the European allies, the White House at last declared itself willing to make trade-offs to achieve arms limitation and accepted the basic requirements of successful negotiation. Even these modest gains might not have been achieved were it not for the political pressures generated by citizen activism. It would take several more years before this more realistic posture would begin to achieve results, but the seeds of this flowering were sown in the transformations imposed on the White House in 1982 and 1983.

Political forces pushed the White House to the bargaining table in the first place and then imposed changes in the U.S. negotiating position twice in the first year and a half. At each juncture, the administration was pushed toward a more conciliatory stance. Initially the administration responded to peace pressures only with words, but soon its actions changed as well. What began as co-option became adaptation as the administration abandoned its nuclear saber-rattling and moved steadily toward moderation and negotiated arms reduction. Citizen activism broke the ice between the United States and the Soviet Union and secured the lines of dialogue that ultimately led to a breakthrough in international understanding and the unraveling of the Cold War.

8

The Zero Solution and the European Peace Movement

In the movie version of John Le Carre's *Russia House,* U.S. intelligence officials question Barley, the irreverent British publisher (played by Sean Connery), about his links to possible subversives.

"Have you made any connections with any peace people in England?"

"Oh hundreds, I should think. You have to stay indoors to avoid them."

Barley's point was well-taken. Not only in England, but in West Germany, the Netherlands, Italy, Belgium, and other NATO countries, "peace people" were everywhere during the 1980s. You really did have to stay indoors to avoid them. The people of Western Europe were aroused as never before by a dangerous escalation of the nuclear arms race.

The immediate catalyst was the NATO decision to deploy new Intermediate-Range Nuclear Forces (INFs) in Western Europe. The public furor sparked by this decision set the stage for the largest peace movement mobilization in modern European history. In the fall of 1981 and then again in October 1983, Europeans took to the streets by the millions to protest the nuclear arms race. Throughout Western Europe, opposition to the new missiles reached enormous proportions and the peace movement enjoyed unprecedented popularity. According to a 1982 poll, approval of the peace movement in the major NATO countries ranged from a low of 55 percent to a high of 81 percent.[1] The result was intense political opposition to NATO and Soviet missiles and powerful pressures not only against INF weapons but the entire Cold War system of East-West competition.

"Irrespective of the SS-20"

The INF controversy and the decision to deploy new missiles in Western Europe derived from several factors. One was the desire, articulated by West German Chancellor Helmut Schmidt, to maintain a strong political and military linkage between the United States and Europe.[2] Another was NATO's drive to improve its capability for "flexible response." Military planners argued that a gap existed between conventional conflict and strategic warfare and that new short- and medium-range nuclear weapons were needed to fill this gap. According to Richard Nixon and Henry Kissinger, these weapons would give NATO the option for "graduated application of its nuclear power"[3] and provide the means for fighting a supposedly limited nuclear war.

The centerpiece of the U.S. effort to achieve flexible response in Europe was the deployment of new intermediate-range nuclear weapons: 464 ground-launched cruise missiles and 108 Pershing II missiles. The Pershing IIs would be deployed in West Germany, and the ground-launched cruise missiles would be stationed in Great Britain, Italy, Belgium, the Netherlands, and West Germany. The 572 new missiles were justified in public as a response to the Soviet SS-20 deployments, but this was not what NATO strategists had in mind. As Nixon and Kissinger later observed, "It is regrettable that ... the deployment of those weapons was justified solely on the ground that they were needed to balance the new SS-20 missiles. ... In fact, these missiles were not needed to offset their equivalents."[4] As General Bernard Rogers, the supreme NATO commander, told a Senate panel: "Most people believe it was because of the SS-20 that we modernized. We would have modernized irrespective of the SS-20 because we had this gap in our spectrum of defense developing and we needed to close the gap."[5]

When the missile deployments were announced in December 1979, the Soviet Union protested loudly. Kremlin leaders objected that the cruise and Pershing missiles upset the military balance in Europe. Although the United States called them theater weapons, the Soviets considered the missiles strategic because they could strike inside Soviet territory. The Pershing II was particularly alarming because it theoretically had the accuracy to knock out Soviet command bunkers. Outraged at what they perceived to be a grave threat to their security, Soviet leaders made the elimination of these new U.S. weapons a top priority. The stage was set for a bruising political struggle between East and West that dominated European politics throughout much of the 1980s.

A "Political Problem" in Europe

Caught in the middle of this feud between Moscow and Washington were the people of Europe. What NATO and Warsaw Pact planners referred to as the nuclear battlefield, the people of Europe saw as their homeland. Although the human aspect was obscured by the objectified language of nuclear planning, the lives and concerns of hundreds of millions of people were nevertheless caught up in this debate. The more military leaders talked about "flexible response" and "limited war," the more Europeans feared they would be the target of nuclear attack. This was especially true in Germany, at the heart of the East-West divide. Even before the INF debate, nuclear phobia was spreading in Europe as it was in the United States. After the December 1979 deployment decision and the Soviet invasion of Afghanistan, fear of nuclear war increased dramatically. The percentage of Europeans believing that nuclear war was "probable in the next ten years" rose from just over 10 percent in 1977 to more than 30 percent in 1980.[6] In West Germany, fear of world war rose from 17 percent in July 1979 to a startling 48 percent in January 1980.[7]

Given these perceptions, it was not surprising that the people of Western Europe overwhelmingly rejected the INF deployments. Nearly every poll conducted on the subject during the 1980s, including those commissioned by the U.S. government, found widespread public disapproval. An October 1981 survey by the U.S. International Communications Agency found opposition rates as high as 57 percent in the Netherlands and 84 percent in Belgium.[8] Subsequent polls showed even greater opposition. In a British survey conducted in October 1982 by the Gallup organization's European subsidiary, Social Surveys Limited, people were asked, "Do you think Great Britain should or should not allow the new American-controlled cruise nuclear missiles to be based here?" In response, 31 percent said "should," 58 percent said "should not," and 11 percent were undecided. In May 1984, after the missile deployments had already begun, the same question elicited a similar level of opposition: 35 percent in favor, 56 percent against, and 9 percent uncertain.[9] When the same question was put to Germans in fall 1983, 25 percent said "should," 48 percent said "should not," and 26 percent were uncertain.[10] A September 1983 poll released by former West German Chancellor Willy Brandt showed 66 percent of the public against deployment if the talks failed and only 31 percent in favor.[11]

For the Reagan administration and its NATO allies, these antinuclear sentiments created a crisis in public confidence. This was brought home to the White House in a 1982 poll by the U.S. Information Agency that showed only 6 percent of the population in the five basing countries "unconditionally" in favor of missile deployment. Approximately 30 percent of the people were "conditionally" in favor of deployment "as a means of getting an agreement," but a solid 25 percent were "unconditionally" against any form of deployment.[12] Reviewing these findings in Washington at the end of the year, chief INF negotiator Paul Nitze told a State Department meeting, "We have a political problem in Europe."[13]

The European Peace Movement Responds

As military planners talked of turning Europe into a nuclear battlefield, the ranks of the peace movement swelled with new recruits. Peace groups suddenly found themselves at the center of a raging political controversy. The first wave of renewed peace mobilization came in 1977 in response to the neutron bomb controversy. The concept of a weapon that destroys people but preserves property was repugnant to many people and prompted widespread protest. The most intense reaction came in the Netherlands. The neutron bomb campaign marked a major turning point for one of the most important peace organizations in Europe, the Dutch Interchurch Peace Council (IKV). Founded in 1966 by the Catholic church and the major Protestant denominations in Holland, the IKV had been relatively innocuous in its initial years and was described by one observer as merely "a debating club about peace."[14] In 1977, however, Ben Ter Veer, IKV chairman, urged greater political activism and brought the council into the neutron bomb campaign. Tens of thousands of Dutch citizens demonstrated in the streets, and more than 1 million people (out of a population of 14 million) signed anti–neutron bomb petitions. In response to these and other pressures, the center-right Christian Democratic government in The

Hague announced in 1978 that it would not accept neutron bombs on Dutch soil.[15] This was followed by President Jimmy Carter's decision to postpone neutron bomb production. These successes gave a tremendous boost to the peace movement. Not just in Holland, but in West Germany, Great Britain, and other European countries, peace groups were experiencing a surge in public support. Even before NATO's December 1979 decision, the peace movement was on the rise and an infrastructure of political opposition was already in place.

The peace movement reaction to the INF decision was immediate. As the formal declaration was issued in Brussels in December 1979, 40,000 people gathered outside NATO headquarters to demand the cancellation of both NATO and Soviet missiles. A few months later, German peace activists launched the Krefeld Appeal, which called on the Bonn government to reject the cruise and Pershing II missiles. The Krefeld Appeal was ultimately signed by more than 4 million people.[16] In fall 1980, the first in a series of major rallies in London organized by the Campaign for Nuclear Disarmament (CND) drew a crowd of more than 80,000 people.

The year 1981 saw spectacular growth and mobilization for the European peace movement. Thousands of new peace organizations were formed all over the continent, and existing groups experienced a phenomenal increase in membership and public support. At CND in Great Britain, national membership increased tenfold in just one year (from 3,000 to 30,000) and the number of local branches jumped from 30 in 1979 to 1,000 in 1981.[17] In addition to its national membership, CND had three times as many additional members organized through its local branches. A similar phenomenon was occurring in the United States as thousands of new groups appeared within the nuclear freeze movement and older organizations such as SANE and the Council for a Livable World grew rapidly. The parallel between the movements in Europe and the United States in this regard is striking. The growth pattern of CND in Britain was almost identical to that of SANE in the United States (see Figure 8.1).

Fuel for the Fire

Support for the peace movement (and public fear of nuclear war) received a major boost in October 1981 when Ronald Reagan made his infamous comment about limited nuclear war in Europe. The "great

FIGURE 8.1   Membership Growth Comparison of SANE and CND, 1980–1985

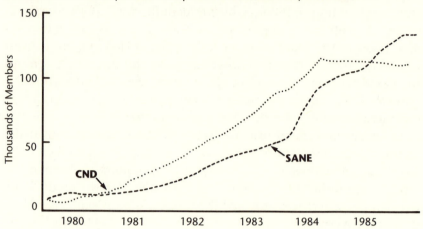

communicator" would commit many rhetorical gaffes during his presidency (see, for example, *Ronald Reagan's Reign of Error* by Mark Green and Gail MacColl), but none was more egregious than his October 20, 1981, statement on nuclear war in Europe. Speaking to a group of out-of-town editors at the White House, Reagan was asked if he thought a battlefield exchange of nuclear weapons could occur without leading to all-out war. The president responded, "I could see where you could have an exchange of tactical weapons against troops in the field without it bringing either one of the major powers to pushing the button."[18] Pressed to explain himself, he tried to elaborate on how a battlefield exchange could be kept limited, but he became entangled in a classic bit of unscripted Reaganesque doubletalk: "Well, I would—if they realized that we—again, if—if we lead them back to that stalemate only because—that our retaliatory power, our seconds, or our strike at them after their first strike, would be so destructive that they couldn't afford it, that would hold them off."[19] Reagan's message was clear, even if his syntax and understanding were not: Limited nuclear war is possible.

News of Reagan's statement landed like a bombshell in Europe and was the subject of feature stories in newspapers and broadcasts all across the continent. Public fears were aroused further when Secretary of State Alexander Haig testified two weeks later before the Senate Foreign Relations Committee. He revealed in his testimony that NATO contingency plans in the event of conventional war in Europe called for the firing of a "demonstration" nuclear explosion, a so-called nuclear warning shot.[20] These and other Reagan administration comments sowed deep doubts among many Europeans about U.S. policy and made the job of defending NATO's deployment decision difficult. Two years later, an embittered Helmut Schmidt told a congress of the Social Democratic party: "I wish some political orators in the West would grasp how very much their ignorant war-like speeches have contributed to this fear ... to this anger."[21]

"Neither Pershings nor SS-20s"

The largest wave of political protest in Western Europe since the end of World War II came in the fall of 1981. On October 10, more than 250,000 people gathered in Bonn for one of the largest peace demonstrations ever held on German soil. More than 3,000 buses and 42 special trains were needed to transport the protesters.[22] Organized primarily by German churches, the rally called for an end to the arms race in both the United States and the Soviet Union and demanded cancellation of both SS-20 and cruise and Pershing II missile deployments. Among the many speakers were Coretta Scott King and Harry Belafonte from the United States. A long list of German peace advocates also spoke, including General Gert Bastian, a tank division commander of the West German Bundeswehr who had been forced to resign for criticizing the proposed missile deployment. Perhaps the most notable speaker was Erhard Eppler, a former government minister of the ruling Social Democratic party. The presence of a prominent leader from the government party and the huge size of the crowd signaled deepening political divisions within Germany over the missile issue.

Two weeks later, similar mass rallies took place in Brussels, Paris, and London. In Belgium, more than 100,000 people marched, and in Paris, the crowd was estimated at more than 50,000. In both demonstrations, the political demands were directed equally at the Soviet Union and the United States. A huge banner carried through the streets of Paris captured the message of the day: "Neither Pershings nor SS-20s."[23] The October 24 demonstration in London was described by the *New York Times* as "the largest of its type ever held in this country."[24] More than 250,000 people clogged the heart of the city, marching north from the bank of the Thames near Trafalgar Square to Hyde Park and creating monumental traffic congestion throughout central London. Among those caught in the traffic jam was U.S. Secretary of Defense Caspar Weinberger, who wrote in his memoirs that he and his wife "had to take a very circuitous route to return to our hotel ... because traffic was effectively blocked for miles by the demonstrators; so, in a sense, we were *caught up* in the demonstration."[25]

While these disarmament campaigns burgeoned in northern Europe, an equally large and quite unexpected peace movement emerged in Italy. Italy had witnessed many forms of political protest over the years, but a mass peace movement had not been one of them. When the Italian government announced in August 1981 that 112 of the NATO cruise missiles would be based in Sicily, however, the situation suddenly changed. The Italian people found themselves for the first time in the front lines of Europe's nuclear battlefield. The public reaction was swift and decisive. A huge peace movement sprang up practically overnight, bypassing the established left-wing parties and trade unions. In October, more than half a million Italians took to the streets in the largest wave of peace protests the country had ever seen.[26] The demonstrations began with an October 10 march of more than 10,000 protesters to the cruise missile base at Comiso in the remote southeast corner of Sicily. On October 31, more than 100,000 demonstrators gathered in central Milan. As elsewhere in Europe, the political demands were directed at both Washington and Moscow. One banner read "No to the Pentagon! No to the Kremlin!"[27] On November 28, more than 200,000 demonstrators converged on the Plaza della Signoria in the historic central district of Florence.[28] The largest of the Italian rallies that fall took place in Rome on October 24, when more than 250,000 people marched past the U.S. and Soviet embassies demanding an end to the arms race and the cancellation of INF missiles on both sides.

At nearly all the rallies and mass demonstrations held across Europe in 1981 and the years following, protesters called for the elimination of Soviet SS-20s as well as NATO's INF weapons. The leaders of the Campaign for Nuclear Disarmament, the IKV, and other major organizations were consistent in criticizing Soviet as well as NATO policy. To be sure, the emphasis was on Western policy, since the demonstrators were citizens of NATO countries and were speaking primarily to their own governments, but Soviet policies were challenged as well. Critics of the peace movement tried to claim otherwise, asserting that the disarmament rallies were somehow Soviet controlled. Caspar Weinberger wrote, for example, that he witnessed several peace rallies in Europe, but that "at no time did I see a single sign, much less a demonstration against the SS-20."[29] The secretary of defense did not look very hard, for banners and signs against Soviet weapons were commonplace at these events.

Much to the chagrin of Weinberger and other NATO officials, the European public tended to hold the United States and the Soviet Union equally responsible for the increased threat of war. According to a 1986 poll in Great Britain, for example, 54 percent agreed that "Russia and America are equally great threats" to world peace; 17 percent saw the United States as the greater threat; and 18 percent viewed the Soviet Union as the greater threat.[30] In a 1982 poll in West Germany, 41 percent agreed that the policies of both the United States and the Soviet Union increased the risk of war.[31] Among supporters of the peace movement, 78 percent found the United States and the Soviet Union equally warlike.[32] For many people, the culprit was not one side or the other but the entire Cold War system of military competition and nuclear escalation.

"We Got the Idea from Your Banners"

When the Reagan administration first came into office, its commitment to negotiation on the INF issue was lukewarm at best. Within the White House, the same bureaucratic infighting that marked the development of START policy raged over the question of INF negotiations. Caspar Weinberger and the Defense Department argued for delay, while Alexander Haig and the State Department urged an immediate resumption of talks (an initial round of INF negotiations had been held in the last months of the Carter administration). National Security Adviser Richard Allen told a press briefing that the White House "would not be stampeded into talks."[33] Enormous political pressures were building among the NATO allies, however. Faced with mounting opposition at home, the European governments were demanding that the White House begin talks for an INF agreement. The Social Democratic government of Helmut Schmidt was particularly concerned and reminded the White House that negotiations were an integral part of the original NATO decision. If a date for the talks were not set soon,

Schmidt warned, Germany and other European countries might not be able to maintain political support for deployment.[34]

Caspar Weinberger explained in his memoirs how these pressures were conveyed by NATO defense ministers and in the process confirmed that peace movement protests had a direct role in advancing the arms control process. European leaders were "concerned by the anti-nuclear demonstrations that regularly took place in their countries" and demanded progress in INF negotiations.[35] Furthermore, "as more and more of the demonstrations were held ... more and more defense ministers at the NATO meetings urged, either as their views or as the opinions being presented to their governments, that more be done on the 'second track' (i.e., negotiations) of the December 1979 resolution."[36] Weinberger elaborated on this point in an interview, explaining that proceeding with negotiations "would solve ... the problems that the defense ministers were having with their own governments in the face of a lot of tumult in the streets."[37] These political pressures from Europe tipped the balance within the White House in favor of early resumption of talks. At a National Security Council meeting in late April 1981, the president approved the recommendation of the State Department, and in early May it was announced that INF negotiations would begin later that year.

Attention now turned to what the U.S. bargaining position should be. Here again peace pressures from Europe became a factor in White House decision making. The initial State Department proposal was that the two sides agree to equal levels of INF weapons. The United States would scale back its planned INF deployment to a specified number if the Soviet Union would reduce its existing missiles to the same number. In Europe, meanwhile, the idea of a "zero solution"—no INF weapons on either side—was steadily gaining political currency. According to Weinberger, NATO officials began to speak of the zero solution in the spring of 1981. Although "the zero option was supported by a number of anti-nuclear groups," wrote Weinberger, the NATO ministers spoke approvingly of the idea.[38] Officials at the White House were decidedly cool to the proposition, however. Haig objected to the zero concept on the grounds that it was contrary to the original intent of the December 1979 NATO decision. In March 1981, National Security Adviser Richard Allen labeled the proposal for zero deployment "illusory."[39] General Bernard Rogers and other commanders emphasized that the new missiles were essential for NATO military strategy and that they should not be traded away under any circumstances. As Haig told a National Security Council meeting in late October 1981, "We wouldn't want a zero option even if we could have it."[40]

If the idea of zero deployment was so contrary to military goals, why did the Reagan administration come to embrace it? The principal factors were politics and public relations. As White House Counselor Michael Deaver put it, the zero option "was our response to the antinuke people."[41] Communications Director David Gergen explained it this way: "We would have been far better off to retain a certain number of INF missiles on the ground in Europe. But in order to win over public opinion, you had to appear that you were for zero-zero. At the time it was a way to buy off a wary Europe."[42] Richard Burt of the State Department confided to author and peace activist Mary Kaldor that the proposal came directly from the peace movement, as she later revealed in an article in the *New Statesman:* "I remember having a drink with a senior Reagan administration official the night the zero option was announced. 'We got the idea from your banners,' he said, chuckling. 'You know, the ones that say 'No Cruise, No Pershing, No SS-20.'"[43]

Although the White House claimed credit for the zero option proposal, the initial concept came not from the Reagan administration but from the people of Europe. It originated in the streets of London, Brussels, and Bonn, not in the boardrooms of Washington. The initiative for turning a demand of the peace movement into a formal bargaining proposal emerged within the Social Democratic party of West Germany. Former Chancellor Schmidt claimed in his memoirs that the zero option proposal was his and that the INF Treaty was a "personal triumph" for him.[44] Schmidt's interest in the zero concept was prompted in part by the intense political pressure he faced at home from the peace movement and from the left wing of his own Social Democratic party. Opposition to the NATO missiles was threatening to split the party and undo the fragile government consensus in favor of deployment. To hold the coalition together, it was essential to get the negotiating process under way and develop an innovative bargaining proposal that could take the heat off NATO and the German government.

When the NATO ministers gathered in Gleneagles, Scotland, in October 1981, they met in the shadow of the massive antinuclear demonstrations then sweeping through the capitals of Western Europe. The meeting focused on the INF deployments and the negotiations that were about to get under way. The Dutch and West German governments proposed that NATO officially adopt the zero solution as its bargaining position. As an official at the meeting told reporters, a "high profile position was necessary to assuage this opposition which has recently staged large demonstrations in West Germany, the Netherlands and other nations."[45] According to the *Washington Post,* the U.S. delegation initially opposed inclusion of zero option language in the NATO communique at Gleneagles.[46] But Secretary of Defense Weinberger and other White House officials soon came to support the idea. Perhaps the rising antinuclear ferment Weinberger encountered during his travels on the continent that fall encouraged his decision. It was certainly a politically popular position. Secretary of State Haig later reported that Weinberger argued in favor of the idea at White House meetings "on the basis of its potential for attracting public support."[47] As Professor Thomas Risse-Kappen has concluded, the "emerging European peace movements were instrumental in inducing NATO and the United States to adopt the zero option as the formal Western negotiating position."[48]

In addition to its political value, the zero option had the advantage of appealing to Ronald Reagan's penchant for simplicity and salesmanship. The idea was easy to explain and had great public relations appeal. It was the stuff of which rousing speeches could be made and had the additional benefit of sparing the often uninformed president the potential embarrassment of trying to explain the details of European missile deployment. Reagan could avoid the specifics and focus on the goal of zero deployment.

A key calculation in the White House's decision was the belief that the Soviet Union would never accept the zero option. Because the original proposal required the Soviets to give up hundreds of missiles in exchange for a promise by the United States not to deploy new ones, it was assumed (and hoped) that the Soviets would flatly reject it. As White House Communications Director David Gergen put it, "They clearly weren't going to accept that."[49] Many officials within the Reagan administration favored the plan precisely because it was seen as nonnegotiable. In this view, adopting the zero proposal was a way to "make sure that the deployment proceeded on schedule."[50]

The zero option solved several political problems at once. On one level, it was a masterful public relations ploy to steal the thunder of the antinuclear movement. At the same time, the proposal was sufficiently one-sided that it was assumed that the Soviets would never accept it. The administration thus could throw the antinuclear movement off balance and satisfy the political demands for negotiations while proceeding with its military buildup and the deployment of new missiles.

On November 18, 1981, the administration unveiled its decision in a dramatic public relations gesture aimed at the people of Europe. Reagan made the announcement himself in a major speech at the National Press Club in Washington. The White House paid for live satellite transmission of the president's announcement to the European Broadcasting Union, and the speech was deliberately timed for maximum exposure in Europe. The 10:00 a.m. presentation in Washington coincided with late afternoon in Europe, thus assuring that the president would have a massive audience and be featured on evening newscasts all across the continent. According to Communications Director David Gergen, "That was the first speech given by an American President planned to coincide with European prime time."[51] Administration officials estimated that the speech was seen by 200 million people in forty nations.[52] It was the largest audience ever to hear a presidential arms control address, and it gave powerful momentum to the administration's campaign to counter the peace movement.

"No Thanks"

If White House officials were anxious to find out how Reagan's speech played in Europe, the answer was not long in coming. Three days later, the largest antinuclear demonstration ever held in Europe took place in Amsterdam. On November 21, nearly 500,000 people jammed the city's narrow streets to demand an end to the arms race and cancellation of NATO missile deployments. A button worn by many of the marchers conveyed a common sentiment: "Nuclear Weapons, No Thanks." Demonstrators marching thirty abreast took three and a half hours to pass a single point. As the crowds streamed past, residents in third and fourth story apartments leaned out of their windows waving and tossing flowers to the peace marchers below. A police spokesperson admitted, "This was definitely the biggest demonstration in Dutch history."[53] Among the participants was a delegation of more than a dozen representatives from the U.S. peace movement who marched behind a huge banner that read "We've Got Hollanditis."[54] Also in the huge throng that day were several hundred long-haired Dutch soldiers in

., many of whom were members of that country's conscripts' VVDM (Vereniging Van Dienstplichtige Militairen), and part of wing antinuclear peace movement within the barracks.[55]

.he European people had a chance to deliver their message personally to Ronald Reagan when he visited the continent in June 1982 for an economic summit in Versailles and meetings with NATO leaders. The president was greeted by demonstrations even larger than those of the previous fall. Once again, hundreds of thousands of people poured into the streets to demand an end to the arms race and the cancellation of INF missile deployments. In Paris, more than 150,000 people gathered for a peace demonstration in late May. On June 5 and 6, more than a quarter of a million demonstrators marched in London and Rome.[56] The largest rally took place in Bonn, where nearly 350,000 people gathered on the banks of the Rhine River on June 10.[57] While Reagan and other NATO leaders met at the West German government chancellery, the huge crowd on the other side of the river basked in unusually sunny weather. The political atmosphere was stormy, though, as speaker after speaker denounced NATO policy and urged continued resistance to INF deployment.

When Reagan traveled to West Berlin the next day, his visit touched off some of the worst political rioting in that city in decades. Local police and courts had banned demonstrations during Reagan's visit "for security reasons," but a crowd of 100,000 protesters gathered in defiance of the ban and attempted to march through the city.[58] Security forces charged into the crowd and fired water cannon and tear gas, and demonstrators responded by overturning cars, erecting barricades, and hurling bricks. A series of pitched battles raged just a few blocks west of Checkpoint Charlie where Reagan was scheduled to appear, and the air was thick with tear gas and the black smoke of burning tires. Reagan was kept away from the street fighting, but the message of the rioting was clear. The policy of pressing ahead with cruise and Pershing II deployment was exacting a high political price in West Germany and throughout Europe.

Women for Peace

One of the most significant responses to missile deployment in Europe came from the women who were involved in the peace movement. Women not only marched against cruise missiles, they "set up house" so to speak on military ground all over Europe. As men throughout history have left their families to go to war, women were now leaving home for peace.[59] By creating peace camps at some of the military bases targeted to receive cruise missiles, large numbers of women began to take an active role in the public debate over nuclear weapons.

The idea of a peace camp emerged in Great Britain in September 1981, when members of the group "Women for Life on Earth" marched 125 miles from Cardiff, England, to the Greenham Common military base.[60] When the women began their walk, they had no idea they would not be returning home. Upon arrival at Greenham, the demonstrators demanded a televised debate with Defense Minister John Nott about the cruise missiles. When their request was denied, they decided to stay. By the end of 1982, there were long-term peace camps in more than a dozen cities in Britain and another dozen scattered throughout Europe. In December, nearly 30,000 women representing these various camps and other peace organizations came to Greenham to surround the base. During the following year, contingents from the camp would dance on missile silos, block the entrance to the base, lie on 10 Downing Street to greet Vice President George Bush, and go to jail.[61]

Although journalists and government officials attempted to dismiss the efforts of the Greenham Common camp and the women's peace movement by portraying them as male-hating lesbians (some of the women were lesbians, some were not), women from the camp refused to be silenced and repeatedly wrote letters and spoke out in an effort to set the record straight. Margaret Bailey and Gill Weeks wrote:

> We shared a feeling of purpose, of hope, along with our fears of what cruise means to our children's future. … We were all at Greenham from a personal belief, not because we had been pressured into going, not necessarily because we are politically motivated, but because we believe that cruise missiles are an unholy and horrific weapon for anyone to contemplate using.[62]

For the first time in its history, the arms control debate would not be left to a coterie of male military analysts, at least not if the women of the European peace movement had something to say about it. As cruise missiles were removed from the Greenham base in 1991, the women of the camp were still there, hoping to transform the base into an ecological park.

The Peak of Protest

Public opposition to the INF missiles reached its peak in 1983 when millions of people all across the continent marched for peace and disarmament in the largest wave of demonstrations in modern European history. The first round of mobilization occurred during Easter weekend, traditionally a time of peace movement activity. In Great Britain, two days of protest ended in a remarkable human chain that extended 14 miles across the English countryside. Stretching from the designated cruise missile base at Greenham Common to the nuclear weapons factory at Burgfield and skirting the nuclear research center at Aldemaston along the way, the human chain wound continuously along highways and narrow country lanes. According to Campaign for Nuclear Disarmament Chair Joan Ruddock, more than 70,000 people participated in the chain and joined hands to demonstrate their desire for peace and an end to the arms race.[63] In West Germany, the Easter events drew more than 400,000 people. Demonstrations and protest actions were held in dozens of cities and towns.[64] Sit-ins and nonviolent blockades took place at a dozen U.S. and West German military bases. In perhaps the largest of these events, 6,000 demonstrators formed a human chain around the U.S. Army's Wiley Barracks at the proposed Pershing II deployment site in Neu-Ulm.[65] In Bavaria alone, nineteen local peace events were organized. The weekend of activity culminated on Monday, a German holiday, when major rallies were held in eleven cities. According to the German Interior Ministry, several hundred thousand people participated in these rallies.[66] One of the largest was in Dortmund, where 100,000 people gathered. The theme in Dortmund and the other cities was the same as it had been for the past two years: "U.S. and U.S.S.R.: Leave Germany in Peace."[67]

By fall 1983, hopes that peace demonstrations might prevent the deployment of new NATO weapons were rapidly fading. With the first cruise and Pershing II missiles scheduled to begin arriving in a matter of weeks and the Geneva talks as inconclusive as ever, few believed that the arms buildup could be stopped. Yet, despite the apparent hopelessness of the situation, millions of Europeans again took to the streets in one last massive statement of political opposition. People seemed to be saying that, whatever the outcome of the debate, they still objected to the new missiles. They wanted to make clear that NATO leaders were acting without the consent of the governed.

The demonstrations began with a "hot autumn" campaign of sit-ins and nonviolent blockades at military bases in West Germany. On September 1, at precisely the hour World War II had begun forty-four years earlier, more than 1,000 people staged a sit-in at the Pershing II base in Mutlangen. Among the protesters blocking the main entrance to the base were novelists Heinrich Böll and Gunter Grass, Green party activist Petra Kelly, and Social Democratic party leader Oskar Lafontaine. Also joining the sit-in were U.S. peace activists Daniel Ellsberg and Phillip Berrigan.[68] The Mutlangen blockade was followed by similar nonviolent sit-ins at numerous military bases. One of the largest of these was a march of 15,000 protesters to Carl Schurz barracks in Bremerhaven.

The culmination of the fall mobilization came in October when nearly 3 million people poured into the streets all across Western Europe to protest NATO missile deployment and demand an end to the arms race. In London, more than 300,000 people assembled in Hyde Park on October 22 for what the *New York Times* called "the largest protest of its kind in British history."[69] Demonstrators were still setting off for the march to Hyde Park four hours after the rally began. Similar demonstrations of hundreds of thousands of people each took place in Rome, Vienna, Brussels, Stockholm, Paris, Dublin, Copenhagen, and other cities.[70] Perhaps the largest single crowd assembled in The Hague, completely filling the streets of the Dutch capital. In this country of just 14 million people, the crowd of nearly 1 million represented seven percent of the total population, equivalent to almost 17 million people in the United States.[71]

The biggest turnout of protesters occurred in West Germany the weekend of October 22. On a single day, 400,000 people marched in Bonn; 250,000 in Stuttgart; 400,000 in Hamburg; and 100,000 in West Berlin. In addition, more than 200,000 people participated in an extraordinary human chain that stretched continuously for 64 miles from the U.S. Army headquarters in Stuttgart to the missile base at Neu-Ulm.[72]

The peace movement enjoyed significant support among the major trade union organizations in Western Europe. Just as many of the member unions of the AFL-CIO in the United States endorsed the nuclear freeze, so most of the major union confederations in Europe supported the campaign to prevent deployment of cruise and Pershing II missiles. In West Germany, the giant DGB union federation (Deutsche

,haftsbund, German Labor Federation) provided financial and
ıtional support for the October 1983 demonstrations. The Ger-
nions also organized a nationwide work stoppage for five min-
ɔn October 4, 1983, to dramatize labor support for peace.[73] In Holland, the major union federation, FNV (Federatie Nederlandse
Vakbeweging, Netherlands Trade Union Federation), likewise served as
a principal sponsor and organizer of the massive October 1983 demonstration in The Hague. In March 1984, the Dutch unions organized a
symbolic fifteen-minute work stoppage for peace. In Great Britain,
nearly all of the country's major trade unions were members of the
Campaign for Nuclear Disarmament.[74]

The October 1983 demonstrations were the largest show of support
for the peace movement in European history. In terms of the numbers
of people involved, the protests were equivalent to the massive demonstrations in Eastern Europe six years later that led to the downfall of
communism. In the democratic West, however, massive political protests seemed to have little effect on government policy, while in the
dictatorial East, similar demonstrations led to political revolution. This
curious anomaly seems to reflect both the weakness of the old Communist system in the East and the inadequacy of representative democracy
in the West. Especially in relation to nuclear decision making, the political system in the West is extremely slow in responding to popular pressures. Over the long run, however, peace movement pressure did indeed help to shape government policy in the West.

Gorbachev to the Rescue

As cruise and Pershing II missiles poured into Europe in 1984 and the
years following, many peace activists felt a deep sense of disappointment and powerlessness. After so many demonstrations and protests,
they had been unable to prevent missile deployment. Washington had
responded to peace pressures by opening arms control talks with the
Soviets, but the negotiations went nowhere. In March 1983, the White
House yielded to further pressures from West Germany and other countries to de-emphasize the zero option and adopt a more flexible bargaining position known as the "interim solution" (a proposal for equal
numbers of INF weapons on both sides).[75] Moscow rebuffed the new
proposal, however, and a few months later walked out of the talks.
NATO went ahead with the nuclear buildup. The long struggle against
INF weapons in Europe seemed lost.

Yet all across Europe, as in the United States, the peace movement remained alive and well. The period of massive street demonstrations had passed, but thousands of peace groups remained active at the community level, educating and agitating for an end to the Cold War and the elimination of U.S. and Soviet weapons. Despite the apparent victory for hardliners, support for disarmament continued to grow. In West Germany, the number of "nuclear pacifists" (those opposed to any use of nuclear weapons, even in retaliation) steadily increased during the 1980s, rising from 29 percent of the population in 1981 to 45 percent in 1987.[76] By the end of the decade, nearly 80 percent of the West German population favored the removal of all nuclear weapons in Europe.[77] The antinuclear current within European society did not go away with the arrival of NATO missiles. Instead, it deepened and became a more permanent feature of society. Hope remained that a disarmament agreement might yet be reached.

A major breakthrough came in 1986, when Mikhail Gorbachev offered to eliminate all intermediate-range nuclear weapons as part of his sweeping proposal for "Disarmament by the Year 2000." Gorbachev's proposal seemed to put the zero option back on the bargaining table, this time at the initiative of the Soviets. A more specific version of the Gorbachev offer was brought to the summit in Reykjavik in October 1986, but it was tied to a restriction on the United States's testing and deployment of the Strategic Defense Initiative (SDI). When the Reagan administration would not compromise on SDI, the discussions at Reykjavik collapsed. Nonetheless, considerable progress had been made during marathon all-night bargaining sessions on the details of an INF settlement, and the possibility of a separate agreement remained alive. U.S. and Soviet negotiators continued to probe for common ground.

The final break came at the end of February 1987, when the Kremlin announced that it would now consider an INF agreement "without reference" to space-based weapons. Suddenly, the obstacles to a separate INF Treaty were removed. Moscow announced that the Soviet Union was now prepared to accept the zero solution—no INF missiles on either side. The White House was faced with the curious and unanticipated dilemma of having to take yes for an answer.

Officials in Washington and other NATO capitals were hardly jumping for joy at this unusual turn of events. Few had anticipated that the Soviets would accept the zero option when it was first proposed. According to Arms Control and Disarmament Agency Director Kenneth

Adelman, NATO leaders had regularly mouthed support for the zero proposal during the 1980s, but few really believed in it.[78] Now they had no choice but to go along with Gorbachev's offer. Helmut Kohl and Margaret Thatcher expressed public support but, according to the *New York Times*, were privately fearful that zero deployment would weaken NATO.[79] Eugene Rostow, Adelman's predecessor as head of the Arms Control and Disarmament Agency, confirmed in an interview that Kohl and Thatcher were uneasy. Their concern, according to Rostow, was that zero deployment would "decouple" the United States from Europe.[80] Henry Kissinger and Richard Nixon wrote an editorial ("speaking out jointly for the first time since both of us left office") warning that the proposed agreement might lead to "the breakdown of the NATO alliance."[81] Future National Security Adviser Brent Scowcroft penned an article (with John Deutsch and R. James Woolsey) entitled "The Danger of Zero Option." Recalling the original arguments for the NATO deployment decision, Scowcroft and his colleagues warned that the zero solution would be a "step toward denuclearizing Europe" and would weaken the "linkage between the United States and Europe."[82] General Bernard Rogers repeated his argument that INF missiles were vital to NATO military strategy.[83] These doubts deepened during the spring and summer, when the Soviet Union went further and accepted the so-called "double zero" concept. This meant the elimination of shorter-range as well as longer-range INF missiles. NATO leaders feared that the antinuclear sentiments they had tried so hard to contain might be reignited.[84]

Despite these reservations, NATO accepted Gorbachev's offer. The White House, in particular, needed the political boost that an arms treaty and a summit would provide. Gorbachev's revival of the zero option came just in time to turn public attention in the United States away from the Iran-Contra scandal (see Chapter 13).

"The Good of Demonstrations"

Throughout the ups and downs of the 1980s—from the exuberance of the giant peace rallies to the disappointment when INF missiles were deployed to the stunning reversals of Soviet policy under Gorbachev—the European peace movement maintained constant pressure for disarmament. The public desire for peace brought the two sides together in the first place, and it kept them focused on the search for a negotiated solution. Through countless acts, large and small, millions of ordinary people affirmed a faith that Europe could find a new path to security without Cold War divisions between East and West. What began as a dream at the beginning of the decade became a reality by its end, thanks in part to the persistent efforts of those who believed in and worked for peace.

With all the twists and turns of the nuclear debate during the decade, some activists lost sight of their contribution to the peace process and could not see their own hand in the writing of the INF Treaty. Yet the document that Reagan and Gorbachev signed was very much a result of their efforts. The third signature on the treaty belonged to the peace movement, to the millions of people who marched through the streets of London, Bonn, and Rome to keep alive the dream of disarmament. As Thomas Risse-Kappen has observed, "European peace movements lost the battle of the Euro-missiles [but] they ultimately won the peace."[85] The INF Treaty was not a victory for peace through strength but the result of new thinking in the Soviet Union and among Western publics. According to Risse-Kappen, "INF cannot be explained without reference to the domestic changes in the Soviet Union and the pressures exerted on Western policy makers by public opinion, peace movements, and center-left parties in Western Europe."[86]

The peace movement did more than help to forge an historic arms reduction treaty. It democratized the discussion of European security in a new and unprecedented way. After a decade of agonizing debate over nuclear weapons policy, public opinion and domestic political considerations were now central factors in military decision making. No longer could nuclear policy be made in the absence of public debate. Because of what happened during the 1980s, antinuclear attitudes became ever more deeply rooted in popular consciousness and the legitimacy of nuclear policy eroded. An example of this came in 1988 when a consensus quickly formed in Europe against the proposed "modernization" of short-range nuclear weapons. This new deployment of nuclear weapons had been proposed by NATO ministers to "compensate" for INF reductions. The public in West Germany and other countries overwhelmingly rejected the idea. Given the state of public opinion, Helmut Kohl informed a disappointed Washington, no German government of whatever political persuasion could deploy new short-range nuclear missiles.[87] A continuation of the old policy of nuclear buildup and East-West military competition was no longer possible. A new politics had been created, and it led inexorably to arms reduction and the end of the Cold War.

When the NATO ministers originally endorsed the zero solution in October 1981, Dutch Defense Minister Jan van Mierlow was asked by reporters if the giant disarmament rallies then taking place in Europe had influenced the ministers' decision. Van Mierlow paused at the question and attempted to draw a fine distinction. It was not the demonstrations, he tried to explain, but the fears that inspired these actions. He paused again and added with a smile: "That's the good of demonstrations."[88]

9

The Stop MX Campaign

The Peace Movement Meets the Mormons

At first nearly everyone was in favor. The U.S. Air Force described it as "a few missiles in the remote deserts of western Utah."[1] Elected officials welcomed the promise of jobs and prosperity. Mormon television and radio stations and a Mormon newspaper, the *Deseret News*, editorialized in favor of the plan.[2] Early opinion polls in Utah and Nevada showed the public solidly behind the project. Supported locally, funded by Congress, and approved by the White House, the MX seemed virtually unstoppable. When a reporter tried to gauge local opposition in August 1979, hardly a dissenting voice could be found. "Isn't anyone against it?" the reporter pressed an aide in the governor's office. "Well, maybe Frances Farley," the aide replied.

An outspoken liberal Democrat in the most conservative Republican state in the union, the first woman elected to the Utah State Senate in twenty years, Frances Farley was accustomed to being in the minority and was not afraid to speak her mind. She had first become involved in politics nearly two decades before while lobbying for a fair housing bill in Minnesota. She said:

> I had always been angry from the time I was a child about the way black people are treated in our country. I remember my mother taking me to Sunday School and seeing this huge picture on the wall of Jesus, hands outstretched from beautiful flowing robes, with children of every color in his arms. Underneath it read, "suffer the little children to come unto me." And I believed it, although maybe I shouldn't have, for I discovered fairly early that people don't always practice what they profess.[3]

Farley's lobbying effort in Minnesota was successful in swaying the votes of three conservative "curmudgeons," as she called them, and the bill passed: "It was my very first demonstration that one person can make a difference. I suddenly realized that I could have some influence on what happened in the world."[4] She remained involved in social activism, not only for the rights of black people, but for women's rights, peace, and the environment.

When Farley and her husband moved to Utah in 1970, she immediately jumped into local politics, eventually helping to elect civil rights and antiwar activist Steve Holbrook to the state legislature in 1974. She said: "Then in 1976 I thought, well now it's my turn. By this time the women's movement had started. I was elected to the state Senate on my first attempt. I decided as I entered office that I would always try to vote my conscience."[5]

Farley's conscience was severely troubled when she and a select group of state officials attended a U.S. Air Force briefing on the MX in August 1979. At the meeting, local officials were given their first glimpse of the enormous project to be built in the Great Basin. It included:

- 200 missiles carrying 10 hydrogen bombs apiece,

- 200 racetracks, each with 23 hiding places 7,000 feet apart, with 4,600 shelters in all,

- more than 10,000 miles of heavy-duty roadway on which a 1-million-pound missile carrier would travel and periodically duck into one of the hardened shelters.

The idea was to stage an elaborate shell game in which missiles would move about constantly and supposedly foil Soviet attempts to target and destroy them. It was obvious that this was more than the "few missiles" originally described and that an enormous amount of land would be required (one authoritative estimate put the total at 40,000 square miles).[6] Farley and others left the briefing room that day in shock. "I was horrified. I felt physically ill. It was insane, and obviously destructive for Utah."[7] She told friends and neighbors what she learned and began working in earnest to stop the program. One of the first persons she talked to was Chad Dobson, an environmental activist who became her partner in fighting the MX and who later moved to Washington to head the National Campaign to Stop the MX. From that point on, Farley said, "The MX fight became dominant in the lives of many of us." A powerful citizens' movement began to emerge against the missile.

The cast of characters involved in the Great Basin MX campaign numbered in the thousands. In Delta, Utah, Sue Dutson, third generation publisher of the *Millard County Chronicle,* meticulously documented the misstatements of U.S. Air Force promoters. In Nevada, Janet Moose of the Western Shoshone and Debra Harry of the Lake Pyramid Piute mobilized Native American people to join the anti-MX battle. In Salt Lake City, Episcopal bishop Otis Charles and Methodist minister Steve Sidorak formed a religious coalition to address the troublesome ethical issues posed by the MX. In Reno, Marla Painter labored long hours to persuade disparate groups, from cattlemen to environmentalists, to work together.[8] Perhaps the most colorful opponent was Utah rancher Cecil Garland, a cowboy and a gifted and educated speaker who was fond of quoting from Cicero. His most famous line, repeated on a two-hour Bill Moyers television special on the MX, deserves quoting: "They're talking about the land mode, the sea mode, and the air mode for basing the MX. I'd like to suggest another solution—let's put it in the commode!"[9]

One of the most influential activists against the MX was Ed Firmage, a respected professor of law at the University of Utah and a great-great-grandson of Brigham Young, founder of the Church of Jesus Christ of Latter-day Saints (LDS). Not only was Firmage a direct descendant of the Mormon prophet but his grandfather had been a member of the church's First Presidency and he himself had served as a bishop and had direct access to the Mormon elite. It didn't take a Ph.D. in political science to see that persuading the church to oppose the MX was a top priority. Firmage therefore focused his energies on educating and lobbying his colleagues in the Mormon community. He began by briefing Gordon Hinckley, then a member of the Council of the Twelve Apostles and chair of the church's Special Affairs Committee, in effect its committee on church and state. Firmage also prepared hundreds of pages of memoranda quoting from Old Testament, New Testament, and Book of Mormon teachings on war and peace. Eventually, Firmage was invited to the inner sanctum to brief church leaders.

The initial set of briefings for the First Presidency took place in the office of Spencer Kimball, then President of the Mormon church, in the headquarters across the street from the temple. I was then due to fly off to the

White House (in an attempt to convince the Carter administration to
back off on MX), but the officials asked me to delay my flight so that I
could conduct a joint briefing for both the First Presidency and the Council of the Twelve.[10]

Ed Firmage was not the only one to brief the Mormon leaders. Chad
Dobson and Frances Farley brought a parade of experts to meet with
church officials and educate local citizens about the consequences of
the MX proposal. Among those who made the trek to Salt Lake City
were retired Admiral Gene LaRocque, director of the Center for Defense
Information in Washington, and scientists Richard Garwin of Harvard,
Sydney Drell of Stanford, and Kosta Tsipis of MIT. Congressman Ron
Dellums (D-CA), the first sponsor of anti-MX legislation in Congress,
spoke before the Utah State Senate. Perhaps the greatest contribution
to this public education effort came from Herbert "Pete" Scoville, former deputy director of the CIA, whose briefings of local officials were
highly influential. Despite a handicap that made walking difficult,
Scoville traveled thousands of miles and spent many long hours in the
last years of his life campaigning against the MX. His patient and authoritative telling of the reasons to oppose the MX played an important
role not only in the Great Basin but also in the corridors of Congress
and in congressional districts all over the country.

The most damaging testimony against the MX came from the government itself. The Air Force's own draft environmental impact statements showed the MX depleting already scarce water resources, causing vast economic havoc (a severe boom and bust cycle), destroying
wilderness and wildlife habitats, and creating a host of other environmental and social problems.[11] The most powerful indictment was contained in an official U.S. Air Force map of the system that gave graphic
proof of the vast scale of the project. Frances Farley explained how it
came to light.

> One day in November 1979, an attorney friend called and said "I've got
> something I think you should see." My husband and I went down to his
> office on a Sunday morning, and he unfolded this huge map showing the
> layout of MX racetracks. We were shocked and overwhelmed. It showed
> the MX covering every desert valley from Salt Lake City to Cedar City and
> a third of the way into Nevada. Every flat place among the mountains was
> covered. I knew if the people of Utah could see this, public opinion would
> turn around.

My friend couldn't give me a copy for fear of losing his job, so I tried to get the map by requesting it under the Freedom of Information Act. The Air Force refused on grounds that this was an "intra-office document." So Chad Dobson, who was working at the time for the local NBC affiliate, began calling around to local Air Force bases to see if he could talk someone into giving us a copy. He found a Captain at Nellis Air Force Base in Nevada who said, "Oh sure, I know that map. I'll send it to you."

That Friday night, while I was at a cocktail party for the legislature, Chad came rushing in and pulled me aside into a separate room. He had the map! The very next morning, we took it down to the *Salt Lake Tribune*, and they published a full-page spread on Sunday. On Monday I presented the map to my colleagues at the legislature, and the local television stations featured it that night.

The impact of the map was devastating. The map showed the MX taking much of the state. People knew this would be a disaster. The next opinion poll showed an immediate change: For the first time a majority of respondents was opposed to the MX.[12]

As doubts mounted and people learned more about the MX, the opposition movement began to pick up steam. A broad coalition of diverse constituencies and interest groups joined to fight the missile, creating an unusual collection of bedfellows. Peace activists opposed the building of a threatening new missile. Religious groups questioned the morality of the program. Environmentalists were alarmed by the vast damage that would result to flora and fauna. Conservative groups such as the National Taxpayers Union spoke out against the waste of money (the official price tag was $33 billion, but independent estimates put the figure at $70 billion).[13] The International Association of Machinists and other unions argued for different federal spending priorities. Cattlemen and sheepmen condemned the use of rangeland for missiles. Native Americans protested the further violation of Indian land rights. Rarely had the peace movement enjoyed the backing of such a broad coalition.

At the national level, SANE and other groups made stopping the MX a top priority. The missile was an inviting target; it was so large and unwieldy that it might collapse of its own weight, especially if given a push by effective citizen action. The primary emphasis for SANE was to encourage and support opposition at the grass-roots level. In October 1979, staff members Marilyn McNabb and Michael Mawby were dispatched to the Great Basin to assist the growing local campaign.

McNabb and Mawby approached their task with a keen sensitivity to local concerns and spent much of their time in the region listening rather than telling. McNabb had been a longtime activist for Nebraskans for Peace and the previous year had helped block Air Force plans for basing the MX in the northern plains. Mawby was a talented young organizer who later became chief lobbyist and political director for SANE. McNabb and Mawby were welcomed by local activists. The information and support they provided in this and several subsequent trips made an important contribution to local empowerment.

Soon the traffic began to flow in the other direction. Instead of bringing national organizers to Utah, local groups now sent grass-roots opponents back to Washington to explain to politicians and the media why a growing number of residents in the Great Basin rejected the MX. A national speaking tour was organized to bring the message to local congressional districts all over the country.

In 1980, the number of groups in Utah and Nevada campaigning against the MX began to multiply. Despite the conservative bent of the area, many people harbored a suspicion about government nuclear programs. This could be traced in part to the bitter legacy of the nuclear testing program of the 1950s, when residents of the region, especially southern Utah, were subjected to harmful radioactive fallout from above-ground testing. The memory of that experience, combined with a resentment at being viewed as the nation's dumping ground for nuclear waste, fed into the growing MX opposition. In Salt Lake City, the MX Information Center was formed. Under the direction of Stan Holmes, it organized numerous educational forums, media briefings, and protest demonstrations. In Nevada, Citizen Alert established itself as a major statewide organization. In Las Vegas, NO MX (Nevadans Opposed to MX) sponsored a wide range of educational and organizing activities. Joe Griggs and Joanne Garrett of Baker, Nevada, worked tirelessly to pull together all of these groups in a single Great Basin MX Alliance.

Gradually, the cumulative impact of this broad citizens' movement began to be felt politically. During the 1980 elections, local organizers in Nevada placed MX referenda on the ballot in eight rural counties. The questions were nonbinding, but the vote nevertheless demonstrated widespread voter rejection of the missile system. Nevadans voted 2-1 against the MX—54,729 against, 26,417 in favor.[14] Where a year before polls had shown only 20 percent of the people opposed to the MX, the 1980 referenda showed two-thirds now against. By 1981, opposition among people in rural Utah had reached 75 percent.[15] Throughout the region, opinion polls showed the public now solidly against the MX.

The most important voice in the region had yet to speak, however. Despite the opposition growing around it, the Church of Jesus Christ of Latter-day Saints had remained officially silent. The question of the MX posed a dilemma for the church. To take a stand only on the MX in Utah could be seen as shallow and undignified, a form of backyard ethics, but to address the larger question of the missile itself and the nuclear arms race would be to go against church tradition. Despite the earlier nuclear testing experience in the region, the church had not previously spoken out on the nuclear issue. Now, however, the weight of potential disruption posed by the MX and the gentle but persistent prodding of Ed Firmage and others prompted the church to act.

Three statements were ultimately issued by the Mormon First Presidency. The first two—at Christmas 1980 and Easter 1981—were general condemnations of the arms race and pleas for negotiated reduction. The Christmas message said, in part:

> We are dismayed by the growing tensions among nations, and the unrestricted building of arsenals of war, including huge and threatening nuclear weaponry. Nuclear war ... spares no living thing within the perimeter of its initial destructive force, and sears and maims and kills wherever its pervasive cloud reaches. ... We are enjoined by the word of God to "renounce war and proclaim peace." We call upon the heads of nations to sit down and reason together in good faith to resolve their differences.[16]

Having established a moral basis for concern about the arms race, the First Presidency then issued a specific MX statement on May 5, 1981:

> We repeat our warnings against the terrifying arms race in which the nations of the earth are presently engaged. We deplore in particular the building of vast arsenals of nuclear weaponry. ... We are most gravely concerned about the proposed concentration [of MX] in a relatively restricted area of the West.[17]

The statement went on to warn that the MX system might actually invite preemptive attack and that the radioactive fallout from such an attack would destroy much of the nation. It spoke of the system's "adverse impact" on water resources, society, and the "fragile ecology" of the area. It concluded:

> Our fathers came to this western area to establish a base from which to carry the gospel of peace to the peoples of the earth. It is ironic, and a denial of the very essence of that gospel, that in this same general area there should be constructed a mammoth weapons system potentially capable of destroying much of civilization.
>
> With the most serious concern over the pressing moral question of possible nuclear conflict, we plead with our national leaders to marshal the genius of the nation to find viable alternatives. [18]

The May 5 statement was the decisive event in the defeat of the MX basing plan. As Ed Firmage observed, "That one act broke the back of the MX. The idea of force-feeding a missile down the throats of 70 percent of the people, that portion represented by the Mormon church, was more than the political process could take."[19]

Mormon opposition to the MX had a major impact on the Reagan administration and contributed substantially to the decision to dump the racetrack plan. Prior to entering office, Reagan had not made a commitment on MX. As a candidate he had spoken derisively of the Carter basing plan, but he did not oppose the missile (and in fact never did) and certainly did not suggest an alternative plan. He was dubious of the racetrack concept but was by no means ready to reject it. The opposition of the Mormons undoubtedly bolstered his skepticism. Here was a constituency the White House could not ignore. As Ed Firmage noted:

> The Mormon people were the rock hard base of Reagan supporters. Our state had gone more heavily for Reagan than any other. When he saw that kind of old line patriarchal leadership, socially and politically conservative, taking that kind of stand, and taking it on an ethical basis, it had to give the Reagan administration pause.[20]

The opposition was also helped by the fact that Nevada Senator Paul Laxalt was Reagan's friend and the chairman of his 1980 Campaign Committee. Laxalt did not commit himself formally on the MX either, but under pressure from his own state's cattlemen and sheepmen he finally announced his opposition in June 1981. Both Frances Farley and Ed Firmage had met with the senator in Washington earlier that year.

They were encouraged by his skepticism and were told that he would convey the depth of local opposition accurately to the president.

The weight of these pressures finally tipped the scales within the White House. Eugene Rostow, head of the Arms Control and Disarmament Agency at the time, confirmed that political opposition in the Great Basin was decisive: "The president ... did make adjustments in response to pressures around the MX. There's no doubt about that. ... When Laxalt came and said he opposed having MX in Nevada, the president listened."[21] In October 1981, the administration announced that the MX racetrack basing plan was being abandoned. The proposal to turn the Great Basin into a home for mobile missiles was at last dead.

Champagne bottles popped on the night of the president's decision. In Salt Lake City, Las Vegas, Reno, and other Great Basin communities, local activists celebrated their victory over the Pentagon. An unlikely coalition of peace activists, environmentalists, religious groups, Native Americans, taxpayer groups, trade unionists, and farmers had defeated the combined power of the White House, the U.S. Air Force, and the military industrial complex. An environmental catastrophe had been averted, and the cause of peace received a major boost. As Frances Farley observed,

> I never doubted for a moment that we would win. We simply were not about to lay 10,000 miles of super missile highway on our deserts. ... We learned from this experience that we had better be involved as citizens in policy making. We learned that we must not swallow whole what our federal government tells us. ... We learned that we have power as citizens.[22]

Celebrations were held in Washington, too, as national organizations rejoiced in the partnership with local groups that had turned back the power of the Pentagon. The euphoria was short-lived, however, for the victory was only partial. The basing plan had been defeated, but not the missile. The MX itself was still alive. The campaign now turned to the second and more difficult task, attempting to defeat a major nuclear weapon system through congressional lobbying.

The Battle in Washington

Defeat of the racetrack basing plan was only the initial step in the MX fight. The MX campaign had always been seen as having several stages.

Once land deployment was prevented and the basing mode blocked, the focus shifted to the missile itself and an all-out lobbying effort to halt MX production funds. Ultimately, the plan was to stop all land-based missiles and begin to reverse the entire arms race. Blocking this one missile was seen only as a first step in the larger effort for disarmament.

The fight against the MX was also a chance to build SANE and other peace movement organizations. The MX campaign was good for raising funds, recruiting and activating members, building coalitions, and strengthening organizational alliances. It also played a key role in forging an effective arms control lobby on Capitol Hill that remains in place to this day. As the MX campaign progressed, SANE, the Council for a Livable World, and other Washington-based groups became increasingly sophisticated and effective in lobbying and grass-roots organizing. Fund-raising increased, revenue grew, and additional lobbyists and organizers were hired. Where previously the arms control lobby on Capitol Hill had consisted of a handful of mostly church-based representatives, the peace community now fielded a formidable team of professional lobbyists who were quickly learning the ways of Capitol Hill politics. It was during the MX fight that the "Monday Lobby Group" was formed. This weekly gathering of peace and nuclear policy groups became (and still is) a central coordinating point for peace lobbying activities in Washington. Formed in the early 1980s, the Monday Group continued to grow throughout the decade, sprouting subcommittees and task forces of all varieties and sponsoring a wide range of field organizing, media relations, and other lobbying activities. The U.S. peace community now had an effective presence on Capitol Hill.

Another key factor in strengthening the anti-MX lobby was the arrival on the scene of the venerable citizens' organization Common Cause. Founded during the Vietnam War, Common Cause had worked throughout the 1970s on issues of "clean government." With the freeze ferment sweeping the country, Common Cause decided to join the antinuclear cause by bringing its considerable resources to bear in the fight against the MX. Common Cause brought not only its 300,000 members and powerful network of local chapters to the campaign, it also added an important element of professionalism and experience to the Capitol Hill lobbying team. While SANE's lobbyists were relatively young and inexperienced (although talented and energetic), the Common Cause lobbyists were seasoned veterans of previous Capitol Hill

battles and were skilled in the ways of pressuring Congress. Led by former Common Cause President David Cohen, the Common Cause lobbyists soon became a dominant force in the MX coalition.

Other groups joined the coalition as well. In all, nearly 100 national
organizations participated in the campaign. The International Association of Machinists, the National Education Association, taxpayer
groups, farmer organizations, national environmental groups, the
YWCA and other women's groups, and most of the major church denominations all joined in the lobbying fight against MX appropriations. By 1984, Monday Lobby Group meetings were drawing more
than fifty people and the conference room of the Washington office of
Stewart Mott where the sessions were held was overflowing. The peace
and arms control community had become, in the words of a veteran
Washington observer, "one of the most effective citizen lobbies ever
wrought."[23]

Arrayed against this coalition was a powerful constellation of forces
including the White House, the Air Force, and major military contractors. For the military industrial complex, the MX was a valued prize.
The missile was important not only to weapons builders eager for new
contracts but to strategists in the Pentagon and the administration.
The missile was described as the centerpiece of the nuclear buildup, an
awesome weapon that would confront the Soviets with overwhelming
nuclear power. Each of the ten warheads on the hydra-headed MX was
thirty-five times more powerful than the Hiroshima bomb. The MX
was also the most accurate intercontinental ballistic missile (ICBM)
ever built. The missile possessed "hard target kill capability"—the ability to deliver a first-strike blow against Soviet weapons.

To preserve their coveted missile, Pentagon and White House officials employed every pressure tactic in the book—and some that were
not in the book. One of the ways Air Force officers promoted the MX on
Capitol Hill was by distributing an elaborate plastic model comparing
U.S. and Soviet missiles. On one side of the model were the huge missiles of the Soviet Union, dark and menacing, while on the other were
the puny, seemingly impotent weapons of the United States. The not-
so-subtle message in the male-dominated world of Congress and the
Pentagon was clear: We need a big one to match theirs. Officials all over
Washington were fixated on the need for a "big missile."

More conventional lobbying tactics were also employed. Whenever
Congress voted on the missile, an army of pro-MX lobbyists was dis-

patched to Capitol Hill. "They were all over the place," reported Congressman Les Aspin (D-WI).[24] Weapons builders mobilized their employees in local districts. Arms negotiators were brought back from Geneva to lobby Congress. Political favors were promised and punishments threatened. Lists were prepared of workers who would be laid off if MX funds were cut. The president and his top cabinet officials personally lobbied legislators who wavered. That the anti-MX coalition was able to hold its own against these powerful forces was a tribute to the strength of the peace movement.

Grass-roots Pressure

The effectiveness of the anti-MX lobbying effort in Washington depended mostly upon grass-roots involvement. No matter how skilled or knowledgeable they might be, peace movement lobbyists on Capitol Hill could not succeed without pressure from the grass roots. SANE lobbyists found that their access to legislators was directly proportional to the amount of heat generated by constituents in the member's home district. In the early phase of the campaign, when local pressures were minimal, lobbyists would cool their heels in the outer office of a member of Congress and have to settle for talking to an aide. Later, as grass-roots networks strengthened, access improved dramatically. Not only in the Great Basin but all across the country the MX became a cause célèbre. An increasing number of activists in the burgeoning freeze movement joined legislative networks to lobby against the MX. When these activists generated pressure at the local level, doors were opened on Capitol Hill. Before long, peace lobbyists were dealing with members of Congress directly. Eventually, they sat in with the speaker of the house and other top legislators in planning strategy and projecting vote counts. Where previously the peace community had little influence, now it was considered a serious and legitimate player. All of this was made possible by the power of citizen action at the local level. More than any other factor, grass-roots pressure defined the effectiveness of the MX lobbying fight.

To mobilize this formidable grass-roots network, an intensive phone-banking operation emerged, run by the Washington offices of Common Cause, SANE, the Coalition for a New Foreign and Military Policy, and other religious and peace groups. Before each crucial vote, volunteers and staff members made hundreds of calls to key activists in local districts. Many of those called at the local level would in turn contact dozens of friends and neighbors on telephone trees. The result would be a flood of last-minute calls and letters to members of Congress. Common Cause also mounted targeted direct mail campaigns, on one occasion sending more than 10,000 letters to its supporters in the district of Vic Fazio (D-CA). The result of these and other grass-roots efforts was a flood of constituent pressure against the MX just before crucial votes.[25] Prior to each vote the phone banks would be activated (sometimes literally overnight), and a deluge of constituent pressure would pour into congressional offices. Prior to the key 1984 votes, for example, Fazio received more than 500 cards and letters from his constituents. In the days before a big vote in 1985, Senator Charles Mathias (R-MD) received nearly 2,000 calls, and Senator Dan Evans (R-WA) received more than 1,000.[26] Backed up by this massive grass-roots support, the lobbyists of the Council for a Livable World, SANE, Common Cause, and other groups were suddenly accorded new respect. The anti-MX grass-roots network was a force to be reckoned with on Capitol Hill. Congressman Aspin said, "The citizens and grass-roots organizations did come up very big time against the MX. That clearly had an impact on forcing the administration to deal with the moderates in the House."[27]

The organizing strategy of the MX campaign focused increasingly on the "swing" votes in the House—those forty or so members who were neither totally for nor totally against the missile but who switched back and forth during the various votes. Eventually, the list of undecided voters was pared down to sixteen Democrats and twelve Republicans. The districts of these members became the focus of intensive grass-roots lobbying pressure. SANE, Common Cause, and other groups in the coalition sent organizers and lobbyists to each of these districts. An example of such efforts was the 1984 visit to the Utica, New York, district of Republican Sherwood Boehlert by Common Cause lobbyist Kathleen Sheekey. In a breathtaking one-day blitz of the city, Sheekey met with local anti-MX organizers, convened a press conference, appeared on two network affiliate television stations, was interviewed on four radio stations, and did a prime-time radio call-in talk show. At the end of the afternoon, she dropped in on Boehlert himself at his local office, accompanied by reporters from local television and radio stations.

Another example of grass-roots lobbying pressure was SANE's door-to-door canvassing drive in the Maryland district of Democratic Representative Steny Hoyer. The SANE canvassing program played an invaluable role in this and other action campaigns. Founded in 1983 by Peter Deccy, former activist with the Connecticut Citizen Action Group, the SANE canvass spread by 1985 to a dozen cities and during the summer employed 200 organizers, mostly young college students. The canvass was an essential tool for recruiting members, raising money, and generating grass-roots political pressure. It was the principal factor in expanding SANE's membership, adding nearly 100,000 contributors to the rolls in just three years. The canvass also provided a ready-made field operation for electoral campaigns and was highly effective in generating petitions and letters from local constituents to members of Congress.

It was this grass-roots lobbying capability that was used to generate anti-MX pressure on Hoyer and other "swing" legislators. In 1984, SANE canvassers delivered to the congressman thousands of anti-MX petitions and letters signed by voters in his district. Hoyer's constituents also were mobilized to show up at local town meetings. Hoyer would appear at these sessions expecting to discuss the usual topics—Social Security and the local post office—and instead would find himself besieged by anti-MX protesters. For months, the beleaguered congressman was hounded mercilessly as peace supporters turned up at nearly every town meeting. On one occasion, which happened to take place on Valentine's Day, several local constituents (myself included) presented the congressman with a huge heart inscribed with the message, "Dear Steny, don't break our hearts, vote against the MX." Religious groups also joined in these lobbying efforts. Hoyer faced pressure not only from SANE canvassers but from clergymen throughout his district, including his own minister. At a service just before one of the crucial MX votes, the congregation in Hoyer's local Baptist church heard a sermon on the nuclear threat and the dangers of the MX missile—a message clearly intended for the distinguished parishioner in the front pew.

The Reagan Administration Stumbles

In the wake of Reagan's cancellation of the racetrack plan, the focus of the MX fight shifted to the administration's attempts to devise a new basing mode. The search for a mobile basing plan had gone on for many years, and Air Force planners had already developed and discarded more than thirty different basing proposals. Some of the plans were wildly bizarre, such as burying missiles in quicksand or lifting them on dirigibles. The seemingly endless and often ludicrous search for MX basing plans became grist for Washington humorists. Chad Dobson produced a booklet of cartoons on the MX that became a hit all over Washington and an effective tool in lobbying against the missile. Jokes about the MX circulated widely. Columnist Art Buchwald once suggested, for example, that if the goal was to keep the location of missiles secret, the easiest solution would be to put them on Amtrak. Since the trains are never on time and no one knows where they are, the Soviets would never be able to find them. It was meant to be a joke, but in the late 1980s, Air Force planners and the Bush administration actually proposed a plan similar to this known as MX rail garrison, which Congress promptly derailed.

The Reagan administration's initial approach to the basing issue was extremely clumsy. Having rejected the Carter racetrack plan, the president and his advisers were unable to come up with a viable alternative. At first, the administration proposed placing the missiles in existing silos as a temporary measure while various long-term basing options were considered. Among the possible scenarios mentioned were placing missiles on large airplanes, the so-called Big Bird plan, or housing them in deep underground missile bases (for which the appropriate acronym was DUMB). Neither Congress nor the public bought these ideas. With grass-roots pressure mounting, Congress rejected the administration's ideas and in effect told Reagan to go back to the drawing board. As Strobe Talbott described it, the MX program was "undergoing a Chinese water torture of public and congressional opposition."[28]

In November 1982, yet another bizarre proposal was announced—the Dense Pack plan. Instead of scattering missiles among widely separated shelters, as in the racetrack plan, the Air Force now proposed packing the missiles close together (this time in the state of Wyoming). The theory was that Soviet warheads attempting to attack the closely packed missiles would destroy each other ("fratricide" it was called in the doomsday lexicon of the Pentagon). The idea was criticized by experts and ridiculed by cartoonists. By this time, according to Kenneth Adelman, "the general public joined Congressional experts in concluding that the Pentagon didn't know what it was doing."[29] Deputy Press Secretary Robert Sims, who was charged with trying to sell the plan, later admitted the impossibility of his task: "I don't care how effective you might be in communicating about fratricide and the benefits of a dense pack system, ... the public wasn't going to buy that. It just was too much of a Rube Goldberg idea."[30]

While the administration was floundering about with this and other MX plans, the White House faced mounting political problems elsewhere. The economic recession that hit soon after Reagan took office brought rising unemployment and declining presidential approval ratings. During the 1982 congressional midterm elections, the Democrats scored important gains, especially in the House of Representatives, where they picked up twenty-six seats. In a few of these races, political participation by peace activists was significant. Democratic advances significantly improved the prospects for arms control in the House of Representatives.[31] In the same election, nuclear freeze referenda were approved in eight states, including California, and in dozens of major cities and counties. Freeze fervor was sweeping the country. With the political tide turning against the military buildup, the new MX plans ran into a storm of criticism.

Thanks to the administration's bungling, the anti-MX legislative fight got off to an auspicious beginning. In the lame duck session of Congress that followed the 1982 elections, the MX Dense Pack plan suffered a humiliating defeat. The House voted 245-176 to reject the administration's proposal and cut off production funds until a new basing plan could be found. The Senate went along with the House action and set procedures for congressional approval of any new MX plan. Congress would have up to forty-five days after receiving the next proposal to decide whether to release production funds. According to Robert McFarlane, the defeat resulted from "a considerable popular backlash ... [from] antinuclear sentiment combined with partisan political opportunism and legitimate military criticism."[32] For SANE, the Council for a Livable World, and the other groups involved in the MX fight, the December vote was an important victory. Production funds had been cut, even if only temporarily, and opponents were guaranteed another congressional vote before MX development could continue. Each additional delay and procedural complication strengthened the opposition and increased the chances that the missile could be halted.

Trading the MX for Arms Control

In the aftermath of the vote on the Dense Pack plan, the struggle began to take on an increasingly symbolic character. The issue became less the missile itself and more the Reagan administration's sincerity (or a lack thereof) in arms negotiation. The MX became a political football that congressional leaders sought to use to force the administration to negotiate seriously with the Soviets. As time went on, the significance of the MX fight became less the cuts in the missile itself and more the political pressures it generated on the Reagan administration.

The idea of using the MX to extract arms control concessions from the White House originated with a group of moderate congressional representatives led by Les Aspin (D-WI), Al Gore (D-TN), and Norm Dicks (D-WA). These and other supporters of approving the MX in exchange for arms control were "swing" votes who had sometimes voted for the missile, sometimes against. Their support was crucial to deciding the outcome of the MX debate. Although Aspin and his colleagues recognized many of the absurdities of the MX, they nonetheless pledged to vote in favor of the missile if the Reagan administration would make a serious commitment to arms negotiation. A similar effort was mounted by moderates in the U.S. Senate led by William Cohen (R-ME), Sam Nunn (D-GA), and Charles Percy (R-IL). By holding the MX hostage to progress in the arms talks, the legislators were essentially redirecting the pressures they were feeling from the peace movement onto the Reagan administration. This congressional effort to force arms control concessions from the White House resulted from the power and effectiveness of grass-roots peace activism. According to Robert Kimmit, who was then executive secretary of the National Security Council, "Gore, Dicks et al. ... were driven in part by what the freeze movement was doing."[33]

The strategy of Aspin and his cohorts had considerable impact on the White House. As Strobe Talbott has pointed out, rescuing the MX from congressional veto was a major preoccupation of the Reagan administration.[34] White House strategists met repeatedly on the MX problem and went to great lengths to preserve this supposed centerpiece of the nuclear buildup. According to Kenneth Adelman, a very high political price was paid for the missile. Adelman calls the MX a "dog, the strategic albatross of the Reagan administration." For five years, the Reagan White House had to battle repeatedly to save the missile, "with the President and the Secretaries of State and Defense doling out staggering political capital each time merely to keep this dubious project alive."[35] Ultimately, it became clear that the MX could not be saved without political concessions. To prevent further losses and avoid a humiliating political defeat, the administration was forced to pledge more serious efforts at the bargaining table. As Robert Sims noted, "The MX seemed to survive in some form ... but at a very great expense in terms of what the administration ... had to agree to with the Congress."[36]

Scowcroft to the Rescue

In early 1983, with the MX gasping for air and its heralded nuclear buildup in disarray, the Reagan administration created the Scowcroft Commission, hoping that this new body of outside experts would bring the missile back to life and restore credibility to White House policy. Composed exclusively of hawks, both Democrat and Republican, the commission was dedicated to the proposition, as Robert McFarlane put it, that "we had to have the MX."[37] Its task was to find a political formula for saving the missile. The appointment of the commission was a direct result of pressures from the movement to stop the MX. According to Les Aspin, "The Scowcroft Commission was created because the administration saw that they were about to lose the whole ball of wax. It was an attempt to put something together politically that would bind up the moderates on the Democratic side. It came about because of the grass-roots opposition."[38] Robert Kimmit agreed that the freeze movement had a "very significant effect" on the MX fight and "probably was one of the factors that contributed ultimately to the Scowcroft Commission being set up."[39]

The Scowcroft Commission issued its report in April 1983. It endorsed the policies of "nuclear modernization" (i.e., buildup), but it also spoke of the need for arms negotiations. On the MX itself, the commission urged that production continue but proposed that the number of missiles be cut in half, from 200 to 100. This was an important concession to the anti-MX coalition. As for the mobile basing plan—the concern that had created so much difficulty for the MX in the first place—the commission simply gave up, recommending that the missile be placed in silos. Scowcroft and his colleagues declared that the "window of vulnerability" (the theory that U.S. missiles were becoming vulnerable to Soviet attack) did not really exist after all—a point the peace movement had been making for years. This abandonment of the vulnerability issue was another important concession. An argument that the Carter and Reagan administrations had emphasized repeatedly was simply dropped in the face of peace movement pressure. The commission also recommended the development of an entirely new land-based system, the small single-warhead weapon known as the Midgetman. Research and development began on the Midgetman, but the program was hampered by congressional opposition and was later abandoned with the ending of the Cold War.

The recommendations of the Scowcroft Commission and the question of renewed funding for the MX were scheduled for a vote in the House of Representatives in May 1983. As the vote approached, congressional moderates renewed their call for a clear commitment from the administration that it would bargain seriously at the Geneva talks. In response, Reagan wrote to members of Congress vowing a serious commitment to arms negotiation and promising to "review" the administration's START proposal.[40] Although MX opponents on Capitol Hill dismissed Reagan's letter as vague and meaningless, the moderates claimed to be satisfied with the White House pledges. A substantial number of "swing" voters dutifully announced their support for the MX. The White House now had enough votes to win, at least for the moment, and the MX passed by a vote of 239-186 in the House and 59-39 in the Senate. This approval of the MX came just three weeks after the House vote in favor of the nuclear freeze resolution that would supposedly halt such weapons. For peace lobbyists, it was a bitter defeat.

Despite the disappointment, the anti-MX coalition continued to mobilize opposition to the missile and the outlook for the next round of MX votes became increasingly uncertain. In July, the House took up the issue again, and while the MX managed to survive, the margin of victory was cut in half. As the deadline for a third round of voting in the fall approached, the fate of the missile became ever more uncertain. Aspin and his partners faced intense anti-MX pressures. A SANE-sponsored advertising campaign against Aspin in his home district in Wisconsin, for example, included a thirty-second radio spot criticizing Aspin's support for the MX that played dozens of times in the local district prior to the key votes. Aspin claimed to be unfazed by the pressure. Michael Mawby remembers that Aspin called to him one day in the halls of Congress, saying, "You guys are helping me out with those ads, keep it up." Despite the congressman's bluster, he faced a steady drumbeat of criticism. Aspin's stand on the MX was so unpopular with his Democratic colleagues in Congress that they voted to unseat him as chairman of the House Armed Services Committee, although he later won back the post. According to Congressman Ed Markey, "All of Les Aspin's problems with the Democratic Caucus resulted from his stand on the MX."[41] As these and other pressures mounted, the moderates became less and less willing to accept the administration's vague promises. They wanted concrete commitments. If the MX was to be saved again, the administration would have to make further concessions.

In a desperate attempt to shore up support for the embattled missile, the White House extended the life of the Scowcroft Commission and renewed its promises of compromise at the bargaining table. Scowcroft was dispatched to Capitol Hill for a new round of discussions with congressional leaders. It is an ironic fact, noted by Strobe Talbott, that negotiations in 1983 were more intense between Congress and the White House in Washington than between the United States and the Soviet Union in Geneva.[42] In October, the White House and Congress reached their "Magna Carta" agreement. In this remarkable and unprecedented development, members of Congress substituted their own proposal for that of the administration and successfully forced the White House to change its bargaining position. As Talbott described it: "The legislative branch of the government had, in effect, fired the executive branch for gross incompetence in arms control."[43]

The congressional attempt to pressure the Reagan administration into accepting arms control was a partial success. The weight of outside political pressure helped to tip the balance within the administration toward greater flexibility at the bargaining table—although it would take several more years before the Geneva negotiations produced concrete results. That the Congress was able to make any change at all in Reagan administration policy was due largely to the pressures generated by the peace movement and the anti-MX coalition. It was grassroots peace activism that created political pressure on Congress, and that pressure ultimately forced the Reagan administration to moderate its positions and make a stronger commitment to negotiated arms limitation.

Continuing the Fight

As the 1984 legislative season opened, the Reagan administration sought to capitalize on its 1983 victories, however narrow, by requesting funds for forty additional missiles, thereby locking in full-scale MX development. Approval of this plan would have given the Air Force a total of sixty-one missiles and created momentum for the full 100 missiles proposed by the Scowcroft Commission. Peace groups feared, moreover, that once the Air Force received the first 100 missiles, it would quickly return to its original request for 200 missiles.

Within the anti-MX coalition, the strategy was not only to deny funding for the new missiles but, if possible, to cancel the twenty-one missiles that had been authorized in 1983. Since there was some disagreement about the latter demand, however, the slogan for the campaign became "No new missiles." The message was sufficiently ambiguous to please those like Common Cause President Fred Wertheimer, who wanted to roll back the 1983 missiles, as well as those like David Cohen, who saw this demand as unrealistic and sought to concentrate instead on stopping just the forty new missiles. Everyone agreed that the May vote was crucial and that an all-out mobilization of anti-MX sentiment was needed.

Throughout the first part of 1984, SANE, Common Cause, the Council for a Livable World, and other groups in the MX coalition intensified their lobbying and organizing efforts. Reports from the grass roots and soundings on Capitol Hill showed the coalition gaining ground. Support for the administration's policies was slipping. The reverse side of the MX-for-arms control gambit was now showing itself: If the administration could not deliver on its promises of arms control, the commitment of moderates would begin to waver. With the Geneva arms talks in suspension and election year criticisms of White House policy mounting, the administration's position on the MX became increasingly untenable. Before long, it was clear that the White House simply did not have the votes to push through the proposed increase in MX funds. Recognizing this erosion of support, the president's allies in Congress began to backtrack. First, the House Armed Services Committee voted to reduce the number of new missiles from forty to thirty. Reagan vehemently objected to this move and even called Chairman Aspin during the committee vote to urge that they hold the line. The congressman listened politely but explained that he did not have the votes for forty missiles and would be lucky to get thirty.[44]

As the lobbying intensified and the day of the May floor vote approached, Aspin saw that he did not have the votes for even thirty missiles. At the last minute, he proposed yet another compromise: reduce the number to fifteen missiles. Attempting to revive his previous strategy, Aspin also proposed that the money for the fifteen new missiles not be spent until the following year, pending the resumption of "good faith" negotiations in Geneva. The definition of what constituted good faith negotiation was to be left to the president. This new compromise seemed to please some MX skeptics in Congress, although the projected vote counts still showed the contest to be extremely close. Throughout this struggle, the anti-MX coalition consistently had a more reliable and accurate vote count than many congressional leaders, and the speaker of the house soon began to rely on its projections.[45] With grass-roots pressure pouring into congressional offices and lobbyists from Common Cause, SANE, and other groups hovering in the Capitol cloakroom, the debate and final vote went late into the night of May 16. When the electronic scoreboard posted the final tally, the Aspin compromise had won—although by the razor thin margin of just six votes.

At any time during the long lobbying fight on the MX, the peace movement forces could have rolled over and given up. It was especially difficult to continue the battle after losing close votes and at times when all of the vast human effort that had gone into the nationwide campaign would come so close and yet still fail. Over the seven years of the MX fight, more than twenty-five major votes occurred on the missile program. Many had the flavor of climactic showdowns, with button-holing by peace lobbyists, arm twisting by the White House, and job blackmail by arms contractors in high gear. Peace movement forces actually won very few of these votes, perhaps just a quarter, although the constant opposition kept missile proponents constantly off balance.

When those of us who were involved in the coalition lost a close vote, as we had done so often in 1983 and then again in early 1984, it was hard to believe that our labors were worth the effort. Often we would gather after these votes at a particular Capitol Hill pub, ironically called the Hawk and Dove. At first we would drown our sorrows and feel depressed and frustrated at losing again by a narrow margin. Gradually the mood would shift, however. After a beer or two, our disappointment would turn to anger and then to determination and we would vow to ourselves not to give up. We were not going to give in to the White House and its Air Force and arms contractor allies. We would leave the pub determined to continue the fight and with a renewed faith that somehow our efforts would bear fruit.

Such was the case after the first showdown in May 1984. The vote had been extremely close, much tighter than many politicians had predicted, and MX opponents had won new respect on Capitol Hill. Convinced that it was gaining strength, the coalition decided to seek an immediate revote. When David Cohen and other senior lobbyists approached Speaker of the House Tip O'Neill with the idea of a new vote, the speaker readily agreed. O'Neill had been impressed with the tenacity and effectiveness of the MX coalition, and he wanted to use the issue as an election year challenge to the Reagan administration. An alternative to the Aspin compromise was crafted: Funds for the MX would be suspended as before, but the determination on what constituted good faith negotiations (and therefore whether funds could be released) would be made by Congress, not by the president.

The coalition groups immediately went back to work and again contacted their members and supporters all across the country for another big push against the MX. At the grass-roots level, as in Washington, the same determination and sense of faith inspired people to gear up their lobbying networks again. Telephone trees were reactivated, and another intensive round of constituent pressure was applied on beleaguered members of Congress. Again the lobbyists worked the corridors of Congress, and again thousands of calls and letters poured in from the grass roots. The vote on what came to be known as the "Common Cause compromise" came on May 31. This time the endless hours of organizing and campaigning paid off. Three separate MX votes were taken that night: The House voted first on the original Aspin proposal, then on another pro-MX proposal, and finally on the Common Cause plan. The MX coalition won the first vote 199-197, the second 198-197, and the third 199-196. The margin of success was extremely narrow, but the victory was sweet nonetheless.

The Final Act

The MX drama continued into 1985 and went through one more cycle of success and failure before culminating in a final compromise and defeat for the administration later that year. The immediate question as the year began was whether Congress would release the MX production funds that had been suspended the previous May. Once again, the fate of the missile hinged on the prospects for arms control in Geneva. The political climate that spring was significantly different from what it had been the previous year. The Reagan administration had made repeated promises of arms control on its way to election victory in November. The Soviet Union had seen the folly of its 1983 walkout at Geneva and had returned to the bargaining table. Perhaps most important (although the full implications of this change were not yet apparent), a new reform-minded leader had been selected to head the Soviet Union. There was a mood of optimism in Washington and a hope that the atmosphere of confrontation that had characterized the first Reagan term might finally give way to an improvement in East-West relations.

Against this background, the MX coalition faced an uphill battle. Nonetheless, the lobbying and phone-banking operations were geared up again. Grass-roots activists responded with a renewed wave of anti-MX pressure, and once again, members of Congress were flooded with demands to stop the MX. Despite the surge of grass-roots pressure, however, the coalition was unable to prevent congressional approval of MX funding. In mid-March, the MX survived four close votes in the House and Senate, and once again missile production funds began to flow. The up and down roller coaster of the MX campaign had come crashing down to rock bottom again.

At this darkest hour, when anti-MX forces had suffered a serious political defeat, a ray of light appeared. Out of defeat came hope for victory, at least a partial one. In a postmortem strategy meeting of senior lobbyists and sympathetic congressional aides, the idea emerged of legislating a permanent cap on the number of MX missiles.[46] The concept was to arrange for a political truce, to stop the MX program where it was in exchange for an end to the constant political squabbling. If a way could be found of freeing Congress from continually voting on the MX, perhaps a majority of legislators would support the idea. When lobbyists began to float the plan on Capitol Hill, it was greeted enthusiastically. Members were so eager to free themselves of the MX albatross that they readily embraced the statutory limit proposal. At last the end of the MX fight seemed in sight.

A key factor in bringing the MX debate to a close was congressional fatigue, a kind of political shell shock among members of Congress weary of facing constant criticism over the MX. After seven years of debate, members were tired of having to vote on the issue and were desperately searching for a way out. This mood was reflected in buttons that anti-MX lobbyists and members of Congress alike sported during the spring debate: "Put Congress Out of Its Misery—Shoot the MX." In a sense, the MX coalition managed to achieve success through sheer perseverance. By refusing to give up, by coming back after each vote, usually stronger and better organized than the last time, the coalition began to wear down the opposition. This relentless pressure and the prospect of seemingly endless debate on the MX no doubt encouraged acceptance of the proposal for a legislative cap.

In truth, peace movement activists were also weary of the MX fight and were eager for a solution that would stop further development and preserve the successes that had been achieved to date. Lobbyists recognized that a cap on missile deployment would halt the MX where it was and prevent additional production or deployment in the future. When the statutory limit was announced, therefore, peace groups also breathed a sigh of relief and signaled a willingness to go along.

The original version of the cap proposal, introduced by Congressman Nick Mavroules (D-MA), was for a permanent limit at forty missiles. The House of Representatives accepted this provision in June. The more conservative Senate adopted a weaker version, however—a one-year cap at fifty. The final version approved by the Conference Committee accepted the House provision for a permanent limit and the Senate proposal for fifty missiles.[47] Liberals and conservatives alike accepted the agreement. By this time, few members of Congress cared about the exact number of missiles. Everyone was relieved that the long and divisive congressional struggle on the MX was finally at an end.

The campaign against the MX was an important success for the peace movement. Despite massive lobbying, first by the Carter administration and then by the Reagan administration, the Pentagon was defeated in its plans for a mobile basing system and managed to obtain only a quarter of the missiles originally sought. A program described as the centerpiece of the nuclear buildup emerged as a pale imitation of its former self. The MX fight also generated pressure on the Reagan administration to negotiate for arms reduction and to adopt a more flexible posture at the Geneva talks. These efforts helped to moderate the positions of the Reagan administration and spurred the negotiations that ultimately led to the INF and START agreements.

Within the peace community itself, the MX campaign provided a vital learning and maturing experience. A relatively sophisticated and professional lobbying presence emerged on Capitol Hill, and the techniques of grass-roots mobilization were refined and strengthened. The benefits of effective coalition building were learned and successfully applied. Perhaps most important, the movement tasted victory and saw that political mobilization at both the national and grass-roots levels could achieve results. The success was only partial, but it was nonetheless real and empowering. The MX Goliath was not slain, but it was cut down to less menacing size.

10

Star Wars
Versus Earth Peace

When Ronald Reagan announced his plan for a Strategic Defense Initiative (SDI) on March 23, 1983, military officials at home and abroad were shocked. Almost no one had been consulted. It was, in McGeorge Bundy's words, "the loneliest presidential decision on nuclear matters in history."[1] White House Communications Director David Gergen called it "a bolt out of the blue."[2] Where did the decision come from? In this and the following chapter I examine the origins and consequences of SDI and assess its relationship to the peace movement.

The SDI program had very earthly origins, to use historian Greg Herkin's phrase.[3] It was the product of many factors—including the persuasiveness of physicist Edward Teller and the "laser lobby" and pressure from High Frontier and other right-wing organizations. It may also have come from the president's days in Hollywood, a fantasy world of heroes and super weapons. In the 1940 film *Murder in the Air*, Ronald Reagan played secret agent Brass Bancroft, who saves the day with a miracle weapon, the "inertia projector," that shoots down enemy aircraft.

As a politician, Reagan had long supported the concept of strategic defense. In 1972, Reagan spoke out against the ABM Treaty negotiated by the Nixon administration and urged instead an acceleration of missile defense programs. The Republican party platform on which Reagan ran in 1980 pledged "vigorous research and development of an effective anti-ballistic system."[4] It was not until early 1983, however, that the president's strategic defense vision began to take shape. Why did the administration wait nearly two years to act on Reagan's cherished dream? Martin Anderson claims that the president was simply too busy,[5] but this excuse is hardly convincing. In fact, the timetable for SDI was dictated primarily by politics, especially the pressures generated by the peace movement. By December 1982, when Reagan first raised the SDI concept with the Joint Chiefs of Staff, the administration's nuclear buildup was in serious trouble. The nuclear freeze movement was at the height of its influence, the MX program was stalemated, a huge disarmament movement was raging in Western Europe, members of Congress were clamoring for progress at the bargaining table, and Roman Catholic bishops and other religious leaders were writing pastoral letters directly challenging White House policy. This mounting antinuclear ferment made SDI not only possible but necessary. The White House desperately needed a creative new political initiative that could overcome and co-opt the rising ground swell of opposition. SDI became the answer. It was a program, in Robert McFarlane's words, that "exploited popular anti-nuclear aspirations" and provided an end run around the political stalemate on earth.[6]

The MX Connection

The most troubling and immediate threat faced by Reagan and his military advisers in early 1983 was the prospect of defeat for the MX missile. The White House's Dense Pack basing plan had just gone down to defeat in the House of Representatives, and the fate of this centerpiece of the strategic buildup was very much in doubt. At a crucial meeting with the military chiefs in February 1983, according to Star Wars proponent Angelo Codevilla, Reagan "heard the grim news that ... political support for new missile programs in the country was fast disappearing."[7] General John Vessey, chairman of the Joint Chiefs, told the president that the United States might not be able to keep pace with the Soviets. According to Sanford Lakoff and Herbert York, Reagan and his advisers "were evidently convinced that while the Soviets were deploying more offensive weapons ... the United States could not keep up—because of political and economic objections" to the nuclear buildup.[8] Faced with these obstacles to an offensive buildup, the administration began to turn toward the option of a strategic defense buildup.

A key figure in promoting the strategic defense plan and shepherding it past the normal process of bureaucratic review was Robert McFarlane, then assistant national security adviser. The manner in which McFarlane bypassed government procedure with the Star Wars decision was similar to the process he and others would follow a few years later in the sale of arms to Iran and the diversion of profits to the Nicaraguan Contras. Almost alone among the president's senior national security advisers, McFarlane encouraged Reagan's missile defense fantasy and worked to make it a reality. A key consideration in McFarlane's thinking was the MX stalemate.[9] He worried that not only the MX but also the newly proposed Midgetman missile would be permanently blocked by a combination of congressional critics, antinuclear activists, and environmentalists. Having seen how the campaign to stop the MX had so effectively derailed the racetrack plan in Utah and Nevada, McFarlane doubted whether mobile missiles could ever be deployed anywhere in the country. These political obstacles made strategic defense seem attractive. In subsequent congressional testimony on the SDI decision, McFarlane made these connections explicit. He said, "After the loss of two proposals for MX basing, and then in December, 1982, the loss again of I think Dense Pack, Admiral Poindexter came in one day and said 'it looks to me like we are going to have trouble … maintaining an equivalent balance with the Russians based on offense alone.'"[10] If an offensive buildup could not be maintained, strategic defenses would have to do.

The Moral High Ground

The administration's embrace of strategic defense also served a broader, more far-reaching political purpose. It was an attempt, as *U.S. News & World Report* observed at the time, to "seize the moral high ground in the struggle with the nuclear freeze movement."[11] The president responded to the nation's nuclear phobia by conceiving a program that would supposedly make nuclear missiles "impotent and obsolete." Never mind that most scientists thought the concept preposterous. The power of the idea was its utopian imagery. Whether it worked or not didn't really matter. The point was to address the public's antinuclear sentiments and convey the impression that the new program would meet these concerns. The White House could thus claim to embrace the goals of the freeze movement—ending the threat of nuclear war—without adopting its means—negotiated disarmament.[12] Instead of the uncertain prospect of bargaining with the Soviets, the president offered a vision of peace based upon the traditional American belief in technological superiority. White House Public Affairs Director

Michael Baroody called the Star Wars decision "a kind of political judo," a means of throwing an opponent off balance.[13] Reagan turned the enormous public concern about nuclear war on its head and used it to leverage support for a new form of military buildup.

The heart of Reagan's SDI message, the line that captured the essential moral appeal, originated with Admiral James Watkins, chief of naval operations. Watkins was part of the White House task force dealing at that time with the Catholic bishops and their troublesome pastoral letter. Watkins, a devout Catholic, may have been influenced by the bishops' injunction against the use of nuclear weapons and the immorality of threatening to kill millions of innocent people. In a meeting between the Joint Chiefs of Staff and the president, Watkins described SDI as a hopeful program that would defend people rather than kill them. According to Caspar Weinberger, who was present, Reagan liked Watkins's "memorable phrase" and jotted it down for subsequent use.[14] Reagan added a stock phrase to his store of aphorisms. "Wouldn't it be better to save lives than to avenge them?" he would frequently intone. Who could argue with such a proposition? Thus did the White House co-opt the moral appeal of the Catholic bishops and the freeze movement. (Of course the White House's SDI program was not what the bishops had in mind in their statement of moral concern about nuclear war. In a 1988 review of the pastoral letter, the bishops stated their support for the ABM Treaty and their opposition to the deployment of an SDI system.)

Star Wars was a masterful political and public relations ploy but was fraught with contradictions that would later create serious problems for the administration's nuclear program. SDI greatly complicated political relations with the Soviet Union and became a major obstacle in arms negotiations. Within the U.S. political establishment, many reacted with shock to the president's announcement, not only because they had been cut out of the decision-making process but because they considered the concept absurd. The major problem was Reagan's insistence on the space dome concept—his belief (contrary to most expert opinion) that SDI could really protect the population against missile attack. Some viewed the concept as dangerous and counterproductive. According to David Gergen,

SDI undercut our nuclear deterrence strategy. It said in effect that nuclear war is immoral, that nuclear weapons are immoral. That was exactly what our opposition was arguing. It badly undercut our conservative friends in European capitals who were trying to tell the Left that nuclear weapons are moral. To go to this SDI-as-an-umbrella concept, and to embrace it as an antinuclear measure, caused real problems in our public communications strategy.[15]

The president's Star Wars vision may have clashed with scientific reality and the established logic of nuclear policy, but the White House pressed ahead regardless. The political requirements of responding to the antinuclear movement led inexorably to the grandiose vision. Star Wars could only overcome public fear of nuclear war if it could promise to eliminate the threat of nuclear war and make missiles "impotent and obsolete." To make an end run around the political obstacles on earth, the White House had to create a fantasy world in outer space.

SDI and Arms Control

Reagan administration officials claim that SDI was crucial in pressuring the Soviet Union to sue for peace. Former National Security Adviser Richard Allen said in an interview that the space defense program was "certainly the most decisive factor" in achieving a breakthrough for peace: "It was SDI that basically broke the resistance of the Soviets and brought them back to the bargaining table."[16] Former White House Communications Director David Gergen likewise stated that "SDI worked magnificently with the Soviets, convincing them that they couldn't keep up with" the United States.[17] Because SDI "would place unacceptable strains on their economy," claimed Martin Anderson, "the only course left to them [was] serious arms reduction negotiations."[18] Many others have made a similar point.

The Soviets showed no sign of being intimidated by SDI, however. On the contrary, they vowed repeatedly that they could and would respond. If the Soviets had attempted to replicate the proposed U.S. technologies—"smart" rockets, laser weapons, and computerized battle management systems—the burden on the Soviet economy might well have been overwhelming. But the Kremlin had no intention of matching these capabilities. Early on in the SDI debate, they recognized the value of what was called an asymmetric response. Moscow proposed to overcome SDI by relying on less expensive countermeasures and an expansion of offensive warheads.[19] As Gorbachev wrote in

Perestroika, "Our response to SDI would be effective. ... A tenth of the U.S. investments would be enough to create a counter-system to frustrate SDI."[20] In 1988, the Council on Economic Priorities (CEP) did a comparative cost analysis of SDI and the likely Soviet response that confirmed Gorbachev's estimate. The CEP study calculated that the cost to the Soviet Union of doubling its ICBM force and building thousands of cruise missiles would be approximately $50 billion.[21] By contrast, cost estimates for SDI began at $400 billion and ranged up to $5 trillion. The Soviet response thus would be from ten to 100 times cheaper. The definitive evaluation of SDI was given by the eminent physicist and Soviet dissident Andrei Sakharov:

> Possibly SDI proponents in the United States are counting on an accelerated arms race, associated with SDI, to exhaust and ruin the economy of the USSR. This policy will not work and is extremely dangerous to international stability. In the case of SDI, an "asymmetric" response (i.e., a push to develop offensive forces and weapons to knock out an SDI system) would most efficiently frustrate such hopes. The claim that the existence of the SDI program has spurred the USSR to disarmament negotiations is also wrong. On the contrary, the SDI program is impeding those negotiations.[22]

SDI played an ambiguous role in the resumption of arms control talks. In the spring of 1984, as Washington and Moscow surveyed the political wreckage from their dispute over INF deployment and the collapse of negotiations the previous November, both sides had reasons to seek an improvement in relations. The Reagan administration remained worried over the president's vulnerability on the nuclear war issue and fretted that the breakdown of arms control talks might be exploited by the Democrats in the fall election campaign.[23] Within the Soviet Union, political pressures were also building for a reopening of talks. The Soviets' strategy of walking out at Geneva and attempting to manipulate Western publics to block the INF deployments clearly had failed. While some within the military and the party bureaucracy continued to argue for a hardline approach, others, including a majority in the Politburo, were looking for a way out of the dangerous deadlock with Washington.[24] As the Soviet leadership cast about for a rationale that would allow them to return to the bargaining table without too much loss of face, their attention focused on the emerging threat posed by SDI. As Lakoff and York have observed: "[SDI] gave the Soviets an excuse to return to the negotiating table. They almost certainly wanted to return for other reasons ... [but] SDI enabled the Soviets to claim that a new and ominous challenge had been added, and that they had compelled the United States to address the issue."[25] The Reagan administration actively encouraged the Soviet hope that negotiations might lead to limits on Star Wars. In his eagerness to resume the Geneva talks, Reagan reportedly told Foreign Minister Andrei Gromyko that the United States would be willing to "consider" restraints on antisatellite weapons testing if the arms control process were renewed.[26] According to Soviet expert Matthew Evangelista, the Soviet "willingness to return hinged on U.S. agreement to negotiate space weapons along with INF and strategic forces."[27] When the talks got under way again in March 1985, strategic defense and space weapons issues were added to the agenda.

Because the Soviet Union appeared to come back to the bargaining table due to concern over SDI, many assumed that SDI would be an effective bargaining chip to force concessions from Moscow. An opportunity seemed to exist for trading SDI limitations for restraints on Soviet strategic missiles. Arms control advocates began to speak of such an arrangement as the "grand compromise." It was an elegant concept that seemed to meet the needs of both sides. For the Soviets, the much-feared prospect of "space strike weapons" could be eliminated, while for the United States, the menace posed by Soviet heavy missiles could be greatly reduced. Enormous efforts went into formulating variations of the concept, including the proposal for a 50 percent cut in strategic forces, elaborated by Paul Nitze, and an innovative plan for percentage annual reductions (PAR), developed by Jeremy Stone of the Federation of American Scientists.[28]

The problem with all of these proposals for compromise, however, was that the Reagan administration stubbornly refused to consider any restraints on its coveted SDI program. Over and over again in public statements and in meetings with Soviet officials, Reagan and his senior advisers repeated that SDI was not a bargaining chip. "We're not going to give anyone a veto over this thing," Reagan declared.[29] Whenever journalists asked about compromise on SDI, which was often, White House spokespersons issued emphatic denials. At every point where an opportunity might have existed to gain concessions through limits on SDI, Reagan insisted that there would be no deals. In November 1985, prior to the first summit meeting with Gorbachev, Reagan vowed to fight any compromise on SDI and said "this isn't a bargain chip."[30] In 1986, prior to the Reykjavik summit, he again emphatically denied rumors circulating in Washington that limits on Star Wars might be part of an arms agreement.[31] "No way. SDI is no bargaining chip," he said.[32]

The Reagan administration's insistence on developing SDI and its refusal even to consider limitations blocked progress toward arms reduction for more than two years. Initially, the White House had offered a promise of compromise as an inducement for the Soviets to return to the bargaining table, but administration officials quickly resorted to a kind of "bait and switch" tactic. The promise of limits on space weapons never materialized, and the Soviets were left with a take-it-or-leave-it proposition. Predictably, the talks went nowhere. According to historian John Newhouse, SDI "became the largest of the obstacles to a strategic arms agreement."[33] In the words of McGeorge Bundy, "Reagan's unbending refusal to accept limits on SDI blocked ... [the] possibility for a new strategic agreement."[34] Sanford Lakoff and Herbert York likewise observed that SDI "seriously complicated the arms control process."[35] Far from being a spur to the ending of the Cold War, SDI was a major obstacle to arms reduction and blocked improvements in U.S.-Soviet relations.

To the Summit

As the 1984 electoral season approached, the White House sought to arrange a U.S.-Soviet summit that would position Ronald Reagan as an arms control candidate. With its touch for the dramatic media event, the administration recognized the political benefits that a well-staged summit could provide. According to Strobe Talbott, administration officials originally planned for such a summit in time to boost Reagan's reelection drive,[36] but Soviet leaders kept dying or were too frail. More important, the chilling of U.S.-Soviet relations resulting from the SDI controversy and the start of INF deployments made direct dialogue between the leaders impossible. Unable to orchestrate a preelection spectacular, the administration had to settle for a September session at the White House with the dour Andrei Gromyko—an effective ploy but not nearly as powerful as a meeting between heads of state.

The resumption of U.S.-Soviet negotiations and the ascent of Mikhail Gorbachev in March 1985 dramatically improved prospects for a summit. Accordingly, the administration laid plans for Reagan to meet the new Soviet leader, and in April it was announced that a summit would take place later that year in Geneva. As the White House prepared for the meeting, a careful game plan was developed. The emphasis would be on atmospherics, not substance. The administration would attempt to create an appearance of improved relations with the Soviets but would carefully avoid any agreements that might restrain their arms buildup. At the Pentagon, Caspar Weinberger and other hardliners dug in their heels against a compromise on SDI, to which the president willingly agreed. White House press officers labored to lower public expectations and dampen media speculation that agreement might result. This was to be just a "get acquainted" session.

To stage the show, it was decided to call in the master of political theater, Michael Deaver, who by this time had left the White House to deal with his problems of alcoholism and influence peddling. Deaver had created many winning images for Reagan in previous campaigns, and it was hoped that he would work his magic again now. After surveying the situation, Deaver quickly saw that the principal press story should be Reagan's personal relationship with Gorbachev. He said, "I started as I always did by asking what we want the newspapers to say the day after the summit and working back from there. The story we wanted was of the personal relationship, Reagan's personal magnetism with Gorbachev." To emphasize this approach, Deaver went to see Reagan in his White House quarters. He later reported:

> I remember the night before he left for Geneva I went up to talk to him. I said, Mr. President, I think it is vital that at the very first meeting, when you walk into the room and sit down, you look at Gorbachev and say, why don't we get rid of these advisers and go talk by ourselves? The most important thing you've got to do is get him to know you and trust you. Well that's exactly what he did. I talked to him afterwards and he said some of the discussions were very deep. He even talked about religion and God.[37]

Deaver and the White House media managers were successful. Press attention focused on Reagan's performance in dealing with his young and formidable Soviet counterpart, and attention was diverted from the substance (or lack thereof) in the negotiations. Ronald Reagan thus emerged triumphant from the summit, although not a single concrete step was achieved to slow the arms race. A number of preliminary discussions were held between U.S. and Soviet negotiators to narrow some differences in the START and INF talks, but the administration's un-yielding position on SDI prevented overall agreement. The disagreement over SDI was too great to allow the progress achieved in other areas to bear fruit.

The Other Meeting with Gorbachev

The Reagan-Gorbachev summit was due in large part to public pressures for arms reduction. Because the peace movement had done so much to generate these pressures, it was only natural that the movement should have a role in the event. Soon after the summit was announced, I met with Jane Gruenebaum, executive director of the Nuclear Weapons Freeze Campaign, to discuss how SANE and the Freeze Campaign should respond. We decided to send a citizens' delegation to Geneva and to seek meetings with Reagan and Gorbachev. An independent group, Women for a Meaningful Summit, also decided to send a delegation. The goal of these efforts was to raise public expectations, thereby countering White House strategy, and to build continuing pressure for concrete steps to halt the arms race. Gruenebaum and I also decided that our SANE/Freeze delegation would be more effective if it carried to Geneva an expression of mass support for disarmament. Accordingly, a national petition drive was launched, the Appeal to World Leaders, with the goal of collecting 1 million signatures by the time of the summit in November. The petition was a simply worded statement that called on Reagan and Gorbachev to achieve progress at the summit and to agree on a mutual halt to nuclear weapons testing.

The decision to focus on the test ban issue was motivated by several factors. A U.S.-Soviet nuclear test ban had long been a goal for the peace movement (SANE was founded in 1957 as part of the movement to halt atmospheric nuclear testing), and it was always seen as an essential part of the nuclear freeze. SANE and other groups began to revive the test ban issue in 1984 as a way of sustaining the momentum of the freeze movement and applying it to a specific, easily verifiable first step toward ending the arms race. These efforts suddenly assumed increased importance in August 1985, when Gorbachev announced that the Soviet Union would begin a unilateral moratorium on nuclear testing. Peace activists quickly recognized the importance of the Soviet action and turned their attention to convincing the Reagan administration to accept the Soviet offer. All the administration had to do, we emphasized, was say yes. The Soviets had already stopped, and the way was now open for the United States to join in a permanent halt to nuclear testing.

The nuclear test ban was (and still is) a great issue for grass-roots organizing. It is a simple, easily understandable proposal that many ordinary people recognize and support. In March 1986, SANE commissioned a nationwide poll with the Opinion Research Corporation of Princeton, New Jersey, to measure this public sentiment. The survey results confirmed that the call for a mutual test ban was highly popular. When asked, "Should the United States stop testing nuclear weapons as long as the Soviet Union also stops?" 60 percent of the respondents said yes and 33 percent said no. An even higher proportion, 80 percent, agreed that the United States and the Soviet Union should refrain from nuclear testing at least until the next summit.[38] Because of the popularity of the test ban, SANE door-to-door canvassers and local organizers asking for signatures on test ban petitions found an enthusiastic response. After Gorbachev announced the Soviet moratorium, the public reaction became even more positive. As a result, support for the Appeal to World Leaders was overwhelming and the goal of obtaining 1 million signatures was reached in just a few months. The SANE canvass played a key role in this effort, collecting nearly half of the 1 million signatures.

In addition to SANE's door-to-door canvass, a special "celebrity canvass" was organized. The idea was to ask prominent entertainers to assist with signature gathering and promotion of the campaign. One of those who helped was model Christie Brinkley. In the midst of the campaign, Brinkley had sent a contribution to the SANE office, which touched off great excitement among the staff. It was decided that I should write to her and ask if she would be willing to participate in the celebrity canvass. Brinkley responded immediately, saying she would be glad to help. To ensure maximum attention, the petitioning table was set up on Fifth Avenue in Manhattan in front of Rockefeller Plaza. At the appointed hour, Brinkley and her assistants arrived in a huge limousine and joined SANE canvassers for a lively and enthusiastic hour of petitioning and campaigning. A large crowd gathered, and reporters and camera crews jammed the sidewalk. The occasion was a great success, generating hundreds of signatures in just one hour, but more important, creating positive publicity for the petition drive and the SANE/Freeze campaign.

By coincidence, the annual nuclear freeze conference in 1985 was scheduled for the weekend of November 15–17, two days prior to the beginning of the Geneva Summit. It was decided to turn the Chicago gathering into a rally to send off the citizens' delegation and the petitions. On the final day of the conference, a huge thermometer was displayed at the front of the hall to tally the number of signatures. As those of us who were participating in the delegation watched from the dais, a roll call of the states began, and SANE and Freeze Campaign representatives from local chapters came forward to present their petitions. As the marker moved steadily closer to 1 million, excitement increased. When the organizers from New York stepped forward with the petitions that put the marker over the top, the convention erupted in cheers. Balloons were released and music blared, and the freeze conference turned into a rollicking celebration. In the midst of the excitement, with delegates cheering and reaching out to us as we passed by, our delegation left the stage and marched out through the hall to depart for O'Hare Airport. It was an exhilarating and inspiring moment. We had the sense of being emissaries on a mission of peace to urge the world leaders to halt the arms race.

The leader of our citizens' delegation was the Reverend Jesse Jackson. Jackson spoke to the freeze convention just before the delegation departed and brought the crowd to its feet with a fiery and impassioned plea "to give peace a chance." Gruenebaum and I had decided to invite Jackson because of his strong support for the freeze movement. We also felt that his participation would help draw public attention to our mission. We looked upon Jackson as a kind of "people's secretary of state" and felt he would be an ideal spokesperson in our hoped-for encounters with Reagan and Gorbachev.

Prior to our departure, we had sent letters and made numerous inquiries to the White House and the Soviet Embassy in Washington requesting meetings. When we arrived in Geneva the night before the summit, however, we still had not received a formal response from either side. Later that evening, the first breakthrough came when we were met by Soviet Central Committee member Georgi Arbatov, head of the Institute for U.S.A.-Canada Studies in Moscow and a top adviser to Gorbachev. Arbatov acknowledged receipt of our requests and said that our delegation could deliver the petitions and meet with a "high official" at noon the next day. Immediately our group was abuzz with excitement and speculation that the official in question might be

Gorbachev himself. We huddled late into the night with Jackson to discuss what to say at the meeting the next day. We had previously agreed that we would urge the Soviet Union to extend its moratorium on nuclear testing, but we also wanted to raise other concerns that would show our independence and challenge the Soviet Union on human rights concerns. Jackson recommended that we focus on the plight of Soviet Jews and other minorities in the Soviet Union, and we quickly agreed.

The next day, as Reagan and Gorbachev began their summit and posed for fireside photographs, our highly expectant delegation made its way to the Soviet Embassy. We were joined by representatives of the European disarmament movement who were also in Geneva, including Monsignor Bruce Kent, the head of the Campaign for Nuclear Disarmament in Great Britain. When we arrived in the hallway of the mission, Soviet protocol officers were nervously scurrying about and trying to position everyone in predetermined places. Our delegation from SANE, the Freeze Campaign, Women for a Meaningful Summit, and the European peace movement numbered more than fifty people. We were told that the meeting would take place right there in the hallway and would probably last only a few minutes. As the preparations became more frenetic and tension mounted, we became increasingly convinced that the "high official" would indeed be Gorbachev. Finally, at a little past 12:30 P.M., a fleet of limousines pulled up to the embassy and the Soviet leader and his entourage swept into the hallway. We gasped in excitement as Gorbachev approached with an outstretched hand to greet Jackson and our delegation.

After introducing Gruenebaum, myself, and several leaders of the Women for a Meaningful Summit delegation, Jackson immediately got down to business and raised the points we had agreed upon the night before. In his lengthy and somewhat rambling response, Gorbachev spoke about the need for "real disarmament" but did not address our concern for the human rights of Soviet Jews and other minorities. At this point, as the interpreter was translating Gorbachev's remarks, Jackson broke in and challenged the Soviet leader to respond on the question of human rights. "We ask you to reply to our concerns," Jackson insisted. Taken aback by Jackson's audacity and obviously shaken by this unexpected challenge from the peace movement delegation, Gorbachev quickly regained his composure and attempted to offer a response. Essentially he denied the issue, saying that Jews have made valuable contributions to disarmament and that the "so-called problem of the Soviet Jews does not exist."

For the rest of the encounter the atmosphere was more cordial. After Jackson and Gorbachev completed their exchange, Justine Merritt, founder of the Ribbon Project, spoke on behalf of Women for a Meaningful Summit and presented Gorbachev with a section of the ribbon embroidered with images of flowers and children. Gorbachev seemed genuinely moved by the ribbon and Merritt's comments. Pointing to the embroidery, he said, "This is a reminder of the diversity and beauty of the world we must save." Jackson then directed Gorbachev to the table where the boxes of petitions were placed, and he and I formally presented them to the Soviet leader. "How many signatures are here?" Gorbachev asked. We told him that the final count was nearly 1.2 million. Impressed at this large outpouring of public concern, Gorbachev responded, "These petitions represent the hopes of millions of Americans." With these final words he again shook Jackson's hand and departed.

It had been a remarkable event. The meeting that was supposed to last just a few minutes had gone on for almost an hour. In the midst of his first encounter with the president of the United States, Gorbachev had taken time for a dialogue and meeting with the peace movement. By contrast, the Reagan administration spurned our requests to meet with the president or a high-level official. When we insisted upon delivering the petitions regardless, we were met at the U.S. Embassy by a low-level official, Deputy Undersecretary of State for European Affairs Charles Thomas.

The next day, international press coverage of the summit focused on the peace movement's meeting with Gorbachev. Because the U.S. and Soviet delegations had decided on a blackout of news coverage on the negotiations themselves, our session with Gorbachev became a major story. Throughout the world, newspapers and broadcast media reported on the Jackson-Gorbachev exchange and the petitions brought by the representatives of the U.S. peace movement. Much of the coverage was highly negative, however, especially that of the *Washington Post* and the U.S. television networks. Many of the stories were critical of Jackson for supposedly upstaging and embarrassing Reagan. The reports mentioned Jackson's challenge to Gorbachev on human rights but ignored his appeal for a U.S.-Soviet testing moratorium.[39] The presence of the peace groups that had sponsored the delegation and collected the petitions was hardly mentioned. Even Bill Moyers, the otherwise liberal commentator for CBS, criticized Jackson and the peace movement delegation for supposedly playing into Gorbachev's hands.

Although much of the national press coverage was negative, local news reporting was more favorable because a major grass-roots component had been built into the summit campaign from the outset. Local groups all across the country had sponsored events to support the efforts of the citizens' delegation in Geneva. Many of the groups that had collected signatures for the Appeal to World Leaders participated in these events. During the first night of the summit, November 19, hundreds of local freeze groups gathered for peace vigils and demonstrations in their communities. The theme of the local actions was "Watching in Hope," and they were designed, as was the entire campaign, to raise public expectations for progress at the summit and generate pressure on Reagan and Gorbachev for an end to the arms race.

The Geneva Summit marked the beginning of a turn by the United States and the Soviet Union away from the era of Cold War competition and toward a new relationship of understanding and cooperation. Under pressure from public opinion, the Reagan administration was slowly, haltingly moving toward a new policy of accommodation with the former "evil empire." The administration's response to the public was limited and contradictory, however. The White House did not abandon its plans for arms escalation but pressed ahead with SDI and plans for a buildup of weapons in space. As long as Star Wars continued to poison U.S.-Soviet relations, the hopes for peace raised at the summit were dashed. It would take another year and a half, and intensive political pressures both in the United States and the Soviet Union, before the Star Wars obstacle would be removed and the way finally opened for progress toward arms reduction.

11
Reykjavik and Beyond

The Reykjavik summit in October 1986 was one of the most remarkable and dramatic events in the history of the atomic age. The leaders of the United States and the Soviet Union approved a plan for the elimination of all ballistic missiles within ten years. They also came breathtakingly close to an agreement on eliminating not just ballistic missiles but all strategic nuclear weapons. For a few incredible hours, the world was on the brink of total nuclear disarmament. At the last minute, however, the deal collapsed and the summit ended in failure. The stumbling block in Reykjavik was the same as it had been in Geneva—disagreement over the Strategic Defense Initiative. The stakes were much higher, though, and the disappointment greater. A decisive turn toward reversal of the arms race was blocked by the continuing controversy over Star Wars.

The peace movement was present at Reykjavik as it had been at Geneva. Delegations from SANE, the Freeze Campaign, and Women for a Meaningful Summit again traveled to the summit to demand progress toward peace. As our group talked with U.S. and Soviet officials in Reykjavik and met with reporters at the international press center, the sense of rising expectations was palpable. At one point, we saw Georgi Arbatov racing past, bleary-eyed from all-night discussions between U.S. and Soviet negotiators. When we asked what was happening, he called, "Can't talk. Very big and historic discussions under way. Very important." Later, our group joined a Women for Peace vigil outside Hofdy House where Reagan and Gorbachev were meeting. As we stood shivering in Iceland's blustery weather, we knew that the talks were continuing well beyond the expected time of adjournment. When an extra, unscheduled negotiating session was added at the end of the second day of talks, anticipation at the press hotel reached fever pitch. After three hours, though, Reagan and Gorbachev emerged from the last session with grim faces, and the message of failure was clear. The talks had collapsed.

In the aftermath of Reykjavik, the Reagan administration was criticized on all sides. Hardliners asked why he had agreed to the hastily called meeting in the first place and were shocked that he had almost given away the store. How could he even consider something as outrageous as nuclear disarmament? Arms controllers were also upset, complaining that a golden opportunity for arms reduction had been lost and that Star Wars was having a disastrous impact on U.S.-Soviet relations. In the pages that follow, I explore the political context of Reykjavik and the continuing controversy over SDI and examine how opposition in the United States and the Soviet Union finally brought Star Wars down to earth and paved the way for the INF Treaty and improved U.S.-Soviet relations.

The Politics of Reykjavik

The decision to go to Reykjavik, like the earlier decision to meet Gorbachev in Geneva, was motivated by politics. The White House hoped that the drama of a summit would distract public attention from mounting political difficulties at home. The administration faced two particularly worrisome domestic challenges in the fall of 1986—a possible Republican defeat in the midterm elections and a growing arms control revolt in Congress. A third political crisis was also brewing that may have influenced White House strategists—what Elizabeth Drew termed "the business about the American cargo plane, carrying weapons, being shot down in Nicaragua."[1] The immediate concern, however, was the approaching vote in November in which Democrats were hoping to regain control of the Senate. White House Chief of Staff Donald Regan hoped that a summit between the president and the Soviet leader would give a boost to Republican candidates. The goal, in the words of Strobe Talbott, was to "remind the electorate that the Republican flag was still firmly planted on the diplomatic high ground."[2] When Gorbachev sent his surprise proposal for a meeting in Reykjavik, Regan seized upon the idea as an important political opportunity. As Regan wrote in his memoirs,

> The decision the President had to make was ... politically complicated. ...
> It was clearly impossible for Reagan to refuse to meet Gorbachev on an is-

sue involving world peace. ... To temporize when he had ... the chance to negotiate could have incalculable consequences in terms of world opinion. The American midterm elections were little more than a month away.[3]

With Regan's encouragement, Reagan was inclined to accept Gorbachev's invitation. Although some administration officials cautioned against a hasty meeting for which the American side would be ill-prepared, the White House decided to proceed. In the end, the gambit proved of no avail politically. After returning from Reykjavik, Reagan went on a thirteen-state tour to campaign for Republican senatorial candidates. At every stop, he promoted SDI and his "success" at Reykjavik in rebuffing Soviet attempts to negotiate limits on the plan.[4] Voters were apparently unimpressed, however, for the Democrats won most of the contested seats and regained control of the Senate.

The other problem for the administration, the mounting arms control rebellion on Capitol Hill, was made possible by persistent pressures from grass-roots peace activists. The freeze movement continued to grow after 1983 and in fact became better organized in subsequent years. Freeze Voter was created as the electoral arm of the movement, and SANE and other groups formed political action committees. Well after the demonstrations and freeze referenda of the early 1980s were gone, the peace movement continued to press for arms reduction. In terms of its influence on the political process, the peace community actually became more effective in the administration's second term than it had been in the first term. The arms control lobby developed a reliable and highly responsive network of grass-roots activists in hundreds of congressional districts throughout the country to generate pressure on legislators. As a result, Capitol Hill efforts to restrain the military buildup were gaining. Congressman Tom Downey (D-NY), a leader in these congressional efforts, traced the growing impact of the arms control lobby in Washington to grass-roots activism:

> The impact of the grass roots was tremendous. It showed up in the SDI debate and in all the fights. During the height of the freeze movement and thereafter ... grass-roots organizers could always be counted on to get the message to their people in the field, who in turn would talk to the members of Congress.[5]

David Cohen, former president of Common Cause, confirmed that peace pressures were having an impact:

Grass-roots pressure played a big role. Our legislative leaders on the Hill were getting reports that other members were hearing from people in the grass roots. This meant that what we were telling the leadership became credible. When we said we were working the grass roots, they knew we weren't faking it, we weren't talking through our hats.[6]

The peak year of peace movement impact on Congress was probably 1986. It was then that the combination of intensive grass-roots pressure from local peace activists and skilled leadership in Congress exerted the greatest influence in challenging administration policy. In the House of Representatives, the arms control lobby scored what was called a "grand slam," winning victories not just on one issue, as had been done in the past with the MX, but on nearly all of the major legislative priorities for the year:

- An amendment was passed to cut off funds for the testing of all but the smallest nuclear weapons.

- A similar amendment was adopted to force the administration to adhere to SALT II weapons ceilings.

- A moratorium on full-scale testing of antisatellite weapons was continued.

- The administration's budget request for the Strategic Defense Initiative was slashed by $2.1 billion, a 40 percent cut.

- The overall military budget was cut by $35 billion, an 11 percent cut, continuing a trend toward lower arms spending that began the year before.

- The production of new binary chemical weapons was blocked. [7]

These actions by the House of Representatives constituted the most severe legislative intrusion into military policy that a U.S. president had ever faced. Although the Senate was much more cautious and did not adopt many of these constraints, the legislative action of the House nonetheless posed a major challenge to administration policy.

White House officials used the Reykjavik summit to counter this challenge and pressure arms control supporters in Congress into dropping their amendments. It was a familiar appeal. "Don't tie the hands of the president while he's negotiating with the Soviets." The administration had used a similar tactic during the first round of START talks to prevent deeper cuts against the MX. Now, the White House complained again that it could not negotiate effectively if Congress limited its options. As administration officials arrived in Reykjavik, their attentions were focused more on the conference room in Capitol Hill than on the discussions with the Soviets. According to Kenneth Adelman, "We spent the first day at Reykjavik not preparing for negotiations with Gorbachev, but conducting active negotiations with the Congress."[8]

Passing the Test Ban

The question of nuclear testing was particularly troublesome to the administration. Peace activists made the testing issue a top priority and were pressing on all fronts to demand that the United States join the Soviet moratorium (now in its second year) and agree to a permanent test ban. American Peace Test, a spinoff group from the Freeze Campaign, and religious activists with the Nevada Desert Experience organized one of the largest civil disobedience campaigns in U.S. history. Thousands of activists (myself included) were arrested at the test site to draw attention to the U.S. refusal to join Gorbachev's moratorium. On Capitol Hill, a parallel effort was mounted by the arms control lobby. The focus was an amendment initially introduced by Representative Patricia Schroeder (D-CO) to cut off funds for nuclear testing so long as the Soviets continued their moratorium. Crafted by lobbyists from the Council for a Livable World, SANE, the Freeze Campaign, and other arms control groups, the test ban amendment was a ground-breaking attempt to use the congressional power of the purse to legislate nuclear policy. The amendment was approved by the House in slightly modified form on August 8 by a margin of 234 to 155.[9] Similar measures were adopted by the House in 1987 and 1988, although in each case the Senate failed to go along and the legislation died.

These efforts in the halls of Congress and on the sands of Nevada had a real impact within the Reagan administration. "Due to pressure from the arms control community, the Congress and the press," wrote Kenneth Adelman, the White House felt compelled to "do something" about nuclear testing.[10] A plan was presented from the Arms Control and Disarmament Agency to reduce the number and the yield of nuclear tests. Ronald Reagan agreed and unveiled the plan with a flourish before the United Nations in September. Another proposal from the nations of the Five Continent Peace Initiative (Mexico, Argentina, Tanzania, India, Sweden, and Greece) offered international help in verifying a test ban. This important initiative was almost accepted by the administration. The idea "lived right up to a White House meeting immediately before ... Reykjavik," reported Adelman, but was scuttled at the last minute by Pentagon official Fred Ikle.[11]

Peace movement pressure on the test ban issue continued into the Bush administration and finally bore fruit in 1992. In September of that year Congress approved a nine-month moratorium on nuclear testing and set limits on the number and types of tests that could be conducted over the next four years. The legislation also imposed a permanent ban on all U.S. nuclear testing after 1996.[12] The measure was a considerable compromise from the original legislative proposal introduced by Senator Mark Hatfield (R-OR) and Representative Mike Kopetski (D-OR), but the goal of ending nuclear tests, at least for a time, was achieved. On October 2, President George Bush reluctantly signed the bill into law. For the first time in history, Congress brought a halt to nuclear testing.

Scientists Say No

As the SDI program began to take shape in 1984 and the years following, a call for help went out from the Pentagon to the nation's scientific community. The challenge faced by military officials was to transform a gleam in the president's eye into physical reality. Since the program required huge—some would say impossible—leaps forward in scientific knowledge, the participation and involvement of the technical community was indispensable. As Weinberger said in an interview, "We needed all the scientific help we could get."[13] Suddenly, hundreds of millions of dollars in research funds were dangled before engineers and researchers to attract their interest. The SDI budget became a "pot of gold" to lure the nation's leading scientists and technicians.

In the spring of 1985, the Pentagon established an Office of Innovative Science and Technology to involve universities in researching the exotic new technologies needed for SDI. The mission of the office, according to its director, was "to get the most brilliant minds in our country involved in this program."[14] The problem for the Pentagon was that many of these brilliant minds were deeply disturbed by the Star Wars program. Instead of being grateful for the Pentagon's largesse, many within the scientific community began to question SDI and protested against it. Their opposition sowed doubt about the feasibility and wisdom of SDI and contributed substantially to the program's political decline.

When Ronald Reagan had announced his plans to fund SDI research, he had hoped that scientists and technicians would rally behind his noble crusade to defend people from nuclear missiles. He once confided to Caspar Weinberger that he understood, although disagreed with, the moral objections that many scientists had to building nuclear weapons. He was no doubt referring here to the fact that some ninety-six Nobel laureates had endorsed the nuclear freeze.[15] He was more hopeful, though, that scientists would be supportive of SDI and would endorse his plan "to save lives rather than avenge them." According to Weinberger, Reagan "expressed the belief that they would work far more eagerly on systems that were not really weapons at all, but were the means of destroying nuclear missiles."[16] Unfortunately for the president, many scientists were not interested. "The most saddening feature of the response to the President's announcement," wrote Weinberger, was that "a very large number of the academic and scientific community, whom we had hoped would give both vocal and scientific support, came out against the idea."[17]

One scientist who disagreed with the president's SDI policy was David Parnas, an unlikely candidate for public protest.Soft-spoken and shy, Parnas is a mathematical research scientist at the University of Victoria in British Columbia, Canada, and one of the world's leading experts on computer software. He was also the first person to resign in protest from the Pentagon's Strategic Defense Initiative Organization (SDIO) in 1985. Parnas gave up his $1,000-a-day consulting job with SDIO after concluding that the Star Wars system could not and should not be built.

When Parnas was selected to work on the SDI project at the age of forty-three, he had already accumulated an impressively long list of scientific publications with indecipherable titles in the world's most prestigious computer science journals. He had also worked on classified projects for the Department of Defense and military contractors for more than a decade and had been a long-term consultant to the NATO Research Laboratory. Parnas was not a self-styled expert, as the president sometimes called his Star Wars opponents, but a Pentagon-styled expert, someone deliberately chosen by the Department of Defense as one of the most brilliant minds available. The resignation of so prestigious a scientist was a major blow to the credibility of the Star Wars program.

Scientists pointed to many problems with SDI feasibility—the limitations of laser and directed-energy technology, the challenge of launching and maintaining numerous satellite battle stations, the vulnerability of the whole system to Soviet defenses and countermeasures—but none was more fundamental than Parnas's critique of the computer software requirements. Parnas's conclusion was that the computerized control systems required to make this complex weapons program work were beyond technical capability. Even if the hardware problems could be overcome, the inability to solve the data management problems would doom the system. "If we can't build the software reliably, all the hardware won't do any good," said Parnas.[18] The problem lay in the nature of software itself and its mathematical limitations.

> You have to be very careful in what you say. It's not that it's impossible to write a program that could carry out all the myriad tracking and processing functions. But it's impossible to know whether it will perform reliably or not. There's no way to check whether the program is correct. There are two reasons for that. One is the property of SDI itself. To do our job we have to make all kinds of assumptions, for example, that Russian missiles will show a certain spectrum. But if the Russians deliberately build missiles with a different spectrum we'll get the wrong answer. There's too much we don't know or can't be sure of.

The other reason we could not know whether the software would work, according to Parnas, had to do with the mathematical nature of computer software. Because it is full of loops and connections and consists of discrete functions rather than continuous functions, software must be based in part on approximations. Even when these are extremely accurate, you can never know if the computer software is completely flawless and free of bugs. This uncertainty would be especially acute with a system as large and complex as SDI, "what may well be the largest software project ever written." Parnas went on:

> Every major programming product, and probably every minor one as well, has had serious errors in it when it was first given to the user. It's cer-

tainly true with military software as well as civilian software. You have to use it first, because you can't systematically analyze it like you can other products.

The problem with SDI was that it would be used only once, if ever, and there would be no way to test the system and its software package ahead of time to see whether it actually worked or not. The result of a weapons program that could not be reliably trusted, Parnas said, would be a further destabilization of the arms race.

Given the weight of these considerations, Parnas felt he had no choice but to resign. He did not object to military-sponsored research per se but to SDI specifically. As he wrote at the time, "My conclusions are based on characteristics peculiar to this particular effort, not objections to weapons development in general."[19] Parnas agonized over his decision. "I worked a full month on nothing else, first trying to convince myself that I could justify staying and finally accepting the fact that I couldn't and explaining why." In his typically careful and systematic way, he submitted a series of fifteen separate memos with his resignation letter explaining the numerous flaws in the SDI program and his reasons for leaving. In the end, he became convinced that he was doing the right thing ("You have to feel pretty certain to resign a $1,000-a-day job") and even agreed to speak out in public and testify before the U.S. Congress and the Canadian Parliament.

Parnas often had to explain to his scientific colleagues why he had taken such an unusual and drastic course of action.

> They thought, we've been given a job, so let's look for ways to spend the money. I thought, I'm being asked to look at the whole big picture, and that picture doesn't make sense, and I don't think I should participate. I asked a different question and got a different answer.
>
> Some said, the government is going to do this anyway, so come and get your part of the action. But I have very strong feelings about that. I think that the world we live in is in pretty bad shape because many of us make decisions as if what we do doesn't count. But if everyone made decisions as if their actions really counted, the world would be in a lot better shape.[20]

Taking the Pledge

Organized scientific opposition to SDI began with the Union of Concerned Scientists (UCS) and the Federation of American Scientists

(FAS). Both groups issued a steady stream of reports critical of the program, and John Pike of FAS became a frequent source of skeptical commentary for newspapers and the broadcast media. The first critique of the project, a study that had significant influence on the early debate, was *The Fallacy of Star Wars,* published by UCS and edited by John Tirman. The March 1984 study questioned nearly all of the assumptions underlying the SDI program and labeled it a complete hoax—unworkable scientifically and dangerous strategically. The criticism reached into the mainstream of the scientific community and academia. A month after the UCS study was released, the congressional Office of Technology Assessment issued a background paper, "Directed Energy Missile Defense in Space," that also challenged the scientific assumptions underlying the program.[21] One of the most damaging and widely quoted assessments of SDI came from the administration itself. In the fall of 1983, Undersecretary of Defense Richard DeLauer, the highest-ranking technologist in the Pentagon, admitted that developing a space-based defense system would require solving at least eight major technical problems, "each of which was as challenging as the Manhattan project or the Apollo project."[22] No wonder that the prestigious scientific journal *Nature* observed in 1984 that "the scientific community knows [the president's proposal] will not work."[23]

A number of efforts were made in the mid-1980s to survey scientific opinion on SDI and obtain statements of collective concern. The following are examples of these expressions:

- Researchers at AT&T Bell Laboratories initiated an open letter to Congress calling for a curb on SDI appropriations and urging that the program be confined to an effort at "exploratory research." Circulated primarily among researchers employed in government and industrial labs, the petition was signed by 1,600 scientists.[24]

- A March 1986 survey of 549 randomly selected members of the American Physical Society commissioned by the Union of Concerned Scientists found 54 percent of the respondents agreeing that SDI is "a step in the wrong direction."[25] Two-thirds of those surveyed considered it very unlikely that a missile defense system would be able to defend selected population centers.[26]

- A poll of National Academy of Sciences members organized by Peter Stein at Cornell University found a 20-1 majority believing it unlikely that an effective and survivable strategic defense program could be built within twenty years.[27]

One of the most significant manifestations of opposition to Star Wars was the "Pledge of Non-Participation" that circulated through the U.S. scientific community from 1985 to 1987 and later spread to Britain, Canada, and Japan. The pledge read, "We, the undersigned science and engineering faculty, believe that the Strategic Defense Initiative ... is ill-conceived and dangerous." The signers agreed "neither to solicit nor accept SDI funds." The pledge was circulated only to those scientists likely to receive funds for SDI—physicists, engineers, chemists, astronomers, and mathematicians. By the fall of 1987, more than 7,000 university scientists and engineers in the United States had signed the pledge. Internationally, the number of signers eventually exceeded 12,000. Among those signing were:

- 57 percent of the faculty of the twenty top physics departments in the United States,

- 50 percent or more of the faculty in each of the 112 physical science and engineering research departments at seventy-one schools, and

- nineteen Nobel laureates in physics and chemistry in the United States.[28]

The idea for the Pledge of Non-Participation evolved in 1985 at Cornell University. One of the initiators was Lisbeth Gronlund, at the time a Ph.D. student in theoretical solid-state physics. When two university vice presidents returned from a trip to Washington, D.C., and convened a meeting of faculty to brief them on how to apply for SDI money, Gronlund and others in the Physics Department became concerned. It was unprecedented that university administrators would call such a meeting, and many faculty members were worried that involvement in SDI would make their department and the university dependent on a highly suspect and dubious enterprise. Gronlund and a number of graduate students tried to attend the session, but the administrators asked them to leave. Undeterred, the graduate students organized to make their voices heard. Soon after the meeting, they joined with members of the faculty to take action. Gronlund said:

One of the worst cuts was ridicule and the renaming of the system as "Star Wars." The first to mock the president's vaunted program in this way was Senator Edward Kennedy. According to Caspar Weinberger, the senator's office "came up with the idea that SDI should be subjected to as much scorn as possible ... as if it were some fantasy that bore no semblance to reality."[36] Administration officials were infuriated by the term "Star Wars." Initially, they tried to prevent the media from using it, but the label stuck and the administration soon had to drop its objections.[37] As a result, Weinberger lamented, "The proponents of what was, and is, the most hopeful strategic concept for at least the last 40 years ... were placed on the defensive, and were hard put to defend the true merits of this imaginative and creative proposal of the President's."[38]

Even more exasperating, and much more damaging to the administration, was the mounting reluctance within Congress to approve SDI budget requests. As Weinberger and other officials went before Congress to ask for more money, SDI opponents subjected them to constant attack. Weinberger wrote in his memoirs that SDI appropriations were "wrung from the Congress after protracted and highly confrontational hearings."[39] He continued, "It is difficult to convey the strength and, as it seemed then and still seems to me, the irrationality and fury of the opposition to SDI in our Congress."[40] As Figure 11.1 illustrates, SDI funding levels were consistently chopped by Congress, and starting in fiscal year 1990, they actually began to decline.

Although SDI spending was enormous, the budget amounts were nowhere near the levels proposed by the Pentagon. Actual spending after five years was nearly 40 percent below what had been originally planned. In fact, total spending for strategic defense programs from 1984 through 1989 was only $3.3 billion more than the Pentagon had projected for these purposes before the SDI program was created.[41] This was hardly the stuff of "unstoppable momentum." These reductions, according to Kenneth Adelman, "took the wind out of research for space-based interceptors."[42] In addition to cutting the overall funding level, congressional opponents also tinkered with various technical and administrative components of the program. These changes ranged from the significant, such as blocking a federally funded research institute for Star Wars, to the frivolous, such as refusing to confirm the promotion of General James Abrahamson, director of the SDIO, to four-star general. The cumulative impact of these congressional pressures

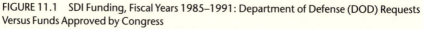

FIGURE 11.1   SDI Funding, Fiscal Years 1985–1991: Department of Defense (DOD) Requests Versus Funds Approved by Congress

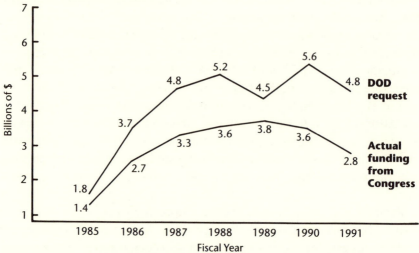

Sources: Weinberger, *Fighting for Peace: Seven Critical Years in the Pentagon* (New York: Warner Books, 1990), p. 313; *Nuclear Times* 8 (Winter 1990-1991), p. 7.

was constant frustration for Weinberger and his fellow proponents and a steady drain on the program's resources. The "fury" that Weinberger complained about was Congress's response to public, grass-roots pressures from peace activists, scientists, and other SDI opponents. The continuous criticisms from the scientific community and the steady lobbying efforts of national groups contributed substantially to SDI's decline.

Stopping Antisatellite Weapons

Perhaps the most important restriction on Star Wars was the successful effort to halt antisatellite (ASAT) weapons testing. The attempt to impose a moratorium on the testing of ASATs began in Congress even before the SDI program got under way. This effort, led in the House by Representative George Brown (D-CA), was motivated by the concern that the destruction of satellites in a military crisis could be extremely destabilizing. Such attacks would knock out vital verification and monitoring systems and thus would "blind" national authorities. Brown and others feared that once ASAT testing began, an arms race in outer space would be unavoidable. These efforts to halt ASAT testing were aided immensely in 1983 when the Soviets ended their antisatellite testing program and announced a unilateral moratorium on further tests. Moscow invited the United States to join in a mutual ban on space weapons tests. The Reagan administration refused the offer.

Beginning in 1983, Brown and his colleagues introduced measures urging negotiations for a verifiable ban on existing and future ASAT systems. When the White House continued to refuse negotiations, the legislators decided to force the issue. In 1984, an amendment was offered to the military authorization bill prohibiting any ASAT tests against objects in space so long as the Soviets also refrained from such testing. The Brown amendment was approved by the House of Representatives, but the Senate refused to go along and the measure died. The Reagan administration had lobbied vigorously to defeat the ASAT amendment. The ASAT program was kept alive, according to Kenneth Adelman, by "umpteen efforts by President Reagan, Secretaries Shultz and Weinberger, and everyone else high in office to save it."[43] The same drama was repeated in 1985, with the House approving the measure and the Senate rejecting it. This time, though, the Conference Committee agreed to a temporary one-year moratorium. The battle was resumed in 1986, and Brown and his colleagues again prevailed upon the House to adopt an amendment extending the ASAT moratorium. This time, the measure survived the Conference Committee to become permanent law.[44]

This successful congressional effort was another example of domestic political pressures impinging upon White House decision making. Despite "umpteen efforts" by top administration officials, the ASAT testing program was brought to a halt by legislative action. Arms control legislators, backed by pressure from grass-roots activists, prevented a dangerous escalation of the arms race into outer space and derailed an important component of the SDI program.

ABM vs. SDI

The crucial battleground in the fight over SDI was the ABM Treaty. Negotiated in 1972, the treaty explicitly prohibited the weapons and strategy at the heart of the SDI program. For Star Wars opponents, saving the ABM Treaty became an essential goal. As long as the provisions of the treaty remained in place, the administration would be unable to develop the proposed strategic defense system.

Given the administration's determination to press ahead with SDI regardless of legal or political considerations, a confrontation over the treaty was inevitable. Many arms control supporters feared that the showdown would occur in 1987, when the treaty came up for its regular five-year review. Concerned that the White House might use the review period to withdraw from the treaty, a coalition of arms control groups and former national security officials formed the Campaign to Save the ABM Treaty. The campaign played an important role in raising public awareness about the significance of the agreement, described as "the most important arms control treaty in history," and helped to ensure broad political support for preserving it. As a preemptive effort to head off a potential move by the administration, the campaign was a great success. There was little or no political support in Washington for withdrawing from the treaty, and the White House had no choice but to live with it.

The administration was not about to give up its SDI obsession, though, so it developed a new strategy. Instead of abandoning the treaty, the White House attempted to rewrite it. If the treaty provisions were too restrictive, the administration would redefine the words and give them a new, more permissive meaning. This approach was similar to that employed in the earlier confrontation with the Catholic bishops. Attempting such a tactic with the ABM agreement, however, was much more difficult, for the treaty was a matter of binding law and its meaning was firmly established through an elaborate record of testimony during the Senate ratification debate. Undeterred, the administration pressed ahead. Perhaps out of frustration with the intense opposition to SDI and the military buildup, the administration also sought to breach the limits on weapons development contained in the unratified SALT II agreement and announced that it would begin a so-called "phased deployment" of actual SDI components.

These White House actions touched off what Strobe Talbott has called a "near-mutiny on Capitol Hill."[45] The administration found itself under mounting criticism not only in the House but in the Senate as well. Now controlled by the Democrats, the Senate became more active in demanding progress at the bargaining table. Senators seeking to remove obstacles to arms reduction increasingly focused their attention on SDI and the attempted reinterpretation of the ABM Treaty. For

Sam Nunn (D-GA), the new chairman of the Senate Armed Services Committee and a respected expert on military affairs, the administration's continued intransigence on SDI was a grave concern. Although conservative on most military issues, Nunn saw the attempted reinterpretation of the ABM Treaty as a disaster for national security and a threat to the constitutional authority of the Senate. In early 1987, he threw his considerable political weight behind the growing effort to preserve the ABM Treaty. His involvement proved decisive in bringing the Star Wars program down to earth. In March 1987, following months of careful examination of the negotiating record of the ABM agreement, Nunn gave a series of historic speeches on the floor of the Senate challenging the administration's proposed reinterpretation.[46] In unusually blunt language, Nunn called the administration's effort a "complete and total misrepresentation" and warned of a "constitutional confrontation of profound dimensions."[47] This reassertion of the traditional interpretation of the ABM Treaty by the senior member of the Senate responsible for military affairs was a powerful rebuke to White House claims.

Not content with just reasserting the traditional interpretation, Senate critics also moved to guarantee their position by writing it into law. The driving force in this effort was Michigan Senator Carl Levin. A liberal Democrat from Detroit, in many ways the very antithesis of Sam Nunn, Levin had earned a well-deserved reputation as an effective legislator capable of achieving results. According to lobbyist David Cohen, "Levin paid attention to the various public interest groups and respected them. Grass-roots pressure played a real part. When the scientists began speaking out, this had a major impact on the Hill."[48] Levin developed the idea of an amendment to the military authorization bill barring tests of any SDI components that would violate the ABM Treaty.[49] Rather than pressing the proposed amendment on his own, Levin approached Nunn and asked him to become a cosponsor. Nunn agreed to support the measure and became its leading Senate advocate. The measure passed the Armed Services Committee in May by a vote of 12-8. When it came to the full Senate, however, Republicans launched a filibuster to block it. Although Senators John Warner (R-VA) and Pete Wilson (R-CA) labored mightily to delete the offending passage, they could not muster the votes to block it. On September 17, 1987, the Senate formally adopted the Nunn-Levin amendment by a 58-38 vote. The House of Representatives approved the same measure by more than 100 votes, and it became law that fall.[50]

The congressional action to prevent SDI testing beyond the limits of the ABM Treaty was a major turning point in the political struggle against Star Wars. It spelled the end of White House efforts to break out of the confines of the treaty and represented a rare and historic assertion by Congress of its rightful constitutional authority in military and foreign policy affairs. In the Senate, it was the first time in history that arms control restrictions had been imposed on a president.[51] Supporters of the White House understood the implications of the amendment and tried vainly to block it. Senator Wilson called the decision "the greatest unilateral concession in the history of arms control."[52] But these and other cries of doom fell on deaf ears. The tide had turned politically against hardline policies, and support for arms reduction was on the rise.

Removing the SDI Obstacle

At Reykjavik, the Soviets shocked their American counterparts by coming into the talks with a proposal essentially accepting Reagan's zero option proposal. They offered to eliminate all their intermediate-range nuclear weapons aimed at Europe in exchange for removal of the recently deployed U.S. Pershing II and cruise missiles.[53] The offer was conditioned on White House acceptance of limitations on SDI testing, however. Since the Reagan administration would not accept such restrictions, the tentative agreement failed to materialize. Just five months later, however, Moscow surprised Washington and the world with the announcement that it would now consider INF issues independently of SDI.

Why did the Soviets change their position? After insisting for more than two years that INF issues must be linked to SDI, why did Gorbachev drop this condition and decide to decouple INF from Star Wars? Many Western observers saw this shift as proof that the Soviets had caved in to overwhelming U.S. military superiority and the pressure of SDI. In fact, the reverse was more likely true. The lessening of the threat from SDI made it easier for the Kremlin to change its position. When the Soviets announced their concession in early 1987, SDI was already in serious trouble politically and was about to be constrained further by the U.S. Senate. Soviet leaders could see that the dangers posed by SDI were diminishing. Alarmist warnings about an imminent first-strike threat from SDI obviously no longer made sense.

Why should they be intimidated by a system that was encountering so much resistance? As it became evident that SDI was not real and that the system would never be built on anything like the scale originally intended, Kremlin leaders began to revise their thinking.

One person who played an important role in this process was Andrei Sakharov. In February 1987, barely two months after he and his wife, Yelena Bonner, were released from internal exile, Sakharov delivered a speech at the Forum for a Nuclear-Free World and the Survival of Mankind held in Moscow. There, he criticized the Kremlin's policy of linking progress on INF and START to limits on SDI:

> I believe that the package approach can and should be revised. A significant cut in ICBMs and medium-range and battlefield missiles, and other agreements on disarmament, should be negotiated as soon as possible, independently of SDI, in accordance with the lines of the understanding laid out in Reykjavik.[54]

Just two weeks after Sakharov's appeal, on February 28, Gorbachev announced the decision to decouple SDI and INF.

The change in the Soviet position was quite dramatic and came as something of a shock to U.S. officials. Accustomed as they were to the usual heavy-handed Kremlin approach, U.S. negotiators now found Gorbachev and the Soviets remarkably accommodating. At the Washington summit in 1987, according to Kenneth Adelman, Gorbachev was "uncommonly calm" about SDI. As Adelman described it, Gorbachev adopted a "Californian (or Siberian) laid-back posture about it all." At his final meeting with Ronald Reagan in the Oval Office, when Reagan insisted that the United States wanted to deploy SDI, "the now mellow Gorbachev ... said simply go ahead."[55]

Progress toward arms reduction was achieved in spite of SDI, not because of it. The Soviets did not change their position to gain any concessions on SDI, and certainly no such restraints were offered by the White House. The Soviets simply gave up on SDI and moved instead to obtain the key concession they had always wanted, the withdrawal of INF missiles in Europe. The Soviets could afford to take this new approach in 1987 because it was clear by then that political pressures within the United States were rapidly bringing the Star Wars program down to earth. The combination of domestic opposition in the United States and a more realistic diplomacy by the Soviet Union removed the

SDI barrier. This process allowed a speedy advance toward the INF Treaty and a dramatic improvement in U.S.-Soviet relations.

Continuing Controversy

In the late 1980s, with the end of the Reagan presidency, SDI fell on hard times indeed. Without its founder and principal patron in the White House, SDI was no longer in favor. From 1989 to 1991, the level of annual SDI funding declined by a billion dollars, a reduction of more than 25 percent in real terms. The Nunn-Levin amendment barring strategic defense testing beyond the limits of the ABM Treaty remained in place. While no program funded at levels of $3 billion a year could be considered dead, the long-term prospects for a Star Wars system even remotely resembling the original plan seemed uncertain at best.

The Persian Gulf War in 1990–1991 gave strategic defense a new lease on life, however. Senators John Warner, Malcolm Wallop, and other SDI proponents cited the presumed success of the U.S. Patriot antimissile system in countering Iraqi Scud missiles as vindication of the strategic defense concept. Opponents countered that even if the Patriot performed as well as claimed (subsequent revelations show that it did not),[56] this in no way proves that SDI could overcome the far greater and more complex threat posed by modern ICBMs. Nonetheless, strategic defense advocates succeeded in pushing through a major boost in spending for the program. The political revival of SDI was aided by a redefinition of its mission. The goal was no longer to guard against a massive attack from Russia but to provide limited protection against ballistic missile attacks from developing countries and accidental or unauthorized launches.[57] The new acronym became GPALS, Global Protection Against Limited Strikes. This new "limited" system would still be gigantic in scale: It would include 1,000 space-based "brilliant pebble" interceptors and 750 ground-based interceptors. In 1992, Congress passed the Missile Defense Act authorizing nearly $4 billion in spending for this program. The act also called for amendment of the ABM Treaty to allow for deployment of the GPALS system.

In pursuit of this objective, the Bush administration attempted to persuade the newly independent government of Russia to accept changes in the ABM Treaty. At their June 1992 summit in Washington, Boris Yeltsin and George Bush issued a statement on a "global protection system," and agreed to establish a high-level group to explore "a concept for such a system."[58] SDI advocates in the United States crowed that the Kremlin had finally come around to the U.S. position and was now willing to renegotiate the ABM Treaty. Secretary of Defense Dick Cheney told the Senate Foreign Relations Committee that the previous Soviet linkage between strategic weapons cuts and adherence to the ABM Treaty had been broken.

Immediately after the Yeltsin-Bush summit, however, officials in Moscow made it clear that the traditional Soviet/Russian position on the ABM Treaty had not changed. On June 23, Russian Defense Minister Pavel Grachev issued a statement in *Izvestia* and the official army newspaper, *Krasnaya Zvezda,* stating that Moscow remained firmly committed to the ABM Treaty and warning that any attempt to go beyond the treaty would jeopardize previously signed arms reduction agreements. Grachev wrote, "The process of strategic offensive arms cuts is tied to observance of the ABM treaty. If the United States tries to step outside the bounds of this treaty, the [START and START II] accords will immediately lapse."[59] In July, following the first meeting of the high-level group set up to discuss strategic defense, Deputy Foreign Minister Grigory Berdennikov repeated the Russian position: "In our view no amendments are needed in the ABM treaty. ... At a time when the strategic offensive systems have been drastically cut back, the treaty has grown even more important, and it is the bulwark of strategic stability."[60]Once again, Washington's drive for a strategic defense system loomed as a potential obstacle to strategic arms reduction.

12

Perestroika and Peace

Paddlewheel for Peace

The grand old riverboat the *Delta Queen* paddles majestically down the mighty Mississippi. The magnificent ship's journey through the American heartland is always special, but this trip in July 1986 is especially significant. The passengers on board include 46 Soviets and 120 Americans—goodwill ambassadors on the Mississippi Peace Cruise—voyaging together to promote U.S.-Soviet friendship.

As the riverboat passes down the river, bedecked with banners reading "No Nuclear Tests" and "Let's Make Peace Together," a crescendo of favorable response rises from local communities. Everywhere the ship is welcomed warmly and enthusiastically. Along the banks, huge crowds of people gather to wave and cheer. Even late at night, people are waiting, often with handmade signs, to welcome the Soviet visitors and express their desire for peace. At the lock in Muscatine, Iowa, hundreds of people are gathered at 1 A.M. to cheer and wave U.S. and Soviet flags. A banjoist strums a Russian folk melody, and the Soviets on board tearfully join in singing the words.

In Dubuque, 2,000 people attend a riverbank rally replete with local marching bands. The mayor presents the keys of the city to the most famous of the Soviet visitors, cosmonaut Georgi Grechko. In Davenport, another huge crowd gathers, including a Brownie Girl Scout troop singing Russian songs. In Hannibal, Missouri, the Soviets impress their American hosts with a thorough knowledge of Mark Twain and his immortal characters Tom Sawyer and Huckleberry Finn. The Americans frequently express their amazement, "Why, they're just like us." As the mayor of LaCrosse, Wisconsin, put it, "You can't tell the Russians from the Americans." The Soviets too are surprised to discover that "you Americans are like we Russians, always joking and smiling."

For those of us lucky enough to be passengers, the Mississippi Peace Cruise was a deeply moving experience. This historic event was a dramatic symbol of a new awakening in U.S.-Soviet understanding and friendship and an eloquent refutation of the logic of the Cold War. Like the churning of the great paddlewheel, the cruise marked a turning in public awareness.

Press coverage greatly enhanced the impact of the cruise. It proved to be one of the most successful peace media and cultural events of the decade. News coverage in river communities was extensive and contributed greatly to the sense of excitement about the Soviet visitors. National coverage was also considerable. United Press International and the Associated Press carried feature stories, and reports appeared in *Time* magazine and the *New York Times*.[1] In all, nearly 500 articles on the cruise were published.[2] Television coverage was also significant, especially in river communities but also nationally. Reports were broadcast on all three network evening newscasts as well as on the "Today Show" and "CBS Morning News." The cruise was extensively reported in the Soviet press as well. *Pravda* and *Izvestia* ran articles, and the television news broadcast "Vremya" featured several stories. "Vremyas'" star newscaster, Svetlana Stardomskaya, was aboard the cruise and reported glowingly on the voyage.

The Mississippi Peace Cruise was a prime example of citizen diplomacy. These direct people-to-people contacts helped to enhance international understanding and overcome the enemy images that blocked peaceful relations. Throughout the 1980s, dozens of organizations sponsored such citizen exchanges. One of the leading groups in these efforts was the sponsor of the cruise, Promoting Enduring Peace (PEP). Under the direction of Howard and Alice Frazier, with able support from media coordinator Lou Friedman, PEP organized not just the Mississippi cruise but more than a dozen similar voyages on the Volga and Dnieper rivers in the Soviet Union. The Volga cruises made a big impression on many people, including Mikhail Gorbachev, who mentioned their symbolic importance on a number of occasions and even referred to them in his book *Perestroika*: "I had once seen a film about a journey made by some American tourists down the Volga. There were shots of our citizens alongside Americans. And it was not easy to tell an American from a Russian. People were talking away and one felt that they were talking like friends, understanding each other."[3]

Many other American organizations too numerous to mention here sponsored U.S.-Soviet citizen exchanges during the decade—sports competitions, youth camps, peace walks, mountain-climbing expeditions, scholarly conferences, professional exchanges of every kind, environmental programs, and a wide range of cultural activities. These efforts had an important impact on popular attitudes. By the latter half of the 1980s, the fear and hostility that previously had marked public perceptions of the Soviet Union began to change, giving way first to curiosity and then to genuine warmth and friendship. In part, this transformation was a natural reaction to the reforms and the new spirit of openness introduced in the Soviet Union by Gorbachev, but it was also a consequence of citizen diplomacy projects like the Mississippi Peace Cruise. As the flow of citizen exchanges and unofficial programs of cooperation increased, Americans began to see the Soviet Union and its people in a different light. The image of an "evil empire" faded, and decades of Cold War hatred began to melt away.

On the last night of the Mississippi Peace Cruise, as the *Delta Queen* approached its final stop in St. Louis, some of the passengers reflected on the meaning of the voyage. Dmitri Agarchev, interpreter for the Soviet group, raised a note of skepticism: "We've worked hard to make this cruise a success, but what good does it do? Will one nuclear bomb be dismantled because of the cruise? For all of our efforts here we haven't done anything concrete to stop the arms race."[4] Karen Jacob, assistant cruise organizer for PEP, disagreed with her Soviet friend: "Just think of how we've helped to change people's attitudes. We can never stop the weapons if we don't change people's hearts. We're turning enemies into friends. I think we've made real progress."[5] The point was well taken. Underlying all the missiles and confrontational policies of the Cold War was a deeply rooted fear and mistrust of the Soviet Union. To the extent that citizen exchanges helped to dispel these fears, they brought real progress in reducing the threat of war.

New Thinking and Old

The task of promoting U.S.-Soviet friendship was made immeasurably easier in the latter half of the 1980s by the rise of Mikhail Gorbachev. The impact of the peace movement during the decade certainly would have been less without the dramatic reforms he introduced in the Soviet Union. He was a catalyst for peace and political transformation throughout the world. When he toured Washington, Bonn, and other Western cities, crowds chanted "Gorby, Gorby." Democratic revolutionaries from Tiananmen Square to East Berlin invoked his name. The Nobel Committee awarded Gorbachev the Peace Prize in 1990 for his "many and decisive contributions" to international cooperation and his "leading role in the peace process."[6] *Time* magazine named him "Man of the Decade" in its issue of January 1, 1990. Under Gorbachev's leadership, the Soviet Union instituted "new thinking" in foreign and military policy and in effect dropped out of the arms race.

Many acknowledge Gorbachev's contributions but claim that the changes in the Soviet Union were the result of military pressures from the West. General Colin Powell, chairman of the Joint Chiefs of Staff, told a congressional committee in 1990, "We are witnessing today the long-term success of policies we put in motion over 40 years ago."[7] *New York Times* columnist William Safire put it more directly: "The U.S. arms buildup sowed the seeds of perestroika." Even liberal columnists gave credit to military toughness. Tom Wicker wrote, "The Reagan arms buildup no doubt speeded reform within the Soviet Union."[8] Such claims became so prevalent that cartoonist Garry Trudeau took up the theme. In his comic strip, "Doonesbury," the character for Eastern Europe says to the U.S. president, "We couldn't have done it without your military buildup, sir."

However widespread it may be, the "peace through strength" interpretation does not hold up to serious scrutiny. The explanations for perestroika and Soviet reform are far too complex to be explained by so simplistic a formula. The sources of change in the East were primarily internal, not external. The Reagan buildup had little or nothing to do with the transformations in Soviet policy and may even have retarded the process. According to Georgi Arbatov, the claim that Western pressures caused perestroika is "absolute nonsense": "Those [reforms] not only ripened inside the country but originated within it. The hostility and militarism of American policy did nothing but create further obstacles on the road to reform and heaped troubles on the heads of reformers."[9]

Soviet history is filled with examples of external military pressures leading not to accommodation but to greater repression and militarism. As Soviet scholar Matthew Evangelista has noted, "There is some precedent, dating back to the 1920s, for Soviet leaders to use 'war scares' for internal political purposes."[10] Belligerence in the West reinforced Kremlin images of a hostile adversary and provided an excuse for intensifying the dictatorial system. Scholars Daniel Deudney and G. John Ikenberry drew a similar conclusion: "Typically the Russian response [to military threats] was a mixture of authoritarian state-building at home and imperial expansion abroad."[11] Only in the Gorbachev era, and for a brief time during the earlier Khrushchev period, did Soviet leaders opt for a different approach.

After Joseph Stalin's death in 1953, the Soviet Union began tentatively to move in a new direction. Nikita Khrushchev and the leadership embarked on a policy of military reform and "serious negotiating on disarmament."[12] From 1955 through 1957, Moscow unilaterally cut its armed forces by 1.8 million men.[13] In 1960, further cuts were announced. Khrushchev also put forward a sweeping disarmament plan in 1955, based on an earlier Western proposal, calling for a total ban on the use and manufacture of nuclear weapons and major cuts in conventional forces. The West rejected this proposal (thus disavowing many of its own ideas) and failed to respond to Moscow's unilateral force reductions. Instead, the Kennedy administration launched a huge ICBM buildup, expanded conventional armed forces, and sent troops to Vietnam. Partly in response, Moscow accelerated its own nuclear buildup, and with the ouster of Khrushchev, launched a major conventional force expansion as well. As Evangelista observed, "the policy of strength-without-serious-negotiation proved counterproductive."[14]

Throughout the Cold War era, buildups by the West led not to concessions and peace on the other side but to similar buildups and hardline positions. NATO's introduction of nuclear missiles in Europe was matched by similar deployments from the Soviets. The Kennedy administration's Minuteman missile program was followed by a massive ICBM buildup by the Soviets. The MIRVing of U.S. missiles in the 1970s was followed by Soviet MIRVing in the 1980s. The two giants were locked in a constant cycle of action and reaction, with each side responding in kind to challenges from the other and neither gaining a commanding lead. Military confrontation was a no-win strategy creating ever greater burdens and risks for both sides.

This pattern of hardline responses to pressures from the West continued into the late Brezhnev era. The initial Soviet reaction to the Reagan buildup, for example, was more of the same—hunkering down in Afghanistan, intimidation of the Poles, continuation of SS-20 and other nuclear deployments, and bluster at the Geneva negotiations.

When NATO began its INF missile deployments in 1983, Moscow accelerated the deployment of short-range missiles and began testing a successor to the SS-20.[15] A political struggle ensued within the Kremlin and continued into the mid-1980s, with representatives of the military and the KGB, supported by some Politburo members, urging a new round of military expansion.[16] Gorbachev and the majority eventually won this debate and proceeded to slow the rate of military investment. The hardline factions remained, however, and attempted to seize power in the failed military coup of August 1991.

An example of hardline policies in the West reinforcing Soviet repression can be seen in the case of Jewish emigration. Human rights for Soviet Jews was a bellwether issue for many Americans during the Cold War, and a great deal of effort went into persuading Moscow to permit freer emigration. The usual approach was highly confrontational, however, and Moscow tended to respond with more repression, not less. The best-known example is the Jackson-Vanik amendment to the Trade Act of 1974, which made U.S.-Soviet economic cooperation contingent on freer emigration for Soviet Jews. The tactic backfired, however, and the Brezhnev regime imposed tighter restrictions. Soviet emigrés who were involved in the policy process in Moscow at the time have argued that the Jackson-Vanik amendment worked against proponents of improved East-West relations.[17] Emigration rates declined after the law's passage, and U.S.-Soviet relations became strained. As Figure 12.1 illustrates, the peaks of Jewish emigration—1973, 1979, and the years following 1988—correspond with periods of successful arms negotiation and improved relations, whereas the lowest rates of emigration occurred during the times of military confrontation and Cold War belligerence. The lesson seems obvious. When confrontation increases, the doors of emigration shut. When hostility lessens, the gates of freedom swing open.

The ironic fact is that military pressures from the West provided political justification for the system of Soviet repression and militarism. As historian and former ambassador George Kennan has observed, "The general effect of Cold War extremism was to delay rather than hasten the great change that overtook the Soviet Union at the end of the 1980s."[18] Whenever Washington resorted to aggressive action, it confirmed the belief of Soviet hardliners that the Americans could not be trusted. When the Bush administration sent troops to invade Panama in December 1989, for example, Georgi Arbatov told Western re-

FIGURE 12.1   Emigration of Soviet Jews, 1971–1989

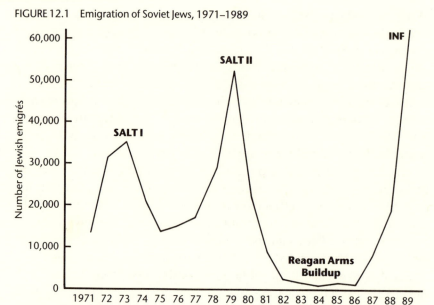

Source: Adapted from "Soviet Jews Leave at a Record Pace, Many for Israel," *New York Times,* December 14, 1989, p. 1.

porters, "Your invasion is helping the opponents of perestroika." As Mary Kaldor has written, "Far from countering a Soviet military threat to Western Europe, NATO legitimized the Soviet presence in Eastern Europe."[19] In this sense, the military establishments of the two sides were symbiotic, feeding off each other and sustaining a right-wing political climate that reinforced the war system on both sides. In the Soviet Union, the vast military industrial complex and repressive apparatus inherited from the Stalin era were justified as a necessary response to the Western threat. In the United States, the military establishment was similarly explained in relation to Soviet power. In the words of Russian poet Evgenii Yevtushenko, "Your hardliners help our hardliners, and our hardliners help your hardliners."[20]

The argument that "peace through strength" worked in the 1980s faces another problem. At the time of the supposed Cold War victory, the Soviet Union was closer to catching up with the West militarily than it had ever been. As Deudney and Ikenberry have asserted, "Far from beginning a decline, the Soviet Union was near the peak of its relative position when Gorbachev came to power."[21] Moscow had steadily modernized and expanded its conventional and nuclear forces since the 1960s and through Herculean effort had managed to stay relatively even with the West in military power. According to Deudney and Ikenberry,

> By the beginning of the 1980s the Soviet deployed military force, both conventional and nuclear, was at an all-time high. ... Given this balance of steadily increasing military capabilities on both sides, it is difficult to attribute the end of the Cold War and Soviet retrenchment and accommodation to an inferior military power position.[22]

The Soviet Union was not forced to "cry uncle" by overwhelming military superiority in the West because no such superiority existed. Despite decades of Cold War competition and the huge spending increases of the Reagan era, the West was unable to achieve a decisive military advantage over the Soviet Union.

The Economic Imperative

The reforms and military concessions of the Gorbachev era resulted primarily from the internal contradictions of the Soviet system. The strongest of these domestic factors were economic. Nearly every commentator, from right to left, has pointed to the chronic economic inefficiency of the Soviet Union as the paramount consideration in the decision to begin the reform process. Gorbachev and his supporters were quite explicit in stating their desire to improve and modernize the stagnant Soviet economy. These imperatives created pressures for dismantling totalitarian political controls. To develop competitive high-technology industries and quality consumer goods and services, initiative had to be encouraged, which meant lifting the leaden hand of state bureaucracy and encouraging freer exchange of information. *Glasnost* and the beginnings of democratization were a necessary accompaniment to the creation of a more open economy.

These same economic considerations led to changes in foreign and military policy. As Gorbachev wrote at the time, "We need lasting peace to concentrate on the development of our society and to cope with the tasks of improving the life of the Soviet people."[23] Gorbachev repeated this point at the International Forum in Moscow in 1987: The Soviet Union sought peace and world stability so that it could focus on domestic priorities.[24] For the program of domestic revitalization to succeed, the Soviet Union had to avoid confrontation and establish a climate of peace and international stability.

Economic reform and changes in military policy were connected in other ways as well. Analysts agree that the introduction of new thinking in Soviet foreign policy was motivated in part by a desire to free up productive resources for civilian needs.[25] Reducing the burden of military spending was seen as a way of benefiting the program of economic restructuring. The "peace dividend" resulting from major military force reductions would make large amounts of capital and skilled labor available for domestic economic needs. The challenge of creating high-tech civilian industries created a special imperative for channeling technical resources from the military sector, where they were previously concentrated, to the domestic economy.[26]

Some analysts concede that economic factors were the primary impetus for perestroika but argue that Soviet economic difficulties were caused by the pressures of the arms race. According to this view, the West won the Cold War by "bankrupting" the Soviet Union. The financial burdens of the arms race became too great, it is claimed, and the Kremlin was forced to sue for peace. There is little doubt that this was one of the goals of Western policy. Throughout the Cold War era, the United States had sought to prevail not by destroying the Soviet Union in a nuclear war (although it seemed at times that the Reagan administration might be moving in that direction) but by forcing the Soviets to divert vast resources into weapons production, thereby overwhelming their industrial capacity. Soviet Foreign Minister Edward Shevardnadze himself once observed, "The arms race can exhaust and bleed the opponent dry, with the goal of undermining its very economy and social base."[27]

The burden of military competition with the West did indeed burden the Soviet economy. The concentration of resources and technology in the military sector robbed civilian industries and ultimately undermined the productive capacity of the entire economy. Certainly these economic problems contributed to Gorbachev's desire to find a new way of dealing with the West. But the burden of militarism was not the only cause of Moscow's economic problems, nor was it the sole impetus for perestroika. The ills of the Soviet economy existed before the Cold War began. They were rooted in the contradictions of the dictatorial system created by Stalin in the 1920s and 1930s, especially in the legacy of collectivized agriculture and the centralized command of industry and commerce. The appalling inefficiency of production, the apathy and low productivity of labor, the suppression of innovation, the emphasis on quantity over quality, the continuing disaster of agriculture—these and other problems of the Soviet economy resulted from the Stalinist system itself. They were endemic to Soviet communism and were not caused by the burdens of the U.S.-Soviet arms race.

The Deeper Roots of Perestroika

To understand the process of perestroika one must look at the underlying social dynamics that radically transformed the former Soviet Union and its people in the mid-twentieth century. As Moshe Lewin explained in his important book, *The Gorbachev Phenomenon,* the Soviet Union changed only recently from a predominantly rural society to an urbanized industrial economy. Despite appalling economic inefficiencies, after World War II the country was radically transformed into a relatively modern industrial society. When the Stalinist system was installed in the 1920s and 1930s, more than 80 percent of the Russian people lived in villages. Today, 70 percent live in cities and the peasantry has been replaced by an urban working class.[28]

Education also advanced rapidly as the socialist system invested heavily in "human capital." In 1959, more than 90 percent of Soviet workers had only an elementary education. By the 1980s, the majority of workers had completed secondary school, and higher education and technical training were widespread.[29] The nature of work changed as well. Three-quarters of the work force was still engaged in peasant or physical labor in 1959.[30] By the 1980s, the Soviet Union was entering the "scientific-industrial-information age," with an increasing number of workers in service, information, and semiskilled professions.[31] An important part of this process has been the rise of the intelligentsia—scientific, political, and administrative "specialists," as they are called. According to Lewin, this group has been the fastest growing part of the Soviet social structure, numbering more than 15 million people in the mid-1980s.[32] Between 1960 and 1986, this class of specialists increased fourfold, more than twice as fast as the rest of the labor force.[33] These highly trained intellectual workers became increasingly important to the political system and to the economy as a whole. This was also the group that chafed most under the restrictions of the old system and that became a primary constituency for perestroika and the process of political renewal.[34]

The combination of these forces—urbanization, industrialization, increasing education, diversification of the labor force, and the rise of the intelligentsia—created a new Soviet society, according to Lewin, and a different kind of social character. The patriarchal authoritarianism of village life was replaced by the greater individualism and anonymity of urban society. New needs and aspirations for autonomy and self-fulfillment arose among the Soviet people. Independent networks and spontaneous social groupings emerged within the old system. The result was the evolution of what Lewin and others term a new "civil society,"[35] a kind of perestroika-from-below that created the conditions for the transformation from above launched by Gorbachev. This new, more independent-minded civil society was evident during the failed coup attempt against Mikhail Gorbachev in August 1991. The people of Moscow, Leningrad, and other cities simply refused to accept the authority of the junta and poured into the streets to face off the tanks in a spontaneous expression of support for a new, more open society.

In a curious way, these changes resulted from the old system's success in accumulating capital. An urbanized, industrial society emerged from old "wooden Russia," but paradoxically, this new society no longer fit within the confining structures of the Soviet model. Karl Marx would say that the forces of production were in opposition to the relations of production. As author Max Watts put it, "Dictatorial socialism, by accumulating human and other capital, created its own grave diggers. Given the new people, new thinking was inevitable."[36]

The consequences of communications technology also deserve mention. Computers, copying machines, faxes, video cameras, cassette recorders—these and other tools of communication in modern society transcended the previous mechanisms of thought control and undermined the foundations of the dictatorial system. They made glasnost almost inevitable. To the extent that information is power, the dispersal of information sources diminished the power of centralized authority. As the systems of internal control weakened, so did the accompanying structures of repression and militarism. These factors reinforced the dynamic of reform and contributed to the evolution of new thinking.

Many observers have noted the generational phenomenon in the Soviet transformation. In a sense, perestroika was the fruition of a process that had begun to unfold more than thirty years before. Gorbachev, Shevardnadze, Yakovlev, and other architects of the new order were young men when Stalin died and were just beginning their professional careers when the first limited reforms were introduced by Khrushchev. They and others had reason to hope that democratization might emerge as the normal course of events.[37] As it turned out, these hopes were premature, and a new orthodoxy descended in the Brezhnev era. Over the next thirty years, however, Gorbachev and his generation of idealists matured, as did the society around them. A new political leadership emerged, surprisingly within the Communist party, determined to make a decisive break with the past. When their turn finally came in the 1980s, Gorbachev and the reformers moved to dismantle the repressive apparatus and unleash the forces of civil society. Once the floodgates were opened, Gorbachev and the Communist system were swept aside and the Soviet Union fell apart.

The Chernobyl Syndrome

One additional factor may have influenced Soviet behavior and the rise of new thinking—the nuclear accident at Chernobyl. According to Sergei Plekhanov of the Institute for U.S.A.-Canada Studies in Moscow, the impact of the April 1986 disaster within the Soviet Union was enormous both politically and psychologically.[38] Gorbachev and his colleagues were severely criticized at home and abroad for their slowness in admitting and responding to the accident. In 1988, Valery Legasov, first deputy chairman of the prestigious Kurchatov Atomic Energy Institute, committed suicide and left a testament, published in *Pravda,* calling Chernobyl "the apotheosis of the whole misguided way of running the economy."[39] Throughout Soviet society, confidence in nuclear technology was shaken. The Kremlin responded to these traumatic events, according to this interpretation, not only by slowing the momentum of nuclear power development but by displaying even greater eagerness for arms reduction. Shortly after the accident, for example, Gorbachev announced another extension of the unilateral nuclear testing moratorium (then in its ninth month). A few months later, he brought a sweeping plan for disarmament to the Reykjavik summit, and in February 1987, he announced the concessions that led to the INF breakthrough. Among American experts, the potential impact of the Chernobyl accident is rarely mentioned. But the world's worst nuclear disaster may indeed have had a significant impact on the rise of antinuclear sentiment in the East.

Outside Influence

Ronald Reagan once claimed that Western peace demonstrations were "all sponsored by a thing called the World Peace Council, which is bought and paid for by the Soviet Union."[40] The president was repeating a claim frequently made by the right wing, that peace movements are controlled and manipulated from Moscow. In the 1980s, however, the opposite was often the case. The nuclear freeze and European disarmament movements exerted some influence over Soviet thinking and contributed a number of suggestions and proposals that eventually became official policy. As Thomas Risse-Kappen has observed, attitudes within the Kremlin "seem to have been influenced more by Western supporters of arms control and detente than by peace-through-strength advocates."[41] Several important disarmament initiatives emanating from Moscow originated with Western peace activists and scholars. Reagan had it backwards. Perhaps it was the Kremlin that was "duped" by the peace movement.

One example of this process was Moscow's 1982 proposal for a partial nuclear freeze. Conservatives sometimes claimed that the freeze was a Soviet idea, but the initiative came entirely from the U.S. peace movement. It was in 1979 that representatives of the American Friends Service Committee and other U.S. groups first presented the idea for what was then called the nuclear moratorium to Soviet officials in Moscow. During the trip, Harvard professor Everett Mendelsohn and former CIA specialist Arthur Macy Cox visited with officials at the Foreign Ministry and with scholars at the Institute for U.S.A.-Canada Studies to urge the Soviet Union to agree to the proposal for a mutual halt to the testing, production, and deployment of nuclear weapons.[42] The Soviets expressed general interest in the idea but made no commitments. Several subsequent appeals were made to Soviet diplomatic representatives in the United States, and additional delegations carried the message to Moscow. The Kremlin finally agreed to a modified version of the freeze in 1982 when it was clear that the issue would have an important impact on public opinion in the West. Even if the Soviet decision to propose the freeze at Geneva was primarily a propaganda gesture, as Strobe Talbott has suggested,[43] Kremlin leaders had to face the possibility that Washington might call their bluff. Regardless of Moscow's motives, the point is that an initiative of the U.S. peace movement influenced Kremlin decision making and was played back to the United States as an official Soviet proposal.

A more important and substantive example of peace movement influence was Gorbachev's nuclear testing moratorium. The concept of unilateral initiatives to break the deadlock of East-West competition was (and still is) central to peace movement thinking and was actively promoted by the Freeze Campaign in the United States, the Campaign for Nuclear Disarmament in Great Britain, and many other Western peace groups. Proponents of the idea often cited the example of John F. Kennedy's test ban moratorium in 1963 that had led to the treaty ending atmospheric nuclear testing. In 1982, Daniel Ellsberg, then a member of the Freeze Campaign Strategy Committee, proposed the idea of a testing moratorium to Soviet policy advisers at the Institute for U.S.A.-Canada Studies in Moscow. The Soviet officials expressed interest in the proposal, but nothing came of the exchange initially.[44] Ellsberg also pressed the test ban concept with Tair Tairov, then secretary general of the World Peace Council in Helsinki. Tairov later left the council and condemned it as a "Stalinist/Brezhnevite structure." In 1985, Tairov urged Kremlin leaders to support the peace movement proposal for a testing moratorium. According to Tairov:

> I myself sent a cable to Moscow saying, please, for God's sake, make an oath not to test for half a year. ... I was reprimanded by the Soviet Peace Committee. They told me, "It's none of your business. No, we will not stop unilaterally."
> I sent another cable: "Please, thousands of people from Australia to Canada are waiting. Bruce Kent, Daniel Ellsberg, CND, SPAS are waiting." ... I sent this two weeks before the moratorium was declared. I know it was read by all the top people, the Ministry of Defence, Gorbachev. When I read in the paper that Gorbachev had announced the moratorium, I felt that I was lucky that day.[45]

Retired admirals Gene LaRocque and Eugene Carroll of the Center for Defense Information in Washington brought the test ban appeal to the White House and the Kremlin in 1984. The Reagan administration responded negatively, claiming that a test ban could not be verified (an assertion contrary to most independent scientific opinion). The two admirals next wrote to Soviet leader Konstantin Chernenko urging that the Soviet Union take the initiative and specifically suggesting that a moratorium begin on August 6, 1985, the fortieth anniversary of the bombing of Hiroshima. Chernenko died before a reply could be sent, but the LaRocque-Carroll letter had an impact, as LaRocque recalled in an interview.

One day in April [1985], I received a call from Ambassador Dobrynin at the Soviet embassy. He asked us to come over to receive a letter from the new Soviet leader. When we arrived, the ambassador greeted us warmly but also chided me gently for not informing him of what was obviously an important matter. He produced a letter from Gorbachev which said that our proposal was given "serious consideration" and agreeing that a testing moratorium should begin on August 6.[46]

The two admirals were encouraged but not satisfied, since there were no specifics in Gorbachev's answer. After a further exchange of letters, LaRocque and Carroll finally received the answer they were seeking. On July 29, the Kremlin announced that a testing moratorium would begin on August 6. According to LaRocque, in subsequent public statements Gorbachev specifically acknowledged the role of the two admirals in recommending the moratorium.[47]

Another example of influence by U.S. citizen groups in the shaping of Soviet policy was the disarmament dialogue project organized by Marcus Raskin, cofounder of the Institute for Policy Studies in Washington. Beginning in 1982, Raskin organized a series of conferences and scholarly exchanges with leading Soviet policy advisors on the need for a comprehensive disarmament approach. At sessions in Minneapolis, San Francisco, and Moscow, Raskin argued that piecemeal arms control efforts were ineffective and that a general disarmament program was the only sure means of ending the arms race. Moreover, he unveiled an elaborate proposal for a U.S.-Soviet agreement on general and complete disarmament. Based on a 1955 United Nations proposal and the 1962 McCloy-Zorin agreement, the Raskin plan called for staged reductions of nuclear and conventional armaments, elaborate inspection and verification procedures, economic conversion of military industries, and a strengthening of the United Nations and other international security mechanisms. Georgi Arbatov and other Soviet academicians who participated in these sessions were greatly impressed by Raskin's sweeping plan and promised to give it careful study. True to their word, they later sent Raskin a detailed response to his proposal and published the plan and their commentary in a leading Soviet journal. More important, some of these ideas began to appear in official Soviet statements and proposals. They emerged in Gorbachev's January 1986 "Disarmament by the Year 2000" proposal, and they made their way into the Soviet documents brought to the bargaining table at

Reykjavik. The degree to which these Soviet proposals were specifically influenced by the Raskin plan is unknown, but the dialogue project clearly reinforced a growing Soviet interest in a comprehensive approach to disarmament. Raskin said, "I'm persuaded that our efforts began to affect their position, which since the early 1970s had been merely a limited arms control approach. By the mid- and late-1980s their positions began to change. Ours was not the only influence, of course, but their interest in our ideas was genuine."[48]

One additional example of this cross-fertilization from West to East deserves mention—the influence of scientists. In both Washington and Moscow, science advisers have sometimes had considerable influence on nuclear policy. Andrei Sakharov wrote, for example, that he and other Soviet scientists helped to persuade Khrushchev to accept the Limited Test Ban Treaty.[49] In the Gorbachev era, Evgenii Velikhov and other scientists had the ear of Kremlin leaders in urging steps toward confidence building and East-West cooperation. Because of the transnational communication and collaboration that are part of the scientific enterprise, ideas that originate in one place may sometimes emerge elsewhere. This was the case with several weapons verification proposals that originated among U.S. scientists but were embraced by leaders in the Soviet Union. In 1988, a delegation of scientists and congressional representatives from the United States visited with Soviet science advisers at the Krasnoyarsk radar station in Central Asia to determine whether the facility was in violation of the ABM Treaty. The event improved the domestic climate for arms restraint in the United States and helped persuade the Kremlin to abandon the questionable site.[50] During the same period, the Natural Resources Defense Council was allowed to set up an independent seismic monitoring station at the Soviet nuclear testing range in the republic of Kazakhstan in an attempt to overcome concerns raised in Washington about test ban verification. Earlier, the Federation of American Scientists (FAS) had developed detailed proposals for the verification of limitations on SDI testing. The White House was unimpressed by the FAS proposal, but the Soviet side was very interested in the plan.[51] It is a curious irony that peace initiatives by U.S. scientists and arms experts received a more sympathetic hearing in Moscow than in Washington.

Soviet leaders had always paid close attention to Western peace movements and tried to manipulate them, but in the 1980s the influence flowed in the other direction. Tair Tairov credited Western peace movements with a decisive role in the evolution of Soviet thinking: "If it wasn't for the peace movements in the West, there would have been no new thinking. ... Gorbachev would never have proclaimed the idea of a nonviolent, nonnuclear world. He knew that the world was already fertile. The peace movements created the historical arena in which he could go ahead."[52]

Peace, and Freedom Too

The peace movement influenced political developments in the East in other ways as well. Many groups applied pressure not only for disarmament but for freedom, too. This was especially true in Western Europe, where activists addressed the dynamics of the Cold War by supporting human rights struggles in the East. During the 1980s, new channels of communication and mutual support were opened between peace groups in the West and human rights advocates in the East. This unofficial dialogue proved of great importance in overcoming Cold War ideology and encouraging democratization in the East. Mary Kaldor has called this process "detente from below" and credits it as a major asset of the disarmament movement: "It established the integrity of large parts of the peace movement. It made it impossible to marginalize the peace movement, as had been done in the past, with the charge that peace activists were agents of the Kremlin."[53]

Perhaps the leading group in this interaction was European Nuclear Disarmament (END), in which Kaldor played an important role. END was a transnational organization facilitating communication and coordination between peace groups in the West and human rights activists in the East. Founded by the eminent British historian E. P. Thompson, END condemned the entire Cold War system of competing blocs and directed its challenges at both Washington and Moscow. END spokespeople felt that in the West, a greater commitment to peace was needed, while in the East, human rights and freedom were paramount. Disarmament and democracy must be achieved together, they asserted. Indeed, it was only through the linkage of the two that genuine peace could be attained. In this respect, the philosophy of END was fully in accord with the view expressed by the future Czechoslovakian President Vaclav Havel in 1985, who said, "Respect for human rights is the fundamental condition and the sole genuine guarantee of true peace. ... Lasting peace and disarmament can only be the work of free people."[54]

It must be admitted that not all Western peace groups acknowledged these connections. Some activists, myself included, tended to give inadequate attention to the underlying ideological conflicts between East and West. We focused our attention on weapons rather than the underlying political conflicts that created the perceived need for such weapons. In the United States, most peace groups either accepted traditional anticommunism or were unwilling to criticize Moscow for fear of encouraging the enemy images that fueled the arms race. Little effort was made to emphasize the symbiotic relationship between militarism and repression or to find a middle ground between condemnation and apologetics. The peace movement sometimes failed to recognize that hostility and mistrust caused the arms race, not the other way around. To the extent that this mistrust was exacerbated by the denial of human rights, such questions were (and still are) a legitimate concern for the peace movement.

Even when the peace movement was not actively campaigning for particular dissidents, it advanced the cause of human rights in the East through its critical stance toward the Soviet Union. The peace movement of the 1980s was more independent than previous movements. Its demands were directed at both sides: Activists wanted a freeze on both U.S. and Soviet weapons and were against both SS-20s and NATO missiles. Soviet officials could not avoid criticisms of their policies even from "friends" in the peace movement. They heard frequent complaints about their military actions, especially in Afghanistan, and also faced constant criticism over human rights. Gorbachev himself got this treatment from Jesse Jackson and the SANE/Freeze delegation at the Geneva Summit in 1985. This critical position toward the Soviet Union not only helped to make the peace movement popular and successful in the West but also aided the cause of human rights in the East.

Perhaps most important were the interactions of the peace movement with prodemocracy groups in the East. END, the Campaign for Peace and Democracy in the United States, the Greens in West Germany, and other Western groups made special efforts to meet with and encourage independent peace and human rights activists in the Soviet Union and Eastern Europe. E. P. Thompson, Joanne Landy, Petra Kelly, and others repeatedly crossed Cold War frontiers to enter into dialogue with both official and unofficial voices for freedom. This solidarity from Western activists gave valuable nourishment to the seeds of democracy that flowered at the end of the decade. Some of the Eastern participants in this dialogue became leaders of the 1989 revolution. In East Germany, Pastor Reiner Eppelmann and other church activists led an independent peace initiative that challenged militarism in both East and West, thus earning the wrath of the East Berlin government and its Stassi security apparatus. END and representatives of British, Dutch, West German, and other West European churches provided important support for Eppelmann and his colleagues. In 1989, the East German churches played a central role in the democratic awakening. During the brief existence of democratic East Germany prior to unification, Eppelmann served as minister of defense—perhaps the first peace activist ever to hold this high military post. In Czechoslovakia, Jiri Dienstbier cooperated with Thompson in coediting a volume of essays on the politics of peace. Dienstbier later became the first foreign minister of new Czechoslovakia. Jacek Kuron, minister of labor in the Solidarity government of Poland, shared the platform with Thompson at the END convention in 1988. In Moscow, historian Roy Medvedev signed the initial END appeal, and later he became a member of the democratic bloc within the Soviet parliament.[55]

Of course, the flowering of freedom in Eastern Europe resulted primarily from internal factors. The people of Eastern Europe played the dominant role in the overthrow of dictatorship. But perhaps the Western peace movement also played a small part in this historic drama. As Mary Kaldor wrote, the peace movement "helped to encourage and provide support for the new peace and human rights groups that emerged during the 1980s all over Eastern Europe, groups that played a key role in the revolutions of 1989."[56] By maintaining autonomy from Soviet influence, by criticizing Soviet as well as U.S. policies, and by insisting upon the linkage between peace and human rights, the Western peace movement may have emboldened independent voices in the East and encouraged the process of ideological realignment that broke through the grip of Cold War consciousness.

The popular movements of East and West reinforced one another. At the beginning of the decade, millions marched in the West for peace, while at the close of the decade, equal numbers marched for freedom in the East. Together, the two movements changed the course of history. Again Mary Kaldor:

The Cold War was ended by a wave of popular movements in both East and West that ... discredited the Cold War idea. It was the Eastern European democracy movement, not Western governments, that brought about the final collapse of Communism. And it was the Western European peace movements that first challenged the status quo in Europe.[57]

13
The Central American Connection

In the early stages of the nuclear freeze movement, a debate raged over the question of political focus. Should the agenda be confined to nuclear issues, or should it be broadened to include Central America? To get the widest possible support for halting the arms race, some argued, the peace movement should concentrate on the freeze and avoid taking a stand on other issues. Opponents argued that the issues are connected, that the nuclear arms race and military interventionism derived from the same policies and assumptions about the use of military force. The former position was identified most often with the national Freeze Campaign, the latter with SANE. When discussions of a possible merger between the two groups began in 1985, differences over this question posed real difficulties.

The issue was a major concern at the December 1986 national freeze conference in Chicago. This was the gathering where the key decision was to be made on merging the Freeze Campaign with SANE. The more than 500 grass-roots delegates in attendance that weekend were being asked to accept a broader political program that, while still focused on nuclear disarmament, now included a commitment to nonintervention and social justice. Would the local freeze groups agree to this change of identity and focus? The answer came in an unexpectedly convincing fashion. As delegates debated the issue and reported on activities at the local level, they discovered that most groups were already working on Central American policy. The issues had already been joined at the grass-roots level. For a growing number of peace activists, the questions of nonintervention and disarmament could no longer be separated. As one local organizer put it, "How can we be concerned about the potential threat of a nuclear war and not care about the actual war under way in Central America?"

Helen Seidman was then president of the Ohio Freeze Campaign, and the evolution in her state was typical of what occurred throughout the country. She explained, "In the early 1980s I was one of those who argued for a narrow agenda, but by the later years the situation changed. People began to work on other issues, and we realized we had no choice but to broaden. Initially we thought of disarmament as a separate issue, but the more we learned, we saw that the issues are connected."[1]

Because of this political evolution, the decision to unite SANE and the Freeze Campaign turned out to be easier than expected. Just prior to the final vote at the 1986 conference, a comedy skit was performed. Written by SANE organizer Ira Shorr and performed by Shorr and Freeze Campaign organizer Gene Carroll, the skit poked fun at the imagined differences that had kept people apart and helped to ease tensions before the big decision.

In the routine, a therapist is counseling a peace activist, who seems to be having problems with a split personality.

Doc: How are we doing today?

Patient: We are in trouble, Doc.

Doc: Of course we're in trouble! With a society mired in militaristic meanderings toward oblivion ...

Patient: I mean me, Doc. Me, your counseling patient. Remember me? Can we talk about me today?

Doc: Of course. I'm sorry. I should never drink coffee when I read the newspaper. Go ahead.

Patient: That's just it. I don't know where to go, what to do.

Doc: I thought we had agreed that it was okay for you to be a peace activist, despite what your mother said about getting a real job.

Patient: Yes, but what kind of peace activist should I be? ... I have a confession to make.

Doc: I won't charge you extra.

Patient: All these years I've told you I was working with a Freeze group ...

Doc: Yes.

Patient: I ... I ...

Doc: Yes.

Patient: I've also been working with SANE.

Doc: So?

Patient: So?! My agenda has broadened, and you just say so? Who am I? What do I believe in? Yesterday I was telling someone about the arms race and I told them that a nuclear war could start because of military intervention in the third world. Military intervention. I mentioned military intervention. I think SANE has taken over my ... taken over my ...

Doc: What's the matter?

Patient: Did you know that 54 cents out of each income tax dollar goes to military-related spending? (hand over mouth) Oh, my god!

Doc: Don't project, I'm only your therapist.

Patient: I'm talking about the military budget now. I'm a walking coalition ... I mean contradiction ... Contras (hand over mouth) I don't know if I'm SANE or Freeze. I've lost my single focus ... I'm bi-focused ... Help me, Doc. Who am I? SANE or Freeze?

Doc: You're Sneeze![2]

With laughter still ringing in the hall, the resolution to merge SANE and the Freeze Campaign was approved overwhelmingly.

Solidarity

The movement to oppose U.S.-sponsored war in Central America during the 1980s was a vast effort. More than 1,000 national and local organizations were involved.[3] The core of the movement consisted of churches and religious organizations, labor-affiliated groups, and human rights organizations, with major support from traditional peace groups such as the American Friends Service Committee, the War Resisters League, and others. An entire book in itself would be needed to give justice to the Central America movement. The purpose here will be to provide an overview, emphasizing the movement's impact on policy and the serendipitous boost it provided for the cause of nuclear arms reduction.

Central America peace activists referred to their cause as the "solidarity movement." The phrase is an apt one, for it helps to describe the motivations that inspired many North American activists to work for peace in Central America. During the 1980s, more than 70,000 U.S. citizens traveled to Nicaragua,[4] and nearly all came away, like a 1984 SANE delegation to observe the Nicaraguan elections, deeply troubled by the pain and suffering inflicted by U.S. policy. The proximity of Central America to the United States and the strong religious and cultural bonds between North Americans and their neighbors to the south created an acute sense of awareness and concern. For many peace activists, solidarity meant "standing with" the people of the region— providing political and material support for the victims of poverty, repression, and war. Clergy and religious people involved in the movement were particularly influenced by the teachings of liberation theology and the doctrine of the preferential "option for the poor." Papal encyclicals, such as *Popularum Progressio* (1967) and *The Social Concerns of the Church* (1987), called for rooting out the structural causes of poverty and oppression in the Third World. Many North Americans believed they were doing this by opposing U.S. imperialism in Central America.

Many tactical and political differences existed within the solidarity movement. Some activists were inspired by religious or moral considerations, while others were motivated by leftist ideology. Some groups emphasized a noninterventionist approach and opted not to take a stand on the Sandinista revolution of Nicaragua and the nationalist movements of the region, while others urged more active support for the popular liberation struggles. Likewise, while some groups emphasized direct action methods, others concentrated on lobbying. Over time, differences even developed within the lobbying community, particularly over whether or not to support proposals by liberal Democrats in the U.S. Congress for so-called nonlethal aid to the Nicaraguan Contras. While these and other divisions existed within the movement, all groups were united in their determination to bring an end to the U.S.-sponsored wars in the region.

The Central America movement was an extraordinarily diverse phenomenon encompassing a wide variety of social action methods and campaigns. One of the most important of these was the sanctuary movement. Modeled after the underground railroad that brought slaves to freedom in the North during the American Civil War, the sanctuary movement helped Central American refugees, mostly Salvadorans and Guatemalans, to escape war and repression in their homelands. The movement provided safety for the refugees in the United States and resisted attempts by the Immigration and Naturalization Service to deport them. More than 400 churches and religious institutions declared themselves sanctuaries during the decade. In Arizona, New Mexico, and Texas, sanctuary leaders were indicted and faced highly publicized trials. Several served jail terms for their activities.[5]

Another important expression of the solidarity movement was Witness for Peace. Founded by the Carolina Inter-Faith Task Force on Central America in 1983, Witness for Peace recruited U.S. citizens to travel to Nicaragua and place themselves in the middle of combat zones threatened by Contra attack. Witness for Peace volunteers assumed considerable personal risk to try to stop the war, providing a kind of human shield against violence. Witness for Peace delegations also documented Contra atrocities and upon their return to the United States engaged in extensive public speaking and media efforts to mobilize public opinion against the war. Ultimately, 4,000 U.S. citizens participated in Witness for Peace delegations.[6]

Activities in the religious community also led to the Pledge of Resistance. This initiative, begun by the Sojourners community in Washington (the same group that had been so influential in the early founding of the nuclear freeze movement), was a response to growing fears of a direct U.S. invasion or bombing attack against Nicaragua. Seeking to put Washington on notice that a high price in political and social disruption would be paid if such a course were pursued, the pledge asked peace activists to commit themselves to engage in civil disobedience in case of an overt U.S. military attack against Nicaragua. In the first four months of the campaign in 1984, more than 40,000 U.S. citizens signed the pledge and committed themselves to civil disobedience in the event of a U.S. invasion. By the end of 1986, more than 80,000 people had signed.[7] Later the pledge broadened its mandate to include resistance to indirect intervention as well. With each new escalation of the Contra war and each increase in U.S. military pressure—such as the war exercises conducted along the Honduran-Nicaraguan border in 1988—the Pledge of Resistance sponsored a wave of civil disobedience and resistance actions all across the country. Hundreds of such protests were held from 1985 through 1988, and thousands of activists were arrested.

Confronting El Salvador

The Reagan administration came into office determined to reverse what it saw as the decline of U.S. influence in the Third World. Immediately it was confronted by a major challenge to U.S. domination in El Salvador. The Salvadoran army and right-wing death squads had mounted a massive wave of terror that left 10,000 people dead, including Archbishop Oscar Romero and many other clergy. In January 1981, the Farabundo Marti National Liberation Front (FMLN) launched a so-called final offensive that threatened to overthrow the ruling oligarchy. With the military situation very much in doubt as they took office, officials of the new administration gathered in the White House to map out a strategy. "There was a very real chance that El Salvador could go over the side," as National Security Adviser Richard Allen put it.[8] Leading the charge for an aggressive U.S. response was Secretary of State Alexander Haig. The secretary saw the conflict as an early test of the administration's mettle and argued strenuously for "a determined show of American will and power."[9] Convinced that the Soviet Union and Cuba were the source of the Salvadoran insurgency, Haig urged a major commitment of military force not only in El Salvador but against Cuba. Haig instructed the State Department to prepare "a plan of action ... to seal off the export of arms from Cuba to Central America."[10] In a dramatic exchange during the very first meeting of the Reagan National Security Council, Haig spoke with "passionate intensity," in the words of Caspar Weinberger, about the crisis in Central America and Cuba.[11] Weinberger reported: "After some time, I broke in to inquire ... where all of this was leading. ... Al, who has never liked to be interrupted, stopped ... [and] turned one of his withering command glares in my direction and said that it was quite clear we would have to invade Cuba."[12] Haig and his supporters were convinced that a show of force "at a high level of intensity" would solve the crisis in El Salvador. During this time the aircraft carriers U.S.S. *Eisenhower* and U.S.S. *Kennedy*, along with thirty escort ships, were sent on maneuvers in Caribbean waters off the Cuban coast. Marine Corps units also staged highly visible amphibious assault exercises in nearby Vieques, Puerto Rico.[13]

Public opinion made the strategy of military escalation untenable, however. As Weinberger told Reagan, "We simply could not expect the American people now to support any kind of military action against Cuba."[14] Each new threat of military pressure in Central America and the Caribbean brought an immediate negative reaction from the American people. As in the case of nuclear issues, hardline signals from the White House created a political backlash.

Organized opposition had begun to form even before the new administration took office. One of the most important groups was the Committee in Solidarity with the People of El Salvador (CISPES), formed in late 1980 and early 1981. With more than 200 local chapters, a strong national office, and an activist network of thousands of committed organizers, CISPES played a key role in mobilizing resistance to U.S. intervention in El Salvador. Along with other solidarity groups, CISPES responded to the administration's talk of military intervention in 1981 with an intensive campaign of organizing and public education. A popular slogan of the time that appeared on many banners and bumper stickers was, "El Salvador is Spanish for Vietnam." A coalition of leftist groups and solidarity and religious organizations called for a demonstration in the spring of 1981. On May 3, in the largest peace and justice demonstration since the Vietnam era, nearly 100,000 people marched to the Pentagon, in part to oppose military aid to El Salvador. Smaller protests were held in local communities all over the country.

As the administration turned up the rhetorical heat, opinion polls showed a sharp increase in the public's disapproval of White House policy on El Salvador—from 32 percent in October 1981 to 50 percent in March 1982.[15] For the next two years, until pollsters stopped asking questions, opposition remained constant. Opponents regularly outnumbered supporters by a two to one margin.[16] Whether people were asked about economic and military assistance or the sending of troops and military advisers, the results were the same—widespread disapproval of U.S. policy.

The president's pollster, Richard Wirthlin, closely monitored these trends and warned the White House of negative political consequences. In response, White House Chief of Staff James Baker reportedly ordered a toning down of Haig's saber rattling and established a more low key approach to the issue.[17] Moreover, the State Department's recommendation to follow a strategy of increased military pressure ran into stiff opposition from the president's political advisers. According to Haig, Reagan was "buffeted by the winds of opinion."[18] Richard Allen admitted that these matters weighed heavily on White House thinking: "Public opinion was a much more important feature of policy formulation in Central America than it was on basic arms ... strategy. ... I would certainly say that public opinion ... would have had major impact on any decisions to go to the source in Cuba."[19] Haig reported that James Baker, Ed Meese, Michael Deaver, and other senior aides "counseled against ... a foreign undertaking that would generate tremendous ... noise in the press and in Congress." The former secretary also offered this revealing observation: "Very nearly the first words spoken on this subject in the councils of the Reagan administration made reference to the danger of 'another Vietnam.'"[20]

Despite its hawkish leanings, the Reagan administration was haunted by the legacy of Vietnam. Public reluctance to support military adventurism limited White House options and made the Haig strategy not only unwise but politically unacceptable. The administration opted instead for a more limited approach and gave up on having a larger U.S. military presence in El Salvador. Congress voted to limit the number of American advisers to fifty-five, and at the end of 1981, the naval task force operating off Cuban waters was withdrawn. The threat of direct U.S. intervention passed.

Although public opinion helped to prevent military invasion, it was unable to halt indirect intervention. The administration imposed its will on El Salvador without invading through a major CIA operation and vast amounts of economic and military aid. U.S. financial support during the decade totaled nearly $4 billion.[21] In 1987, the amount of U.S. aid surpassed the entire Salvadoran state budget.[22] Intervention by proxy remained (and continues to be) less susceptible to public control than direct intervention is.

Despite the difficulties, the solidarity movement worked throughout the decade to pressure Congress to cut military aid to El Salvador and to demand a negotiated political solution. Religious, peace, human rights, and labor groups worked together to lobby specific legislators and generate grass-roots pressure in targeted congressional districts. The Coalition for a New Foreign and Military Policy played a central role in coordinating these efforts in Washington. Initially the campaign was successful in restraining U.S. intervention and persuading Congress to reduce White House military aid requests, but the administration managed to circumvent these restrictions by invoking executive authority. After 1983 and the election of Napoleon Duarte as Salvadoran president, Congress became less concerned about events in El Salvador and shifted its attention to the Contra war in Nicaragua. In

November 1989, the political focus returned to El Salvador when six Jesuit priests, their housekeeper, and her fifteen-year-old daughter were
murdered in San Salvador. As CISPES Director Angela Sanbrano put it,
"Congress could no longer justify funding an army that goes around
killing priests."[23] Members of Congress now listened to reports that human rights groups were circulating on abuses by the Salvadoran military and links between the army and right-wing death squads. In May
1990, the House of Representatives voted to withhold 50 percent of
U.S. military aid, and in October the Senate followed suit. The long legislative fight to reduce U.S. military involvement in El Salvador finally
had brought results. A few months later, in part as a result of this congressional action, negotiations began between the Salvadoran government and the FMLN toward a political solution to the crisis. In January
1992, an agreement was reached to end the war in El Salvador.

The Quest for Peace in Nicaragua

Bill Callahan didn't start out in life as someone likely to lead a major
humanitarian aid campaign. He said, "I was terribly slow on everything. I never had a socially conscious thought until I was in my early
thirties. I got my degree from Johns Hopkins and was a physicist for ten
years. I thought that's what I would always be doing."[24] But while
studying for the priesthood, Callahan became embroiled in a major religious debate: "I was studying theology during the time of the Second
Vatican Council. It was an exciting time, because I thought the liturgi-
cal changes were wonderful. There were big fights in the seminary,
though, and I became the center of a lot of controversy."[25] From these
initial debates over theology, Callahan moved on to social and political
controversies. First came organizing against racial discrimination in his
native Boston. Then, in 1971, he participated in the Vietnam antiwar
movement. Later came the struggle against gender discrimination in
the Roman Catholic church.

When newspapers leaked reports in 1982 of a "secret" CIA war
against Nicaragua,[26] Callahan became deeply concerned. In January
1983, he traveled to Nicaragua and lived there for four months "to
make up my own mind about what was going on and to learn some
Spanish." After returning to the United States, Callahan became increasingly involved in the growing Central American solidarity movement. Later that year, a friend, Maryknoll Sister Helene Sullivan, came

back from a visit with the religious orders of Nicaragua to deliver an urgent request for humanitarian aid. The Jesuits and other clergy in Nicaragua were reaching out to their colleagues in North America for help. Callahan's life was about to change abruptly. He recalled:

> The aid campaign needed a coordinator, so Helene called me up and stuck it to me. She said, "You people say you'll help if the cause is just. Well the people are desperate, so how about it?" I hemmed and hawed and said we don't do that kind of thing. We Jesuits are more intellectual. But I had a bit of time on my hands, and it seemed like a short-term effort, so I said all right. That was December 1983, and I'm still at it eight years later.[27]

Working from modest offices in Mt. Ranier, Maryland, near Washington, D.C., Callahan and his religious community began to collect medicines and other supplies for delivery through the Institute of John the 23rd, located on the Jesuit campus in Managua.

As the U.S. war against Nicaragua expanded, so did the aid campaign. When Congress voted in June 1985 to approve $27 million in military aid for the Contras, Callahan and his colleagues boldly vowed to match it. Callahan said, "That's when we launched the Quest for Peace, a citizens' policy of peace and friendship with Nicaragua. We pledged to gather and send to Nicaragua an equal value in donated humanitarian aid as Congress sent in military aid to the Contras."[28] In the next year, the Quest for Peace succeeded in raising $27 million in humanitarian aid, all of it in the form of cargo containers shipped from local groups around the country. In 1986, when Congress approved a further expenditure of $100 million for the Contras, the Quest responded in kind, pledging to deliver $100 million in humanitarian aid. Once again they succeeded, providing $60 million in physical aid and $40 million in donated services from Americans working in Nicaragua. Over the next several years, the Quest for Peace launched two additional $100 million campaigns, ultimately delivering more than $327 million worth of aid to the Nicaraguan people.

The Quest for Peace also had an important political dimension, as Callahan describes: "From the very beginning the message to local groups was 'send your boxes to Nicaragua and your letters to Congress.' The goal was to use physical aid to keep the Nicaraguans alive but also to rally Americans to learn what was going on and to lobby Congress to stop the war."[29] The aid campaign also had a significant psychological and even spiritual impact within the movement: "It had a holistic effect, helping people to survive the very frustrating days of Congress voting support for the war. Gathering boxes of physical aid was something positive and reinforcing. It helped to sustain people for the long haul."[30]

In 1991 Callahan did an analysis of the vast human effort that went into Nicaraguan solidarity work. Placing a dollar value on the many hours of donated labor by tens of thousands of activists lobbying, speaking in public, and collecting humanitarian aid, Callahan arrived at an estimate of $250 million a year. In dollar terms, this was a greater effort than that of the administration. "In a sense it was also a more effective effort," claimed Callahan, "because so much of official U.S. aid went to sustain the bureaucracy and for graft."[31] His conclusion was hopeful:

> Even though the odds seemed unequal, with a popular president at the peak of his powers, with his most obsessive foreign policy, we were successful. Because of the long hours spent and the quality of the services provided, the citizens' movement actually outspent the administration. At the level of public opinion, the solidarity groups won the struggle.[32]

The Contra Aid Battle

In its first year in office, the Reagan administration focused on the precarious situation in San Salvador, but by 1982 the center of attention had shifted to Nicaragua, and it remained there for the rest of the president's term in office. For the Reagan White House, Nicaragua was an obsession. It occupied an enormous amount of the administration's time and energy and became a kind of personal crusade for the president. The White House, determined to turn back the Sandinista revolution, launched a massive campaign of military pressure to destabilize and overthrow the Nicaraguan government.

Initially, the White House claimed that the Nicaraguan operation was designed solely to interdict the flow of arms to El Salvador. Many congressmen were skeptical (since the 1980 Republican party platform pledged "to support ... efforts ... to establish a free ... government in Nicaragua"[33]), and they decided to hold the administration to its word. In the fall of 1982, Congress passed what became known as the Boland I amendment—named for its sponsor, House Intelligence Committee

Chairman Edward Boland (D-MA)—prohibiting the use of CIA and Defense Department funds for the purpose of overthrowing the government of Nicaragua.

The Boland I amendment signaled the beginning of congressional opposition to the Contra war and set the stage for a protracted legislative battle over U.S. policy in Nicaragua. The struggle over Contra aid became one of the most divisive and bitter political fights of the decade. Climactic legislative battles on the issue littered the Washington landscape. From 1982 through 1989, Congress voted dozens of times on Contra aid. As in the MX fight, the peace movement lost many of these votes, especially in the Senate. But the opposition won often enough to complicate and obstruct the administration's planning and for a time during 1984–1985 actually succeeded in outlawing military operations altogether. An increasingly frustrated White House responded by going underground and embarking on the illegal Contra support operation run by Oliver North, touching off the administration's worst political crisis.

The lobbying campaign against the Contra war was a massive effort that involved more than 150 national organizations and tens of thousands of grass-roots activists. The Coalition for a New Foreign and Military Policy served as the legislative nerve center. The Caribbean Basin Information Project, aided by Fenton Communications, focused on communications and press strategy. The Center for National Security Studies marshaled expert opinion and the support of former high-level policymakers. Most important were the churches. They not only activated their local congregations and social action networks but provided the core national leadership in Washington. The United Church of Christ, the Presbyterian church, and the American Baptists were the major players, aided by the Protestant-based Inter-Religious Task Force on Central America in New York and the Catholic-based Religious Task Force on Central America in Washington.[34] These efforts were bolstered after 1983 by the growing involvement of disarmament groups that applied the lobbying skills acquired in the nuclear freeze and MX debates to the Contra aid struggle.

By 1985, the Contra aid campaign had begun to rival the MX coalition in size and effectiveness. Weekly legislative coordinating meetings of the Central America Lobby Group attracted as many as sixty peace and human rights lobbyists. Targeting lists were developed of members of Congress needing additional pressure, and activist networks in the districts of these members were alerted to turn up the heat. As in the MX campaign, the Lobby Group became a major player on Capitol Hill. The Democratic leadership of the House sent staff members to the weekly coordinating meetings, and a smaller group of lobbyists met frequently with Representative David Bonior (D-MI), chairman of the House Democratic Task Force on Nicaragua, to share vote counts and plan legislative strategy.[35] Although this relationship between lobbyists and legislators deteriorated in later years as Democrats began to embrace proposals for nonlethal aid to the Contras, the collaboration showed the growing political strength of peace forces on this issue.[36]

In the early years of the legislative battle over Contra aid, the House of Representatives consistently opposed Reagan administration policy. After passage of the first Boland amendment in 1982, the House returned to the issue in 1983 and approved a more comprehensive prohibition, the Boland II amendment, barring all military and paramilitary operations against Nicaragua. The Republican-controlled Senate refused to go along with this provision, and the Conference Committee allowed for the continuation of funding for the Contras—although at substantially lower levels than the administration had requested. The initiative for the Boland amendment came out of the Human Rights Working Group, a precursor of the Central America Working Group that consisted of Washington-based human rights groups and legislative aides on Capitol Hill. With staff support from the Coalition for a New Foreign and Military Policy and its chief lobbyist, Cindy Buhl, the Working Group played a key role in mobilizing support within Congress for restrictions on the war in Nicaragua.

In early 1984, the White House requested a supplemental appropriation for the Contras and the battle began again. During the debate, the CIA's involvement in the mining of the Nicaraguan port of Corinto was revealed, creating acute embarrassment for the administration and a political furor in Congress. Even the hawkish Senate approved a nonbinding resolution in April calling for a halt to the mining of Nicaraguan harbors. In this atmosphere of controversy, the House voted 241-177 to ban aid for the Contras. With opposition rising, the Senate acceded to the House position and agreed to withhold additional funding for the Contras until 1985. With the funds from the previous year exhausted, U.S. support for the Contras officially came to an end, at least for a time.

As was subsequently revealed during the Iran-Contra scandal, it was during this period of rising congressional opposition that the Oliver North operation began. By the time the flow of aid from Congress stopped, North and company were already in business, assuring a steady flow of support to the Contras from third countries, private donors, and profits from the sale of arms to Iran.

In 1985, the Reagan administration renewed its bid for Contra aid. Newly confident after its landslide reelection victory, the White House demanded that Congress release the funds withheld the previous year. Central America peace groups responded with a huge lobbying effort, concentrating on the House of Representatives. With grass-roots pressure pouring into congressional offices, the House held firm, voting 248-180 on April 23 to reject further aid to the Contras. The peace movement's victory celebration was short-lived, however, for the Democratic leadership immediately began devising plans for humanitarian aid to the Contras. Although a majority still opposed the Contra war, many Democrats were frightened by Reagan's crushing defeat of Mondale in November. The electoral results had a powerful intimidating effect on many members of Congress. Moderate and conservative Democrats from the South felt especially vulnerable, since Reagan had rolled up huge majorities in many of their districts. These members wanted an alternative proposal that did not entirely abandon the Contras and that would protect them from being criticized by the president.[37] After a complicated and confusing series of votes that spring, the House decided in June to approve an amendment by Representative David McCurdy (D-OK) for $27 million in nonlethal assistance. The Senate agreed, and the flow of authorized aid resumed, although the ban on weapons and military equipment remained in place.

In 1986, the White House upped the ante, requesting a $100 million aid package that removed all previous restrictions on lethal aid and CIA involvement. Intensive personal lobbying by Reagan and continued vacillation by moderate Democrats allowed the administration to win. The U.S. government was now officially back in the war against Nicaragua. Ironically, Congress voted to resume funding for the Contras just a few months before the Iran-Contra scandal and the revelations of North's illegal resupply operation hit the press.

Peace and solidarity groups were disheartened by this reversal of fortune, but they did not give up. Lobbying pressure in Washington and at the grass-roots level continued. In 1987, two new campaigns were launched. Focusing primarily on activist groups, the "Days of Decision" campaign organized national days of protest and grass-roots lobbying prior to major congressional votes. The second coalition, "Countdown 87," was designed to create a high level of professionalism and political sophistication within the anti–Contra aid campaign. Countdown 87 existed for only one year, from June 1987 to May 1988, but during that time it spent more than $1 million for expanded field operations in sixteen targeted congressional districts, including local polling and direct mail campaigns, and a major public relations and media advertising effort.[38]

The opposition to Contra aid was aided a great deal by the Central American peace process initiated by Costa Rican President Oscar Arias. In August 1987, five Central American presidents signed the Esquipulas Agreement calling for free elections in the region, a halt to outside support for insurgents, and reconciliation between armed opponents. The Arias peace plan caught the Reagan administration off guard and pulled the rug out from under the president's Contra war policy. It also created a positive political alternative that congressional moderates could support. While claiming to welcome the Arias plan, the White House refused to accept a halt to outside aid and proceeded to request additional military support for the Contras. As Congress prepared to vote on the proposal in early 1988, the intensified lobbying efforts of peace groups began to pay off. Tens of thousands of letters and phone calls inundated congressional offices.[39] In February, the House of Representatives voted to reject the White House's request. Two months later, it approved a Democratic substitute proposal that provided food and medicine for the Contras and aid for war victims inside Nicaragua but no military support. In May, a last attempt by Representative Henry Hyde (R-IL) to resurrect military aid for the Contras was defeated 190-214.[40] By the time the Reagan administration left office, U.S. support for the Contra war had again been halted.

The Failure of Public Diplomacy

Oliver North asserted during the Iran-Contra hearings in Congress that the Reagan administration did not effectively communicate its case to the American people. Perhaps not, but it was not for lack of trying. The administration went to extraordinary lengths to sell the Contra war, but the public simply wouldn't buy it. The president gave six full-length speeches on behalf of the Contras, beginning with a dramatic address before a joint session of Congress in April 1983. Three of his addresses were broadcast live by the television networks.[41] He spoke often of his Nicaragua policy in press conferences and made many statements on behalf of the Contras. One of his more outrageous assertions came in March 1985 when he hailed the Contras as the "moral equivalent of the Founding Fathers."[42] The White House also set up a new Office of Public Diplomacy to mobilize public opinion on behalf of the president's policy. The National Security Council and other government agencies were mobilized for a nationwide campaign of more than a thousand speaking engagements and hundreds of editorial commentaries.[43] The operation was similar to the public relations campaign conducted against the nuclear freeze movement.

Despite these efforts, opinion polls consistently showed widespread public opposition to White House policy. Nearly every survey conducted during the decade showed that the American people were against military aid for the Contras and that they opposed U.S. policy in Nicaragua.[44] Disapproval of military aid for the Contras consistently stood above 60 percent.[45] The Gallup poll found opponents of Contra aid outnumbering supporters by two to one. According to authors Jane Mayer and Doyle McMannus: "Nowhere was public opinion less in tune with Reagan's policy than on the issue of Nicaragua. Richard Wirthlin ... told others in the [1984] campaign that the issue was 'pure poison.'"[46] When the question of overthrowing the Nicaraguan government was posed, opposition was even higher. Disapproval of such a policy stood at 72 percent in March 1985, according to the ABC/*Washington Post* poll.[47] Public opinion on these issues remained stable through the decade. The American people wanted no part of the Contra war against Nicaragua.

Ronald Reagan himself was deeply disappointed at his inability to win support for the Contras. He later wrote:

> During the eight years of my presidency, I repeatedly expressed my frustration (and sometimes my downright exasperation) over my difficulties in convincing the American people and Congress of the seriousness of the threat in Central America. The White House staff regularly received

the results of polls that measured what Americans thought of administration policies. Time and again, I would speak on television, to a joint session of Congress, or to other audiences about the problems in Central America, and I would hope that the outcome would be an outpouring of support from Americans. ... But the polls usually found that ... few cared enough ... to apply the kind of pressure I needed on Congress.[48]

Hard Measures

As the Contra war kicked into high gear in 1983 and the years following, CIA Director William Casey and other hardliners pressed the White House for intensified military pressure against Nicaragua. The CIA-directed attacks against oil storage facilities in Corinto were part of a deliberate strategy to cut petroleum supplies. The mining of Nicaraguan harbors was a further attempt to strangle the economy. Military bases were opened in neighboring Honduras, combat exercises involving U.S. National Guard units were conducted along the border, and the Contras launched frequent forays into rural areas inside Nicaragua. These actions caused enormous suffering for the Nicaraguan people and undermined many of the social gains of the 1979 revolution, but they had little military impact. At no time was Sandinista power threatened militarily. In fact, these attempts to impose a military solution backfired politically, prompting sharp criticism in Congress and spurring efforts to rein in administration policy.

Frustrated by the ineffectiveness of their Contra policy and the lack of military success against the Sandinistas, administration officials began to explore the option of direct U.S. intervention. In December 1984, Deputy CIA Director Robert Gates wrote a memo to Casey concluding that the Contras "cannot overthrow the Sandinistas" and proposing a series of "hard measures" to increase the pressure against Managua.[49] Among Gates's recommendations were a number of steps that Washington subsequently implemented, including the imposition of economic sanctions and the encouragement of efforts by the Contras to "maximize the economic dislocation." Gates also recommended "the use of air strikes to destroy a considerable portion of Nicaragua's military buildup."[50] The second highest official in the CIA was proposing a massive U.S. bombing raid against Nicaragua.

This was not the first time national security officials considered air strikes against Managua. In September 1984, the National Security

Planning Group, a select group of National Security Council officials, had met to discuss the use of U.S. military force to prevent the delivery of MIG fighter jets to Nicaragua.[51] The White House openly threatened military action if the jets were delivered. The option of direct U.S. intervention came up in other ways as well. In early 1985, in a policy statement accompanying a request for renewed military aid to the Contras, the White House warned Congress that the introduction of U.S. military force in Nicaragua would be an "eventual option" if the Contras failed.[52] When Representative Lee Hamilton (D-IN) confronted the president over this passage at a White House meeting, Reagan and his senior aides backed away and disavowed the statement.[53]

Proposals for the direct use of U.S. forces ran into fierce opposition whenever they were raised. Gates had written in his 1984 memo that the hard measures he was proposing "probably are politically unacceptable."[54] He was right. Resistance to overt intervention existed in Congress, among the American people, and within the administration itself. Foremost among the opponents of military intervention were the Joint Chiefs of Staff and the Defense Department. A 1983 RAND Corporation study had estimated that 100,000 or more U.S. combat troops would be required to defeat the Sandinistas and that such an operation "could bog the United States down in a prolonged military occupation and counterinsurgency campaign."[55] The armed forces had learned during the Vietnam War that the lack of political support could have disastrous consequences for their own institutions, and they had no intention of jumping into another unpopular military adventure. As Caspar Weinberger told the president during a discussion of military intervention in the region, the administration could not impose a war on the American people and "expect to have their support."[56] Since such support did not exist, the option of direct military intervention was out of the question. As Professor Alexander George has observed: "The Reagan administration's ability to engage in stronger coercive diplomacy against the Sandinista regime was severely constrained by domestic political opposition."[57]

Robert McFarlane confirmed this assessment in testimony before the congressional Iran-Contra Committee in 1987. Attempting to explain what he called the "failure" of administration policy in Nicaragua, McFarlane identified the lack of political support as a key factor. If you are going to "engage in conflict" with another nation, McFarlane observed, "you must have the American people and the U.S. Congress solidly behind you."[58] In the case of Nicaragua, the necessary political support was lacking. This left the White House no other option but to rely on the Contras and the unsatisfactory and ultimately unsuccessful use of covert action. McFarlane said, "I think it is safe to say that no one making these important decisions in the Reagan administration viewed covert action as the best way to pursue our aims in Nicaragua. People turned to covert action because they thought they could not get Congressional support for more overt activities."[59]

Many presidents in U.S. history would not have hesitated to send the marines to overthrow an unfriendly government in Nicaragua. But in the post-Vietnam era, public opinion was solidly against military intervention in Central America. Congress and an active social movement opposed every attempt at military escalation. Domestic political opposition became an obstacle to more overt military pressures. The option of military invasion that had been available to so many U.S. presidents in previous eras of history was blocked by the strength of antiwar opposition.

The Link to Disarmament

The Central American solidarity movement and the disarmament movement were linked in many ways. The same activists often participated in both, especially at the local level. An activist might join a local nuclear freeze effort one week and an action against Contra aid the next. Both movements were working toward the same general goal—preventing war and creating a more peaceful world—and it was only natural that they would draw support from the same constituency. The two movements not only overlapped but reinforced one another, for it was the combined impact of the two that helped bring about the INF Treaty.

When news of the Iran-Contra scandal broke in 1986, the White House was plunged into political crisis. Reagan's approval ratings plummeted more than 20 points, from 67 percent in October to 46 percent in November, according to the CBS/New York Times poll.[60] This was the steepest one-month drop in presidential approval ever measured.[61] In March 1987, the ratings dropped even lower, to 42 percent. Support for the administration's foreign policy also fell sharply, from 57 percent in October to 29 percent in March.[62]

How did the White House respond to this crisis? Daniel Ellsberg and other administration critics have contended that Ronald Reagan tried to diffuse the Iran-Contra scandal in the same way that Richard Nixon sought to overcome Watergate twelve years before—by pursuing arms control and summitry with the Soviet Union.[63] According to this interpretation, the White House finally got serious about arms control in part to deflect attention from the Iran-Contra crisis. Focusing on arms control and the historic treaty with the Soviet Union was a way to project a positive image of the president as a leader in command. It was also a way to bolster the standing of the Republican party in time for the 1988 presidential campaign season.

Other observers have noted this connection between arms control and the Iran-Contra scandal as well. Historian John Newhouse wrote that "Reagan's interest in arms control [grew] as his domestic problems worsened."[64] Social scientist Bruce Russett likewise concluded that senior White House political advisers were motivated by such considerations in urging the president to conclude the INF agreement.[65] Several administration officials interviewed for this book agreed that overcoming Iran-Contra was a factor in the White House desire for an arms agreement in 1987. Given the "obvious erosion in approval," according to Public Affairs Director Michael Baroody, "dealings with the Soviet Union inevitably would have been influenced ... in terms of a stronger desire to prove the bona fides of the administration."[66] In an interview, Richard Wirthlin would not disclose his political advice to the president on this matter:

A. I don't want to get into the kind of things that I suggested.

Q. But would you admit that the strategy during the Iran-Contra crisis was to push the agenda in other areas?

A. The classic political axiom is you deal to your strengths. He did that beginning in 1987 until he left office.

Q. Was one of those strengths negotiating with the Soviets?

A. Absolutely.[67]

Some officials who criticized the INF agreement on military grounds conceded that it was a sound move politically. Brent Scowcroft and his colleagues were unhappy with the treaty but admitted that it made "tactical sense ... to help demonstrate that the President's recent political wounds had not impaired his ability to function."[68] Arms Control and Disarmament Agency Director Kenneth Adelman likewise observed that the agreement with Moscow came "just when the Reagan administration most needed CPR as it was rocked by ... Iran-Contra revelations."[69]

Concluding a treaty to reduce nuclear weapons was a sure means of regaining political popularity. The White House could be certain that arms control and improved U.S.-Soviet relations would enhance the president's approval ratings and the standing of the Republican party. Opinion polls conducted at the time showed that presidential approval ratings always increased following summit meetings with Mikhail Gorbachev and at times when arms control talks showed the greatest promise. Each gesture toward a thaw in the Cold War improved the president's political standing. The boost in Reagan's ratings was considerable after the Geneva Summit and then again after the Washington summit in December 1987.[70] Other social science studies have also found a pattern of higher approval ratings following peaceful gestures.[71] Such information was available to White House strategists and no doubt affected decision making during the crisis. When the administration needed a political boost, arms control provided the answer.

But how did arms control become so popular? Why was it good politics in 1987 when it had been so out of favor just six years before? Here we return to the central concern of this book: the role of the peace movement in shaping public consciousness and creating a new political dynamic. The demonstrations, lobbying campaigns, grass-roots organizing, public education, and media efforts of the disarmament movement helped to create a new climate of opinion conducive to arms control and improved U.S.-Soviet relations. When Reagan "played to his strength," it was in a political context partly defined by the peace movement.

The solidarity movement played its part by placing roadblocks in the way of Central America policy and raising the political costs of continuing the Contra war. When these political restrictions became too tight, the administration went "off the shelf" to the illegal Oliver North operation, thereby creating the political crisis that propelled the White House toward arms control. The two movements—disarmament and solidarity—worked in tandem to place limits on Reagan administration policy.

A Loss But Not a Defeat

When the Sandinistas were voted out of office in February 1990, Reagan administration supporters declared victory. Elliot Abrams, former assistant secretary of state, called the results "spectacular." Oliver North claimed that the success would not have been possible "without the bravery" of the Contras.[72] Columnist James Kilpatrick wrote, "Reagan was right all along about Nicaragua. If it had not been for the former President's unrelenting support of the anti-communist Contras, Sunday's election never would have happened."[73]

But the initiative for the 1990 elections came from Oscar Arias and his colleagues in Central America, not from the Reagan administration. The proposal for elections and peaceful political reform tied to the dismantling of the Contras was crafted independently of the White House by the Central American presidents as a substitute for the administration's war policy. As *Congressional Quarterly* noted at the time, the Reagan administration had "little control over events in Central America ... [and] only marginal influence over the peace plan." It was Arias and his fellow presidents "who were largely responsible for pressuring the Sandinistas to carry out the political reforms they promised."[74] The February 1990 elections were accepted by Managua only on the condition that the U.S.-sponsored war would come to an end and that the Contras would be demobilized. The political transformation in Nicaragua was achieved by negotiation, not confrontation, by ballots, not bullets.

Administration supporters claimed that the military pressures of the Contra war were necessary to bring about the electoral process. But the Sandinistas had agreed to elections previously, in 1984, and were pledged to do so again in the future. Most international observers, including those of us who participated in the SANE delegation, considered the 1984 vote open and honest, for the most part. Opposition parties were given full access to the media and had complete freedom to campaign. Right-wing parties chose not to participate in 1984, but that was their decision (urged on by the White House), not the government's. Free elections would have been held again in Nicaragua without the Contra war. Indeed, the country's entire political and social evolution would have been freer had it not been for the burden of military and economic hostilities imposed from the United States.

The 1990 election was hardly "free." The Nicaraguan people voted with a gun to their head, quite literally, knowing that the United States would continue the Contra war if Daniel Ortega was reelected president. They also knew that Washington's trade embargo would continue if the Sandinistas remained in office. A vote for Violeta Chamorro and the opposition coalition thus was a vote for more food on the table. It was also a vote to stop the war and end military conscription. As if this pressure were not enough, the U.S. government poured $8 million into Nicaragua, through the Endowment for Democracy, to support anti-Sandinista electoral activities. This was a formidable expenditure for so small and impoverished a country. That the Sandinistas managed to get 40 percent of the vote under these circumstances was a remarkable testament to their core support in Nicaragua.

Reagan officials achieved their objective of removing the Sandinistas from office, but the means by which this happened were not of their choosing. Nor were the results as definitive as hardliners had hoped they would be. The Sandinistas lost an election, but they were not defeated. After the election, they remained the largest political party in the country and continued to exert considerable influence in the army, in parliament, among unionized workers, and elsewhere in society. Moreover, by demonstrating a genuine commitment to democracy and free elections (contrary to what the Reagan administration had always insisted), the Sandinistas enhanced their political legitimacy and improved their public image. If Nicaragua is allowed to continue evolving toward parliamentary democracy free of interference from the United States, the Sandinistas may one day occupy the presidential palace again. Whether this happens will depend in part on the strength of the North American solidarity movement.

14

Who Won
the Cold War?

Is it true that the West "won" the Cold War? On the surface it is easy to see why so many people think so. Since action A, the Reagan arms buildup, was followed by action B, the fall of the Berlin Wall, many assume that A caused B. As noted in Chapter 12, however, the reasons for the historic transformations in the East are extraordinarily complex. The sources of change were primarily internal, not external. Hardline policies from the West did not cause these events and may even have impeded the process.

A central tenet of the peace-through-strength interpretation is that arms expansion was necessary to bring the Soviets to the bargaining table. Reagan officials claim that their military buildup forced the Kremlin to negotiate seriously for arms reduction. In fact, the Soviets were eager to begin negotiations from the very first days of the new administration. It was not Moscow but Washington that blocked the opening of serious talks. As Alexander Haig reported in his memoirs: "The Soviets were eager to enter into arms control talks. ... [Soviet Ambassador] Dobrynin raised the subject in his first talk with me and never failed to mention it in subsequent encounters."[1] The White House spurned the Soviet overtures because, in Haig's words, "there was nothing substantive to talk about, nothing to negotiate."[2] It was only when political pressures in the United States began to build that the White House became serious about negotiations.

The immediate impact of the administration's missile deployments and confrontational approach in the early 1980s was not a breakthrough for peace but a complete breakdown in negotiations. When the United States proceeded with deployment of the cruise and

Pershing II missiles in Europe, the Soviet Union responded by walking out of Geneva and ending all arms talks. For the first time since such negotiations had begun in 1969, in the words of Strobe Talbott, arms talks were "shut down across the board."[3] The hardline rhetoric and confrontational policies of the early Reagan years worsened U.S.-Soviet relations and heightened international tensions. It was not until 1984 and afterward, when the administration softened its rhetoric and Congress eased up on the military buildup, that relations between the two powers began to improve and negotiations resumed in a more businesslike manner.

Those who argue that the easing of Cold War tensions resulted from the Reagan military buildup must answer the question: Could a similar or better result have been achieved through other means? The answer almost certainly is yes. It was not necessary to deploy INF weapons and other missiles to get an arms treaty. Agreements as good as or better than the INF Treaty were available in earlier years and could have been achieved if the United States had been interested.

Even during the Brezhnev years, opportunities existed for arms limitation. In 1982, the Kremlin announced a policy of no first use of nuclear weapons and invited the United States to join in a mutual no-first-use pledge. Washington turned a cold shoulder. The Soviet Union also announced in 1982 that it would be willing to adopt a partial freeze on the deployment of nuclear weapons.[4] The Soviet proposal, which was not the same as the more comprehensive freeze plan of the U.S. peace movement, urged that strategic armament be "frozen quantitatively ... and that modernization be limited to the utmost."[5] By contrast, the original freeze proposal required a complete halt to weapons modernization. Nonetheless, the Soviet plan would have been a step forward. The White House rejected it. In 1981 and 1983, the Soviets introduced draft treaties at the United Nations to restrict the militarization of outer space, and in 1983, Moscow declared a unilateral moratorium on the testing of antisatellite weapons. Washington rejected these offers and proceeded with its massive SDI program.

Many additional arms control opportunities presented themselves after Gorbachev's ascent to power. The most significant was the Soviet nuclear testing moratorium, which began in August 1985 and continued for eighteen months. Here was a golden opportunity for the United States to enter into an important and easily verifiable agreement to achieve substantial arms limitation. Unlike previous Soviet offers, this was a plan of action, not merely words, a unilateral restraint that the Kremlin extended four times. The testing moratorium was also Gorbachev's first foray into nuclear arms policy and a bold departure from previous Soviet policy. The Reagan administration's repeated rejection of the testing moratorium could not have helped the reform process.

Gorbachev's most grandiose proposal was the January 1986 plan for "Disarmament by the Year 2000" presented at the Reykjavik summit. Gorbachev called for the complete elimination of all nuclear weapons by 2000, beginning with a 50 percent cut in strategic weapons within five years, followed by second- and third-stage agreements that would bring nuclear weapons down to zero. Although Reagan briefly flirted with the concept of disarmament at Reykjavik (much to the chagrin of his advisers), the Gorbachev plan was dismissed. The U.S. government was not interested in disarmament and had no plan for dealing with Gorbachev's peaceful overtures. It was only in 1987, when the Soviet leader offered to accept the zero option with no strings attached and when the White House faced its most severe political crisis at home, that the administration finally decided to take yes for an answer and proceed with negotiating the INF Treaty.

The Broader Context

Although this book has focused on the role of the peace movement, domestic peace pressures were not the only influence acting on policymakers during the 1980s. Many other factors were also at work. These included perceptions of external threat or opportunity, the influence of allies, calculations of economic costs and benefits, and of course the actions of adversaries. To gain a complete picture of the arms control process, one must weigh all the pressures impinging upon both U.S. and Soviet policymakers. In doing so, one gains a better understanding of the overall development of relations between the two powers and, more specifically, of how the peace movement fits into the picture.

At the beginning of the 1980s, nearly all of the influences acting upon Washington and Moscow were pushing the two sides apart and heightening military tensions. Abroad, U.S. policymakers saw hostile trends—the Nicaraguan and Iranian revolutions, the Soviet military buildup, the hostage crisis in Iran, and the Soviet invasion of Afghanistan. At home, right-wing groups fanned the flames of militarism and pressured first the Carter presidency and then their friends in the Reagan administration to boost military spending. The NATO allies went along with these trends and in some cases encouraged them. Calculations of economic cost were largely ignored, as political leaders deluded themselves that an accelerated arms race (combined with tax breaks for the rich) would not cause economic damage. The Kremlin, too, saw a threatening external world and, moreover, was troubled by the rejection of SALT II and rising militarism in the United States. Soviet leaders, like their U.S. counterparts, denied the huge and steadily rising economic costs of the arms race, and the ossified political structures of the country tried to silence alternative voices.

By the latter half of the decade, the influences acting on the two sides were changing. U.S. leaders faced fewer challenges overseas (in part owing to the early effects of Soviet policy shifts). For some, the enormous military budget increases pushed through in the first half of the decade created the illusion of greater strength (although in fact actual U.S. military capability changed relatively little during the buildup[6]). Domestically, the sharp rise in federal budget deficits and a deepening financial crisis created pressures to limit federal spending (the Gramm-Rudman law), which in turn restrained military expenditure. Political pressures for arms limitation and U.S.-Soviet detente, initiated by the peace movement, were mounting in Congress and among the American people. The NATO allies, under intense peace pressure themselves, also urged greater effort toward arms control.

Within the Soviet Union, Gorbachev's rise to power led to dramatic changes, especially in foreign policy, as the leadership espoused new thinking and began a long-term process of arms reduction and military disengagement. The easing in Washington's previous hostility and its greater interest in arms talks made these steps easier. Domestically, the now-acknowledged economic crisis and the burdens of the arms race reinforced the drive to scale back military spending. Glasnost and the beginnings of internal democracy added new domestic pressures for restraint. In both East and West, influences that earlier pushed the two sides apart now brought them closer together. These trends are depicted graphically in Figure 14.1.

The peace movement played an important role in shaping several of these influences. The nuclear freeze movement and other peace efforts in the United States influenced public opinion and created political pressures in Congress and elsewhere for arms control and military re-

FIGURE 14.1 The Direction of Factors Influencing Foreign Policy

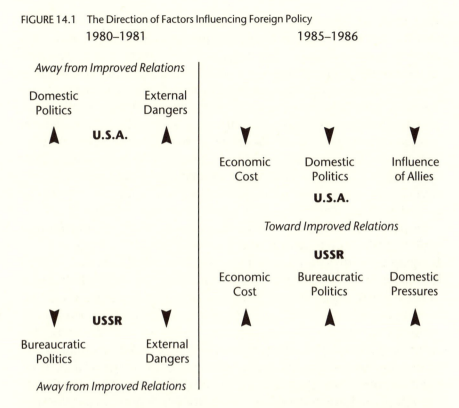

1980–1981   1985–1986

Away from Improved Relations

Domestic   External
Politics   Dangers

▲   **U.S.A.**   ▲   ▼   ▼   ▼

Economic   Domestic   Influence
Cost   Politics   of Allies

U.S.A.

Toward Improved Relations

USSR

Economic   Bureaucratic   Domestic
Cost   Politics   Pressures

▼   **USSR**   ▼   ▲   ▲   ▲

Bureaucratic   External
Politics   Dangers

Away from Improved Relations

straint. The European disarmament movement generated similar pressures on their governments, which in turn redirected them onto the White House. The peace movement was not the whole picture, but it played a significant and legitimate part in securing the nuclear peace and ending the Cold War.

A Final Assessment

To assess the impact of the peace movement on Reagan administration policy, we need a scorecard that measures goals to results. What were the specific policy aims of the administration and how were these altered or redirected by peace movement pressures?

Ronald Reagan came into office on a Republican platform explicitly pledging the new government to achieve "technological and military superiority" over the Soviet Union. The White House was unwilling to accept parity with the Soviets and sought instead to alter the strategic balance by confronting the Soviet Union with overwhelming military and nuclear power. As described in Chapters 2 through 6, however, public opinion became increasingly hostile to the radical philosophy of the Reagan administration and a political climate in favor of arms limitation quickly developed. More concerned about the threat of nuclear war than the need to achieve superiority, the American public favored negotiation over military confrontation. Popular culture became increasingly antinuclear as the freeze movement swept the country. Faced with this unreceptive political climate, the Reagan administration largely abandoned its harsh rhetoric and quietly dropped the concept of superiority. The principles of nuclear brinkmanship never gained public acceptance.

As part of its design for nuclear confrontation, the Reagan administration dusted off long-discredited notions of civil defense and attempted to create a nationwide program of bomb shelters and evacuation planning to protect against nuclear attack. The declared objective of these plans was to save 80 percent of the American population and thereby ensure rapid social and economic recovery after nuclear war. As noted in Chapter 3, these plans were met with widespread public skepticism and hostility. The Physicians for Social Responsibility held forums on the medical horrors of nuclear war, officials in dozens of communities rejected federally mandated evacuation plans, and Congress refused to fund much of the White House's program. The administration had to settle for a significantly scaled-down federal emergency program.

Left to their own devices, Ronald Reagan and his hardline advisers might have waited a very long time to begin arms negotiations. Reagan campaigned for office on his opposition to the SALT agreements and had opposed every previous nuclear weapons treaty. Defense Secretary Caspar Weinberger and other administration officials talked of delaying negotiations until the arms buildup was completed. Nonetheless, the White House was forced to begin INF talks by the end of 1981 and strategic negotiations during the summer of 1982. As described in Chapter 7, political pressures in the United States and Europe pushed the administration to the bargaining table. Once talks with the Soviets began, the White House eased its negotiating stance on several occasions in direct response to political pressures from Congress and the NATO allies. Nonetheless, hardliners in the administration succeeded in obstructing progress at Geneva well into the second term. Peace pressures could force the administration to the bargaining table but could not guarantee results.

No objective was more important to the United States and NATO during the 1980s than the deployment of INF missiles in Western Europe. U.S., British, and West German officials made it seem at times that the fate of Western civilization hinged on deployment of cruise and Pershing II missiles, and they spared no effort to ensure that the new weapons were deployed on schedule beginning in December 1983. The peace movement responded with a massive resistance campaign, the largest mobilization of popular opposition in the modern history of Western Europe. Millions of people poured into the streets, and opinion polls showed broad popular opposition to the new missiles. Despite the huge campaign, however, military officials succeeded in ramming through the INF deployments. Peace movements managed to delay the process in the Netherlands and Belgium, but they were unable to block the missiles. What seemed a political defeat, though, contained the seeds of victory. U.S. and NATO officials had appropriated the peace movement's proposal for a zero solution—no INF missiles East or West—as their official bargaining position in the Geneva negotiations. They had done so as part of the political maneuvering necessary to win public acceptance of the missiles. Many NATO officials did not favor the zero solution but felt it safe to offer, since the Brezhnev regime would surely reject it. When Gorbachev turned the tables several years later and unexpectedly accepted the zero solution, NATO leaders were stuck with their own proposal and had no choice but to remove the missiles they had labored so hard to install. In the end, the peace movement's position prevailed.

Pentagon officials saw the MX missile as the centerpiece of the strategic nuclear buildup. The peace movement made the mobile missile program a prime target of political opposition, and a diverse coalition of environmentalists, religious activists, taxpayer groups, trade unions, Native Americans, and farm organizations emerged to battle the MX. The Reagan administration, like the Carter presidency before it, expended enormous political capital trying to save the beleaguered missile. Despite these efforts, the anti-MX coalition succeeded in blocking plans for mobile basing and reduced the number of deployed missiles to one-quarter the original plan. The stop MX campaign was a partial victory for the peace movement. It also generated political pressures on the administration that moderated the U.S. bargaining position in the

START talks. While the Pentagon was stalemated on the MX program, other elements of the nuclear buildup—Trident submarine missiles, B-1 bombers and strategic cruise missiles—proceeded on schedule with relatively little opposition. The peace movement gave relatively little attention to these other weapons.

Another White House priority, an obsession that came to dominate the second half of the Reagan presidency, was the Strategic Defense Initiative. The president's March 1983 Star Wars proposal originated in part as a response to the nuclear freeze movement and the stalemating of the MX missile. The proposal was greeted with widespread skepticism, and intense opposition to SDI developed within the peace community, among scientists, and within Congress. As a result, the Star Wars program was constrained by budget cuts and legislative restrictions and the testing and development of SDI components in space was prohibited. The Reagan administration was unable to move toward development of SDI. The testing of antisatellite weapons was barred. Nonetheless, vast amounts of money continue to be spent on the program, especially in the wake of the Persian Gulf War, and the ultimate outcome of the controversy remains uncertain.

Perhaps no concern was more passionately felt by Reagan and his senior national security aides than the struggle to overthrow the Sandinistas in Central America. Not just in Nicaragua but in El Salvador as well, the Reagan administration organized and funded proxy wars and on occasion threatened direct U.S. intervention. Despite the administration's efforts to gain public approval, however, the American people never supported this White House policy. A solidarity movement based largely in the religious community emerged to contest administration efforts, and polls consistently showed public disapproval of U.S. policy. Partly as a result, the administration rejected the strategy of military confrontation advocated by the State Department and the option of direct U.S. intervention, so often used in previous administrations, was foreclosed. Congress passed the Boland amendments temporarily blocking military aid for the Contras, which led the administration to go underground and resulted in the disastrous Iran-Contra scandal. The Sandinistas were voted out of office in 1990, but this was the result not of Contra military prowess but an independent Central American peace process. Solidarity forces in the United States played an important role in restraining the excesses of Reagan administration policy, although they were unable to end the proxy wars in the region or prevent indirect U.S. intervention.

TABLE 14.1 Scorecard: Reagan Administration Intentions, Peace Movement Impacts, and the Outcome of Policy

Administration Goal	Peace Movement Influence?	Administration Success?
Create political climate that favors "peace through strength" philosophy	Creation of nuclear freeze movement; Physicians for Social Responsibility campaign; organization of religious leaders against concept of nuclear superiority; showing of *The Day After*	Forced to abandon rhetoric and concept of nuclear superiority
Develop national civil defense plan	Physicians and others spread notion of prevention, not protection; local officials reject nuclear war evacuation planning; Congress limits funding	Public resistance forces administration to abandon large-scale civil defense plans
Delay arms negotiations	Pressure from peace movements in the United States and Europe pushes the administration to the bargaining table and moderates U.S. positions	Although forced to begin negotiations, the White House delays serious bargaining until the second term
INF deployment in Europe	Massive peace mobilizations unable to halt deployment, but peace movement proposal for zero solution adopted in INF Treaty	NATO successful in pushing through deployment, but missiles later abandoned in treaty
MX missile; strategic "modernization"	Partial success of stop MX campaign in blocking mobile basing and reducing number of missiles; pressure generated for arms control	MX stalemated, but other new weapons advanced
Strategic Defense Initiative	Opposition by peace groups and scientists; Congress cuts funds and imposes restraints	Vast sums spent on development, but no systems deployed; goals of early deployment and reinterpretation of ABM Treaty rebuffed
Overthrow the Sandinistas in Nicaragua and prevent FMLN victory in El Salvador	Large-scale solidarity movement; public opinion solidly against direct intervention and military aid; partial success in blocking Contra aid and preventing direct U.S. intervention	Contra war maintained through illegal means; FMLN stalemated and Sandinistas voted out of office, but neither defeated militarily
Increase military spending and strengthen U.S. military power	Little direct peace movement focus on the military budget and war system in general, although public mood shifts against spending increases after 1985	Largest peacetime military spending rise in history and support for overall strategy of military confrontation sustained

Although the peace movement influenced some areas of policy, it was ineffective in altering the larger structures of militarism. Despite the massive peace campaigns of the 1980s, the Reagan administration was successful in bolstering the war system and reinforcing the power of military institutions. It not only enlarged the military budget but also strengthened the CIA and other national security agencies and enhanced the legitimacy of military force as an instrument of foreign policy. The peace movement was unable to prevent the largest peacetime military spending increase in U.S. history. The continuing force of militarism in U.S. politics and culture was graphically illustrated by the Bush administration's mobilization of public support for the Persian Gulf War in 1991. The peace movement achieved success at the margins but did not alter the core structures of the war system.

Table 14.1 summarizes the foregoing discussion and offers a balance sheet of peace movement impacts during the 1980s.

For all of its limitations, the peace movement had a real impact on Reagan administration policy. The decision to begin arms control negotiations, the changes in administration rhetoric and declaratory policy, the shaping of the zero option and other bargaining positions at the Geneva talks, the stalemating of the MX missile, the rejection of civil defense planning, the end of ASAT testing, the limitations imposed on SDI funding and testing, the prevention of overt military intervention in Central America—these were important achievements. They helped to shape the history of the decade. The pressures generated by peace groups pushed the political system toward military restraint and blocked many of the Reagan administration's hardline policies.

During the freeze movement, when doubters questioned the worth of such efforts, activists sometimes replied, "Think how much worse things would be if there were no peace movement." The point was well taken. If citizen groups had not campaigned constantly to prevent nuclear war, the military standoff between East and West might have become much more dangerous. The peace movement played a significant role in restraining the Reagan administration and pulling the United States and the world back from the brink of nuclear destruction. In a very real sense, we helped to save the world.

Chronology of Events
in the Peace Movement

1979 December 12: NATO ministers approve the deployment of INF weapons; 40,000 protest in Brussels.

1980 November 4: Ronald Reagan is elected president; the first nuclear freeze resolutions are approved in western Massachusetts; referenda against the MX missile are approved in Nevada.

November 17: The first Women's Pentagon Action is held in Washington, D.C.

1981 March: The founding convention of the Nuclear Weapons Freeze Campaign is held in Washington, D.C.

May 3: About 100,000 demonstrate at the Pentagon against military intervention in El Salvador and for peace and justice.

May 4: In Salt Lake City, the Church of Jesus Christ of Latter-day Saints issues a statement against the MX missile.

September: A women's encampment begins at Greenham Common in England.

October 2: The Reagan administration cancels the plan to base the MX in Utah and Nevada.

Fall: Massive demonstrations against INF and SS-20 missiles take place in Bonn, London, Brussels, Rome, Amsterdam, and other European cities.

November 18: Reagan announces the zero option proposal in a speech broadcast live to Europe.

1982 March 10: The Kennedy-Hatfield freeze resolution is introduced in the U.S. Senate.

March 12: The Reagan administration announces a plan to begin strategic arms negotiations.

June: Massive demonstrations in Bonn, London, Paris, and other cities greet Reagan during his visit to Europe.

June 12: Nearly 1 million people gather in New York's Central Park to demand an end to the arms race in the largest political rally in U.S. history.

August 4: The freeze resolution loses in the U.S. House of Representatives by a vote of 204-202.

November: Nearly 11 million voters approve nuclear freeze referenda in eight states and dozens of cities and counties.

December: The MX Dense Pack basing plan is defeated in the U.S. Congress.

1983   March 23: Reagan announces the SDI program.

April: Easter demonstrations against Euromissiles draw hundreds of thousands of protesters in West Germany and Great Britain.

April 11: The Scowcroft Commission recommends flexibility in arms control and halves the MX program.

May 3: The U.S. Catholic bishops release a pastoral letter entitled *The Challenge of Peace.*

May 4: The nuclear freeze resolution passes in the U.S. House of Representatives.

October: The "Magna Carta" agreement is established between Congress and the White House to modify the START proposal.

October 22: The largest political rallies in modern European history occur as 3 million people demonstrate against Euromissiles in London, the Hague, Rome, Hamburg, and dozens of cities.

November 20: "The Day After" airs on ABC television to an audience of 100 million viewers.

1984   January 16: In a "curtain raiser" for the 1984 electoral campaign, Reagan says that Washington is ready for "mutual compromise" with the Soviets.

May 31: The Common Cause compromise to suspend MX funding is approved by House of Representatives.

Fall: Congress approves the Boland II amendment barring aid for the Nicaraguan Contras.

1985   March 11: Mikhail Gorbachev becomes leader of the Soviet Union.

March 12: U.S.-Soviet arms negotiations resume in Geneva.

June: The Quest for Peace is launched; it ultimately raises $327 million in humanitarian aid for the people of Nicaragua.

July 17: House-Senate conferees approve a legislative cap on the MX, limiting the program to one-quarter of its original size.

August 6: Gorbachev announces a unilateral Soviet nuclear testing moratorium.

October 11: The Nobel Prize for Peace is awarded to International Physicians for the Prevention of Nuclear War.

November 18: A peace movement delegation led by Jesse Jackson meets with Gorbachev at the Geneva Summit.

1986   April 26: Nuclear disaster occurs at Chernobyl.

May: The Pledge of Non-Participation with SDI is announced to the press; 12,000 scientists eventually sign.

July: The Mississippi Peace Cruise builds U.S.-Soviet friendship.

Fall: An arms control "grand slam" in the U.S. House of Representatives limits nuclear testing, SDI funding, ASAT testing, and other programs.

October 12: In Reykjavik, Reagan and Gorbachev nearly agree on elimination of nuclear weapons.

November: Eighty thousand people sign the Pledge of Resistance vowing nonviolent direct action in the event of U.S. military intervention in Nicaragua; the Iran-Contra scandal is disclosed, wounding the Reagan administration politically.

1987   February 28: Gorbachev announces acceptance of the zero option proposal without linkage to SDI.

May 5: The Senate Armed Services Committee adopts the Nunn-Levin amendment barring SDI tests that would violate the ABM Treaty.

August 7: Five Central American presidents sign the Esquipulas Agreement calling for free elections and an end to outside support for insurgents in Central America.

December 7: The Reagan-Gorbachev summit in Washington marks the signing of the INF Treaty.

Notes

Chapter 1

1. Quotation taken from public statements. Confirmed in a communication with David Cortright, March 25, 1993.

2. Quotation taken from public statements. Confirmed in a communication with David Cortright, March 29, 1993.

3. "The 1992 Campaign: Transcript of First TV Debate Among Bush, Clinton and Perot," *New York Times,* October 12, 1992.

4. See John Lewis Gaddis, "Arms Control, Hanging Tough Paid Off," *Bulletin of Atomic Scientists* 45 (January/February 1989): 11–14.

Chapter 2

1. Fox Butterfield, "Anatomy of the Nuclear Protest," *New York Times Magazine,* July 11, 1982, p. 14.

2. See "New York Rally Draws Half-Million," *Washington Post,* June 13, 1982, p. 1; and Neal R. Peirce and William R. Anderson, "Nuclear Freeze Proponents Mobilize on Local Referendum," *National Journal,* September 18, 1982, p. 1602.

3. Interview, David Cortright with Leslie Cagan, July 3, 1990.

4. Strobe Talbott, *Deadly Gambits: The Reagan Administration and the Stalemate in Nuclear Arms Control* (New York: Vintage Books, 1985), p. 7.

5. See Douglas Waller, *Congress and the Nuclear Freeze* (Amherst, Mass.: University of Massachusetts Press, 1987), p. 14.

6. Talbott, *Deadly Gambits,* p. 18.

7. Martin Anderson, *Revolution: The Reagan Legacy* (San Diego: Harcourt Brace Jovanovich, 1988), p. 74.

8. Alexander Haig, *Caveat: Realism, Reagan, and Foreign Policy* (New York: Macmillan, 1984), p. 228.

9. Jim Castelli, *The Bishops and the Bomb: Waging War in the Nuclear Age* (New York: Doubleday, 1983), p. 83.

10. Quoted in Robert Scheer, *With Enough Shovels: Reagan, Bush and Nuclear War* (New York: Vintage Books, 1983), p. 90.

11. Gerald Felix Warburg, *Conflict and Consensus: The Struggle Between Congress and the President over Foreign Policy Making* (New York: Harper and Row, 1989), p. 281.

12. This and other quotations are contained in the factsheet "Nuclear War Fighting Quotations by Reagan Administration Officials and Supporters," Center for Defense Information, Washington, D.C., September 1983.

13. Richard Halloran, "Pentagon Draws Up First Strategy for Fighting a Long Nuclear War," *New York Times,* May 30, 1982, p. 1.

14. "Brezhnev and Reagan on Atom War," *New York Times,* October 21, 1981, p. 5.

15. Richard Barnet, "U.S.-Soviet Relations: The Need for a Comprehensive Approach," *Foreign Affairs* 57 (Spring 1979): 779–795.

16. Pam Solo, *From Protest to Policy: Beyond the Freeze to Common Security* (Cambridge, Mass.: Ballinger, 1988), p. 44.

17. Frances McCrea and Gerald Markle, *Minutes to Midnight: Nuclear Weapons Protest in America* (Newbury Park, Calif.: Sage Publications, 1989), pp. 97–99.

18. Randall Forsberg, "A Bilateral Nuclear-Weapon Freeze," *Scientific American* 247 (November 1982): 52–61.

19. The Call to Halt the Arms Race (Brookline, Mass.: Institute for Defense and Disarmament Studies, 1981).

20. Quoted in J. Bern, "The Changing Nuclear Debate in the 1990s," *Origins: CNS Documentary Service* 19 (March 1990): 631.

21. David Meyer, *A Winter of Discontent: The Nuclear Freeze and American Politics* (New York: Praeger, 1990), p. 172.

22. McCrea and Markle, *Minutes to Midnight,* pp. 101–102.

23. Solo, *From Protest to Policy,* pp. 49–50.

24. Peirce and Anderson, "Nuclear Freeze Proponents Mobilize," pp. 1062–1063.

25. Ibid.

26. Solo, *From Protest to Policy,* p. 66.

27. Meyer, *Winter of Discontent,* pp. 105–107.

28. Solo, *From Protest to Policy,* p. 88.

29. The Topsfield Foundation, *Grass Roots Peace Directory* (Pomfret, Conn.: The Topsfield Foundation, 1986).

30. *PSR Reports* 1 (November 1984), p. 8

31. Interview, David Cortright with John Isaacs, June 25, 1990.

32. Interview, David Cortright with Jo Sedeita, June 21, 1990.

33. Ibid.

34. Quoted in *PSR Newsletter* 3 (Spring 1982), p. 11.

35. Interview, Jo Sedeita.

36. Butterfield, "Anatomy of the Nuclear Protest," p. 38.

37. See Mark Hertsgaard, *On Bended Knee: The Press and the Reagan Presidency* (New York: Shocken Books, 1989), p. 280.

38. Interview, Jo Sedeita.

39. Interview, David Cortright with Ed Markey, August 28, 1991.

40. See Solo, *From Protest to Policy.*

41. See Waller, *Congress and the Nuclear Freeze.*

42. Interview, Ed Markey.

43. Ibid.

44. Solo, *From Protest to Policy,* p. 75.

45. Quoted in Meyer, *Winter of Discontent,* p. 224.

46. John Martilla and Thomas Kiley, *Turnabout: The Emerging New Realism in the Nuclear Age* (Boston: WAND Education Fund, 1986), p. 24.

47. "Freeze Debate Founders as House Bickers," *Washington Post,* April 24, 1983.

48. Interview, Ed Markey.

Chapter 3

1. Interview, David Cortright with Jennifer Leaning, July 24, 1990.

2. Ibid.

3. Helen Caldicott, *Missile Envy: The Arms Race and Nuclear War* (New York: Morrow, 1984), p. 6.

4. *PSR Reports* 1 (November 1984), p. 8

5. Interview, Jennifer Leaning.

6. Ibid.

7. Ibid.

8. Interview, David Cortright with Michael McCally, June 12, 1990; with Mary Lord, June 21, 1990.

9. Interview, Mary Lord.

10. Interview, Jennifer Leaning.

11. *PSR Newsletter* 3 (Fall 1982), p. 1.

12. Interview, Mary Lord.

13. Ibid.

14. *PSR Newsletter* 4 (Winter 1983), p. 2.

15. *PSR Newsletter* 3 (Fall 1982), p. 1.

16. "Nobel Peace Prize Citation," *New York Times,* October 12, 1985, p. 14.

17. Interview, Mary Lord.

18. Interview, Jennifer Leaning.

19. Ibid.

20. Robert Scheer, *With Enough Shovels: Reagan, Bush and Nuclear War* (New York: Vintage Books, 1983), p. 105.

21. Ibid., p. 261.

22. Ibid., p. 111.

23. Editorial, "The Shelter Fraud," *New York Times,* April 3, 1982, p. 24.

24. Scheer, *Shovels,* p. 108.

25. Ibid., pp. 108–109.

26. Interview, David Cortright with Marilyn Braun, July 31, 1990.

27. Ibid.

28. Ibid.

29. SRI International, *Crisis Relocation of the Population at Risk in the New York Metropolitan Area* (Stanford, Calif.: Stanford Research Institute, 1978).

30. Interview, Marilyn Braun.

31. Ibid.

32. Jennifer Leaning and Langley Keyes, eds., *The Counterfeit Ark: Crisis Relocation for Nuclear War* (Cambridge, Mass.: Ballinger, 1984).

33. *PSR Newsletter* 2 (Winter 1981).

34. Interview, Jennifer Leaning.

35. *Congressional Quarterly Weekly Report,* May 1, 1982, p. 983.

Chapter 4

1. Bruce Van Voorst, "The Churches and Nuclear Deterrence," *Foreign Affairs* 61 (Spring 1983): 830.

2. Ibid., p. 828.

3. Quoted in *The Challenge of Peace: God's Promise and Our Response* (Washington, D.C.: United States Catholic Conference, 1983), §139, p. 59.

4. Ibid., §140, p. 59.

5. Interview, David Cortright with William Sloane Coffin, December 3, 1990.

6. Interview, David Cortright with Cora Weiss, February 8, 1991.

7. For a detailed history of the program, see Marjorie K. Horton, *The Disarmament Program of the Riverside Church: A History, 1978–1988* (Birmingham, Ala.: EBSCO media, n.d.).

8. Interview, William Sloane Coffin.

9. Horton, *The Disarmament Program,* p. 6.

10. Interview, Cora Weiss.

11. Interview, William Sloane Coffin.

12. Jim Castelli, *The Bishops and the Bomb: Waging Peace in the Nuclear Age* (Garden City, N.Y.: Doubleday, 1983), p. 60.

13. Interview, William Sloane Coffin.

14. Castelli, *Bishops and the Bomb,* p. 26.

15. Interview, David Cortright with Mary Evelyn Jegen, February 11, 1991.

16. Ibid.

17. Ibid.

18. Castelli, *Bishops and the Bomb,* pp. 128–129.

19. All citations from *The Challenge of Peace,* United States Catholic Conference, 1983.

20. Castelli, *Bishops and the Bomb,* p. 150.

21. Van Voorst, "The Churches," p. 382.

22. *Commonweal* 110 (May 20, 1983): 291–292.

23. George F. Kennan, "The Bishops' Letter," *New York Times,* May 1, 1983, sec. 4, p. 21.

24. Interview, David Cortright with Father Dick Warner, December 5, 1990.

25. Ibid.

26. "I Am Just a Symbol," *Time,* November 29, 1982, p. 78.

27. Interview, David Cortright with Robert Sims, December 21, 1990.

28. I am indebted to columnist Mary McGrory for her use of this famous quote in the *Washington Post,* November 18, 1982, p. 3.

29. Interview, Robert Sims.

30. Van Voorst, "The Churches," p. 845.

31. Ibid.

32. "Will Pope Stop Nuclear Heresy?" *Washington Post,* November 8, 1982, p. 15.

33. Van Voorst, "The Churches," p. 847.

34. Ibid., p. 846.

35. Castelli, *Bishops and the Bomb,* p. 119.

36. Ibid., p. 120.

37. Hedrick Smith, "Reagan Is Pressed Anew on Weapons," *New York Times,* May 5, 1983, p. 13.

38. News Session Transcript, *New York Times,* May 5, 1983, p. D22.

39. *New York Times,* March 28, 1982, p. 18.

40. Castelli, *Bishops and the Bomb,* p. 61.

41. Interview, David Cortright with Robert K. Musil, February 14, 1991.

42. Interview, Vienna Colucci with Dan Juday, March 20, 1991.

43. Robert McClory, "Peace Pastoral Headed for Graveyard?" *National Catholic Reporter,* December 28, 1984, p. 15.

44. Ibid.

45. Phil Berryman, *Our Unfinished Business: The U.S. Catholic Bishops' Letters on Peace and the Economy* (New York: Pantheon, 1989), p. 139.

46. Interview, William Sloane Coffin.

47. Van Voorst, "The Churches," pp. 841–842.

48. Quoted in The United Methodist Council of Bishops, *In Defense of Creation: The Nuclear Crisis and a Just Peace* (Nashville, Tenn.: Graded Press, 1986), p. 41.

49. Ibid., p. 48.

50. Ibid., p. 15.

51. Van Voorst, "The Churches," p. 845.

52. Frances Beal and Ty dePass, "The Historical Black Presence in the Struggle for Peace," *The Black Scholar* 17 (January/February 1986): 2.

53. Interview, William Sloane Coffin.

54. Cardinal Joseph Bernardin, "The Changing Nuclear Debate in the 1990s," *Origins: CNS Documentary Service* 19, no. 39 (March 1, 1990): 631.

55. Ibid., p. 632.

Chapter 5

1. The author was present at this meeting.

2. Dean Smith, North Carolina SANE advertisement, written by David Cortright and Norris Frederick, produced by the SANE Education Fund of Pennsylvania.

3. Ibid.

4. See, for example, *Raleigh News and Observer,* February 8, 1983, p. 1C.

5. Interview, David Cortright with Norris Frederick, July 3, 1990.

6. Mark Hertsgaard, *On Bended Knee: The Press and the Reagan Presidency* (New York: Shocken Books, 1989), pp. 35–36.

7. Interview, David Cortright with Les Janka, August 23, 1990.

8. Hertsgaard, *On Bended Knee,* p. 6.

9. Interview, David Cortright with Betsy Taylor, June 3, 1991.

10. Milton Katz, *Ban the Bomb: A History of SANE, the Committee for a Sane Nuclear Policy* (New York: Praeger, 1987), pp. 42–43.

11. Interview, David Cortright with Jimi Kaufer, December 3, 1990.

12. Sting, "Russians," from *The Dream of the Blue Turtles,* 1987.

13. Ibid.

14. R.E.M., "Hyena," from *Life's Rich Pageant,* 1986.

15. "Say Goodbye to Glasnost Ad Themes," *New York Times,* August 20, 1991, p. C8.

16. Interview, David Cortright with David Johnson, December 3, 1990.

17. *New York Times,* November 27, 1983, p. 11.

18. John W. Wright, ed., *The Universal Almanac 1990* (Kansas City: Andrews and McNeil, 1990), p. 279.

19. David Meyer, *A Winter of Discontent: The Nuclear Freeze and American Politics* (New York: Praeger, 1990), pp. 124–125.

20. Interview, David Cortright with David Gergen, October 8, 1990.

21. Interview, David Cortright with Robert Sims, December 21, 1990.

22. Roger L. Shinn, "The Day After 'The Day After,'" *Bulletin of Atomic Scientists* 40 (February 1984): 44.

23. Interview, David Gergen.

24. Interview, David Cortright with Nicholas Meyer, January 24, 1991.

25. Ibid.

26. Ibid.

27. Ibid.

28. Interview, David Cortright with Timothy Hayes, January 23, 1991.

29. Ibid.

30. Ibid.

31. Lawrence Weschler, "ABC Drops the Big One," *The Nation* 237 (November 26, 1983): 542.

32. Interview, Nicholas Meyer.

33. Interview, David Gergen.

34. Ibid.

35. Robert K. Manoff, "The Week After," *The Nation* 237 (December 10, 1983): 588–589.

36. Interview, David Gergen.

37. Interview, Nicholas Meyer.

Chapter 6

1. Jerry Yeric and John Todd, *Public Opinion: The Visible Politics* (Itasca, Ill.: F. E. Peacock Publishers, 1983), pp. 17, 107.

2. C. Wright Mills, *Power, Politics, and People* (New York: Ballantine, 1967).

3. Noam Chomsky and Edward Hermann, *Manufacturing Consent: The Political Economy of the Mass Media* (New York: Pantheon, 1988).

4. Charlotte Ryan, *Prime Time Activism* (Cambridge, Mass.: South End Press, 1991).

5. Benjamin Page and Robert Shapiro, "Effects of Public Opinion on Policy," *American Political Science Review* 77 (1983): 181–187.

6. Benjamin Page, Robert Shapiro, and Glenn Dempsey, "What Moves Public Opinion?" *American Political Science Review* 81 (1987): 23.

7. Page and Shapiro, "Effects of Public Opinion," p. 181.

8. W. Caspary, "The Mood Theory: A Story of Public Opinion and Foreign Policy," *American Political Science Review* 64 (1970): 536–547; and Michael Leigh, *Mobilizing Consent: Public Opinion and American Foreign Policy, 1937–1947* (Westport, Conn.: Greenwood, 1976).

9. James Rosenau, *Public Interest and Foreign Policy* (New York: Random House, 1961), p. 61.

10. Benjamin Page and Robert Shapiro, "Foreign Policy and the Rational Public," *Journal of Conflict Resolution* 32 (1988): 211–247.

11. Bruce Russett and Thomas Graham, "Public Opinion and National Security Policy: Relationships and Impacts," in *Handbook of War Studies,* ed. Manus Midlarsky (London: Unwin Hyman, 1989), p. 243.

12. Richard Beal and Ronald Hinckley, "Presidential Decision Making and Opinion Polls," *Annals of the American Academy of Political and Social Science, Polling and the Democratic Consensus* 472 (1984): 74.

13. Ronald Hinckley, "Public Attitudes Toward Key Foreign Policy Events," *Journal of Conflict Resolution* 32 (1988): 296, 298.

14. Beal and Hinckley, "Presidential Decision Making," p. 74.

15. Ibid., p. 84.

16. Interview, David Cortright with Michael Deaver, June 16, 1990.

17. Interview, David Cortright with Robert Sims, December 21, 1990.

18. Robert Mandel, "Public Opinion and Superpower Strategic Arms," *Armed Forces and Society* 17 (Spring 1991): 415.

19. "Poll Finds 7 out of 10 Imagining Outbreak of Soviet Nuclear War," *Washington Post,* September 27, 1981, p. 17.

20. David Gergen, "Following the Leaders: How Ronald Reagan Changed Public Opinion," *Public Opinion* 8 (June/July 1985): 57.

21. *Voter Options on Nuclear Arms Policy: A Briefing Book for the 1984 Elections* (New York: The Public Agenda Foundation, 1984).

22. Daniel Yankelovich and John Doble, "The Public Mood: Nuclear Weapons and the USSR," *Foreign Affairs* 63 (Fall 1984): 33–35.

23. Ibid., p. 36.

24. Tom W. Smith, "Nuclear Anxiety," *Public Opinion Quarterly* 52 (Winter 1988): 559.

25. Yankelovich and Doble, "The Public Mood," p. 37.

26. Ibid., p. 44.

27. Kenneth P. Adler, "West European and American Public Opinion on Peace, Defence, and Arms Control in a Cross-National Perspective," *International Social Science Journal* 38 (1986): 590.

28. Gergen, "How Ronald Reagan Changed Public Opinion," p. 57.

29. Yankelovich and Doble, "The Public Mood," p. 46.

30. Page and Shapiro, "Foreign Policy and the Rational Public," p. 243.

31. Interview, David Cortright with Richard Wirthlin, September 5, 1990.

32. Notes from Peace Media Briefing, New York, April 11, 1984. The briefing for national peace organizations was hosted by Rockefeller Family Associates and included presentations from pollsters Peter Hart, Dottie Lynch, Michael Kagy, Stan Greenberg, Mark Melman, and Ed Diamond.

33. Pam Solo, *From Protest to Policy: Beyond the Freeze to Common Security* (Cambridge, Mass.: Ballinger, 1988), p. 24.

34. Notes from Peace Media Briefing, 1984.

35. Ibid.

36. Interview, Michael Deaver.

37. Interview, David Cortright with Les Janka, August 23, 1990.

38. See, for example, Miroslav Nincic, *United States Foreign Policy: Choices and Issues* (Washington, D.C.: Congressional Quarterly, 1988), p. 70; see also Benjamin Page and Richard Brody, "Policy Voting and the Electoral Process: The Vietnam War Issue," *American Political Science Review* 66 (September 1972): 979–995.

39. The survey was funded by philanthropist John A. Harris IV (a registered Republican), not the Democratic party.

40. Briefing by Peter Hart, Washington, D.C., June 28, 1984; see also *Boston Globe,* June 11, 1984.

41. Interview, Michael Deaver.

42. Ibid.

43. The author was present at the meeting in Washington on January 23, 1984.

44. Interview, David Cortright with David Johnson, December 3, 1990.

45. Ibid.

46. Interview, David Cortright with David Gergen, October 8, 1990.

47. Page, Shapiro, and Dempsey, "What Moves Public Opinion?" p. 38.

48. Ibid.

49. Roy Behr and Shanto Iyengar, "Television News, Real-World Cues and Changes in the Public Agenda," *Public Opinion Quarterly* 49 (1985): 39.

50. Ibid., pp. 47–48.

51. Page, Shapiro, and Dempsey, "What Moves Public Opinion?" p. 38.

52. David Meyer, *A Winter of Discontent: The Nuclear Freeze and American Politics* (New York: Praeger, 1990), pp. 124–127.

53. Howard Schuman, Jacob Ludwig, and John Krosnick, "The Perceived Threat of Nuclear War, Salience, and Open Questions," *Public Opinion Quarterly* 50 (Winter 1986): 530.

54. Meyer, *Winter of Discontent,* p. 127.

55. Bernard Kramer, S. Michael Kalick, and Michael Milburn, "Attitudes Toward Nuclear Weapons and Nuclear War," *Journal of Social Issues* 39 (1983): 14.

56. Solo, *From Protest to Policy,* p. 66.

57. Kramer et al., "Attitudes Toward Nuclear Weapons," p. 10.

58. Ibid., pp. 9–10.

59. Ibid.

Chapter 7

1. "White House Has Little to Say on Atom Protest," *New York Times,* June 14, 1982, sec. 2, p. 6.

2. Richard Nixon, *RN: The Memoirs of Richard Nixon* (New York: Grosset and Dunlap, 1978), pp. 393–405.

3. Daniel Ellsberg, "Introduction: A Call to Mutiny," in *Protest and Survive,* ed. E. P. Thompson and Dan Smith (New York: Monthly Review Press, 1981), pp. xv–xvi.

4. Melvin Small, *Johnson, Nixon and the Doves* (New Brunswick,N.J.: Rutgers University Press, 1988), p. 225.

5. Interview, David Cortright with Michael Baroody, July 20, 1990.

6. Interview, David Cortright with Richard Wirthlin, September 5, 1990.

7. Interview, David Cortright with Aram Bakshian, July 16, 1990.

8. Ibid.

9. John Martilla and Tom Kiley, *Turnabout: The Emerging New Realism in the Nuclear Age* (Boston: WAND Educational Fund, 1986), pp. 26–27.

10. Mark Hertsgaard, *On Bended Knee: The Press and the Reagan Presidency* (New York: Shocken Books, 1988), pp. 280–281.

11. Jon Sawyer, "Reagan Moves to Blunt Nuclear Freeze Drive," *St. Louis Post-Dispatch,* October 17, 1982, pp. 1, 5.

12. Frank Donner, "The Campaign to Smear the Nuclear Freeze," *The Nation* 235 (November 6, 1982): 456.

13. John Barron, "The KGB's Magical War for Peace," *Readers Digest,* October 1982, p. 211.

14. *Weekly Compilation of Presidential Documents* 18, no. 40, p. 1260.

15. Interview, David Cortright with Michael Deaver, July 16, 1990.

16. Ibid.

17. Ibid.

18. Interview, Aram Bakshian.

19. Interview, Michael Baroody.

20. Interview, David Cortright with David Gergen, October 8, 1990.

21. Interview, Aram Bakshian.

22. Quoted in "President Rejects a Nuclear Freeze but Calls for Cuts," *New York Times,* April 1, 1982, pp. 1, 23.

23. Ibid.

24. *Weekly Compilation of Presidential Documents* 18, no. 16, pp. 503–504.

25. *Weekly Compilation of Presidential Documents* 18, no. 19, p. 602.

26. "The Reality Principle," *New York Times,* May 13, 1982, p. 27.

27. "U.S.-Soviet Meeting on Arms Cutbacks Will Begin June 29," *New York Times,* June 1, 1982, pp. 1, 13.

28. Editorial, "Leadership on the Lawn," *New York Times,* June 12, 1982, p. 30.

29. "Reagan at U.N.," *New York Times,* June 18, 1982, pp. 1, 16.

30. "President Rejects a Nuclear Freeze but Calls for Cuts," *New York Times,* April 1, 1982, p. 1.

31. Martilla and Kiley, *Turnabout,* p. 27.

32. Ibid.

33. *Weekly Compilation of Presidential Documents* 20, no. 3, p. 58.

34. John Newhouse, *War and Peace in the Nuclear Age* (New York: Alfred A. Knopf, 1989), pp. 369–370.

35. Interview, David Gergen.

36. Henry Grunewald, "Foreign Policy Under Reagan II," *Foreign Affairs* 63 (Winter 1984–1985): 227.

37. *New York Times,* November 8, 1984, p. 1.

38. Kenneth Adelman, *The Great Universal Embrace: Arms Summitry—A Skeptic's Account* (New York: Simon and Schuster, 1989), p. 126.

39. Martilla and Kiley, *Turnabout,* p. 27.

40. Newhouse, *War and Peace,* pp. 369–370.

41. Interview, Michael Baroody.

42. Alexander Haig, *Caveat: Realism, Reagan, and Foreign Policy* (New York: Macmillan, 1984), p. 223.

43. Strobe Talbott, *Deadly Gambits: The Reagan Administration and the Stalemate in Nuclear Arms Control* (New York: Vintage Books, 1985), pp. 15–17.

44. Talbott, *Deadly Gambits;* and Strobe Talbott, *The Master of the Game: Paul Nitze and the Nuclear Peace* (New York: Vintage Books, 1989).

45. Talbott, *Deadly Gambits,* p. 229.

46. Ibid.

47. Interview, David Cortright with Les Janka, August 23, 1990.

48. Interview, David Cortright with Martin Anderson, July 10, 1990; see also Martin Anderson, "The Reagan Legacy," introduction to the paperback edition of *Revolution: The Reagan Legacy* (Stanford, Calif.: Hoover Institution Press, 1990).

49. See John Lewis Gaddis, "Hanging Tough Paid Off," *Bulletin of Atomic Scientists* 45 (January/February 1989): 11–13.

50. Quoted in *New York Times,* May, 14, 1982, p. 16.

51. Talbott, *Deadly Gambits,* p. 273.

52. Ibid., p. 274.

53. "U.S. Forging a New Concept for Curbing Strategic Arms," *New York Times,* May 2, 1982.

54. Strobe Talbott, "Buildup and Breakdown," *Foreign Policy* 62 (Winter 1983–1984): 605.

55. Interview, Les Janka.

56. Talbott, *Deadly Gambits,* p. 247.

57. Adelman, *Great Embrace,* p. 35.

58. "The Anti-Antinuclear Battle Plan," *Washington Post,* May 9, 1982, p. D4.

59. Quoted in Talbott, *Deadly Gambits,* p. 247.

60. Ibid.

61. Interview, Richard Wirthlin.

62. Ibid.

63. Interview, David Cortright with Caspar Weinberger, September 23, 1991.

64. Editorial, "Leadership on the Lawn," *New York Times,* June 12, 1982, p. 30.

65. Talbott, *Deadly Gambits,* p. 247.

66. Ibid.

67. Ibid., p. 251.

68. Ibid.

69. Ibid., p. 267.

70. Adelman, *Great Embrace,* p. 34.

71. Talbott, *Deadly Gambits,* p. 302.

72. Ibid., p. 305.

73. Ibid., p. 308.

74. Ibid., pp. 325–326.

75. Ibid., p. 338.

76. Ibid., p. 263.

77. Ibid., p. 339.

Chapter 8

1. Thomas Rochon, *Mobilizing for Peace: The Antinuclear Movements in Western Europe* (Princeton, N.J.: Princeton University Press, 1988), p. xvi.

2. Helmut Schmidt, *Men and Powers: A Political Retrospective* (New York: Random House, 1989).

3. Richard Nixon and Henry Kissinger, "A Real Peace," *National Review* 39 (May 22, 1987): 33.

4. Ibid.

5. "Statement of General Bernard Rogers," *Hearings Before the Subcommittee on Strategic and Theater Nuclear Forces, Department of Defense Authorization for Appropriations for Fiscal Year 1984, Part 5: Strategic and Theater Nuclear Forces, Senate Armed Services Committee,* March 15, 1983, p. 2370.

6. Rochon, *Mobilizing for Peace,* p. 47.

7. Ibid., p. 46.

8. Connie deBoer, "The Polls: The European Peace Movement and Deployment of Nuclear Missiles," *Public Opinion Quarterly* 49 (Spring 1985): 126–127.

9. Ibid.

10. Ibid.

11. "Germans Enlist Poll-Takers in Missile Debate," *New York Times,* September 23, 1983, p. 10.

12. Strobe Talbott, *Deadly Gambits: The Reagan Administration and the Stalemate in Nuclear Arms Control* (New York: Vintage Books, 1985), p. 163.

13. Ibid.

14. Maarten Huygen, "Dateline Holland: NATO's Pyrrhic Victory," *Foreign Policy* 62 (November 12, 1984): 171.

15. Ibid.

16. Rochon, *Mobilizing for Peace*, p. 5.

17. "'Ban the Bomb' Movement Is Bouncing Back in Britain," *New York Times*, November 13, 1981, p. 3.

18. "President Fumbled on Arms Question; News Analysis; Excerpts of Reagan's Remarks," *Washington Post*, October 22, 1981, p. 24.

19. Ibid.

20. "Allied Contingency Plan Envisions a Warning Atom Blast, Haig Says," *New York Times*, November 5, 1981, p. 1.

21. Quoted in R. Jeffrey Smith, "Missile Deployments Shake European Politics," *Science* 223 (February 17, 1984): 666.

22. "250,000 at Bonn Rally Assail U.S. Arms Policy," *New York Times*, October 11, 1981, pp. 1, 9.

23. "50,000 March in Paris to Protest Weapons Build Up," *New York Times*, October 26, 1981, p. 11.

24. "'Ban the Bomb' Movement Is Bouncing Back in Britain," *New York Times*, November 13, 1981, p. 3.

25. Caspar Weinberger, *Fighting for Peace: Seven Critical Years in the Pentagon* (New York: Warner Books, 1990), p. 338.

26. "In Italy, the Bomb's a Political Issue for First Time," *New York Times*, November 14, 1981, p. 2.

27. "100,000 in Milan Peace March," *New York Times*, November 1, 1981, p. 6.

28. *New York Times*, November 29, 1981, p. 16.

29. Weinberger, *Fighting for Peace*, p. 338.

30. David Yost, "The Delegitimization of Nuclear Deterrence?" *Armed Forces and Society* 16 (Summer 1990): 492–493.

31. Rochon, *Mobilizing for Peace*, p. 60.

32. Ibid.

33. Talbott, *Deadly Gambits*, p. 49.

34. Ibid., p. 47.

35. Weinberger, *Fighting for Peace*, p. 335.

36. Ibid., p. 338.

37. Interview, David Cortright with Caspar Weinberger, September 23, 1991.

38. Weinberger, *Fighting for Peace*, p. 337.

39. Talbott, *Deadly Gambits*, pp. 56–57.

40. Alexander Haig, *Caveat: Realism, Reagan, and Foreign Policy* (New York: Macmillan, 1984), p. 229; see also Talbott, *Deadly Gambits*, p. 71.

41. Interview, David Cortright with Michael Deaver, July 16, 1990.

42. Interview, David Cortright with David Gergen, October 8, 1990.

43. Mary Kaldor, "We Got the Idea from Your Banners," *New Statesman* 113 (March 18, 1987): 14.

44. Schmidt, *Men and Powers*, p. 109.

45. "NATO Ministers Support Possible Missile Curbs," *Washington Post*, October 22, 1981, p. 1.

46. Ibid.

47. Haig, *Caveat,* p. 229.

48. Thomas Risse-Kappen, "Did 'Peace Through Strength' End the Cold War?" *International Security* 16 (Summer 1991): 181.

49. Quoted in Mark Hertsgaard, *On Bended Knee: The Press and the Reagan Presidency* (New York: Shocken Books, 1989), p. 273.

50. Strobe Talbott, *The Master of the Game: Paul Nitze and the Nuclear Peace* (New York: Vintage Books, 1989), p. 170.

51. Hertsgaard, *On Bended Knee,* p. 273.

52. "Audience for Speech Is Put at 200 Million," *New York Times,* November 19, 1981, p. 16.

53. "350,000 in Amsterdam Protest A-Arms," *New York Times,* November 22, 1981, p. 3.

54. Interview, David Cortright with Gene Carroll, December 21, 1990.

55. See David Cortright and Max Watts, *Left Face: Soldier Unions and Resistance Movements in Modern Armies* (Westport, Conn.: Greenwood Press, 1991), Chapter 7.

56. Rochon, *Mobilizing for Peace,* pp. 5, 95.

57. "200,000 Are Drawn to a Bonn Protest," *New York Times,* June 11, 1982, p. 18.

58. *New York Times,* June 12, 1982, p. 8.

59. Alice Cook and Gwyn Kirk, *Greenham Women Everywhere: Dreams, Ideas and Actions from the Women's Peace Movement* (Cambridge, Mass.: South End Press, 1983), p. 30.

60. Ibid., p. 91.

61. Ibid., pp. 56–58.

62. Ibid., pp. 101–102.

63. "Protest in Britain Stretches 14 Miles," *New York Times,* April 2, 1983, p. 3.

64. "No Nukes Drive Stronger Than Ever," *U.S. News and World Report* 94 (April 25, 1983): 22.

65. "West Europe Says Soviet Arms Move Is Not Last Word," *New York Times,* April 4, 1983, p. 13.

66. *New York Times,* April 5, 1983, p. 9.

67. Ibid.

68. "Quiet Protest at U.S. Base in Germany," *New York Times,* September 2, 1983, p. 3.

69. *New York Times,* October 23, 1983, p. 16.

70. *New York Times,* October 23, 1983, p. 1; and *New York Times,* October 30, 1983, p. 3.

71. Rochon, *Mobilizing for Peace,* p. 6; Huygen, "Dateline Holland," p. 176.

72. Rochon, *Mobilizing for Peace,* p. 6.

73. *New York Times,* October 5, 1985, p. 5.

74. Rochon, *Mobilizing for Peace,* pp. 141–142.

75. *Weekly Compilation of Presidential Documents* 19 (March 30, 1983).

76. Yost, "Delegitimization," p. 488.

77. Ibid., p. 494.

78. Kenneth Adelman, *The Great Universal Embrace: Arms Summitry—A Skeptic's Account* (New York: Simon and Schuster, 1989), p. 83.

79. *New York Times,* March 1, 1987, p. 1; *New York Times,* March 3, 1987, p. 3.

80. Interview, David Cortright with Eugene Rostow, October 15, 1991.

81. Nixon and Kissinger, "Real Peace," p. 32.

82. John Deutsch, Brent Scowcroft, and R. James Woolsey, "The Danger of Zero Option," *Washington Post,* March 31, 1987, p. 21.

83. Elizabeth Drew, "Letter from Washington," *The New Yorker,* October 27, 1986, p. 131.

84. Adelman, *Great Embrace,* pp. 208–209.

85. Risse-Kappen, "Did 'Peace Through Strength' End the Cold War?" p. 182.

86. Ibid., p. 187.

87. Thomas Risse-Kappen, "Odd German Consensus Against New Missiles," *Bulletin of Atomic Scientists* 44 (May 1988): 14–17.

88. "NATO Ministers Support Possible Missile Curbs," *Washington Post,* October 22, 1981.

Chapter 9

1. Frances Farley, "The MX: A Case Study of Citizen Involvement," n.d., unpublished manuscript, p. 1.

2. Interview, David Cortright with Ed Firmage, July 29, 1991.

3. Interview, David Cortright with Frances Farley, August 16, 1991.

4. Ibid.

5. Ibid.

6. Herbert Scoville, *MX: Prescription for Disaster* (Cambridge, Mass.: MIT Press, 1981), p. 28.

7. Interview, Frances Farley.

8. Interview, David Cortright with Marla Painter, August 17, 1991.

9. Quoted in Farley, "MX: A Case Study," p. 10.

10. Interview, Ed Firmage.

11. *Missile X: Description of the Proposed Action and Alternatives; Missile X: Weapons System Environmental Program;* and *Missile X: Operational, Environmental, and Geotechnical Considerations* (Washington, D.C.: U.S. Air Force ICBM Program Office, August 1979).

12. Interview, Frances Farley.

13. Patrick Ziska, "MX: Missile Experimental or Mammoth Expenditure," *The Machinist,* August 1979, p. 5. The Council on Economic Priorities estimated an ultimate price tag of more than $200 billion. See Council on Economic Priorities, *Misguided Expenditure, An Analysis of the Proposed MX Missile System* (New York: CEP, 1981).

14. SANE MX Campaign archives, Swarthmore Library Peace Collection, Swarthmore, Penn.

15. *Aviation Week and Space Technology,* June 22, 1981.

16. "LDS First Presidency Christmas Message," December 20, 1980, the

Church of Jesus Christ of Latter-day Saints, Public Communications Department, Salt Lake City, Utah.

17. "First Presidency Statement on the Basing of the MX Missile," May 5, 1981, the Church of Jesus Christ of Latter-day Saints, Public Communications Department, Salt Lake City, Utah.

18. Ibid.

19. Interview, Ed Firmage.

20. Ibid.

21. Interview, David Cortright with Eugene Rostow, October 7, 1991.

22. Farley, "MX: A Case Study," pp. 2, 12.

23. Michael Pertschuk, *Giantkillers* (New York: W. W. Norton, 1986), p. 187.

24. Interview, David Cortright with Les Aspin, August 1, 1991.

25. Pertschuk, *Giantkillers,* p. 205.

26. John Isaacs, "MX: Reagan's Pyrrhic Victory?" *Bulletin of Atomic Scientists* 41 (June/July 1985): 5.

27. Interview, Les Aspin.

28. Strobe Talbott, *The Master of the Game: Paul Nitze and the Nuclear Peace* (New York: Vintage Books, 1989), pp. 191–192.

29. Kenneth Adelman, *The Great Universal Embrace: Arms Summitry–A Skeptic's Account* (New York: Simon and Schuster, 1989), p. 172.

30. Interview, David Cortright with Robert Sims, December 21, 1990.

31. William Sweet, "The 1982 Elections," *Bulletin of Atomic Scientists* 39 (January 1983): 56–57.

32. Robert McFarlane, "Effective Strategic Policy," *Foreign Affairs* 67 (Fall 1988): 37.

33. Interview, David Cortright with Robert Kimmit, December 21, 1990.

34. Strobe Talbott, *Deadly Gambits: The Reagan Administration and the Stalemate in Nuclear Arms Control* (New York: Vintage Books, 1985), p. 217.

35. Adelman, *Great Embrace,* p. 173.

36. Interview, Robert Sims.

37. Elizabeth Drew, *Campaign Journal: The Political Events of 1983–1984* (New York: Macmillan, 1985), p. 80.

38. Interview, Les Aspin.

39. Interview, Robert Kimmit.

40. "Reagan Eases Toward Shift in Stand on Strategic Arms," *New York Times,* May 14, 1983, p. 3.

41. Interview, David Cortright with Ed Markey, August 28, 1991.

42. Strobe Talbott, "Buildup and Breakdown," *Foreign Affairs* 62 (Winter 1983–1984): 609.

43. *Wall Street Journal,* July 18, 1985, p. 6; Talbott, "Buildup and Breakdown," p. 610.

44. Pertschuk, *Giantkillers,* p. 218.

45. Interview, David Cortright with David Cohen, August 23, 1991.

46. Ibid.

47. *Wall Street Journal,* July 18, 1985; letter, Michael Mawby to David Cortright, May 31, 1990.

Chapter 10

1. McGeorge Bundy, *Danger and Survival: Choices About the Bomb in the First 50 Years* (New York: Random House, 1988), p. 570.

2. Interview, David Cortright with David Gergen, October 8, 1990.

3. Gregg Herken, "The Earthly Origins of Star Wars," *Bulletin of Atomic Scientists* 43 (October 1987): 20.

4. Quoted in Martin Anderson, *Revolution: The Reagan Legacy* (Stanford, Calif.: Hoover Institution Press, 1990), p. 87.

5. Ibid., p. 93.

6. Robert McFarlane, "Effective Strategic Policy," *Foreign Affairs* 67 (Fall 1988): 40.

7. Angelo Codevilla, "How SDI Is Being Undone from Within," *Commentary* 81 (May 1985): 25.

8. Sanford Lakoff and Herbert York, *A Shield in Space? Technology, Politics and the Strategic Defense Initiative* (Berkeley, Calif.: University of California Press, 1989), p. 23.

9. Strobe Talbott, *The Master of the Game: Paul Nitze and the Nuclear Peace* (New York: Vintage Books, 1989), p. 202.

10. Testimony, Defense Policy Subcommittee, House Armed Services Committee, May 17, 1988, quoted in Lakoff and York, *Shield in Space?* pp. 165–166.

11. Joseph Fromm, "Behind Reagan's Star Wars Strategy," *U.S. News and World Report* 94 (April 4, 1983): 28.

12. Lakoff and York, *Shield in Space?* p. 39.

13. Interview, David Cortright with Michael Baroody, July 20, 1990.

14. Caspar Weinberger, *Fighting for Peace: Seven Critical Years in the Pentagon* (New York: Warner Books, 1990), p. 304.

15. Interview, David Gergen.

16. Interview, David Cortright with Richard Allen, December 4, 1991.

17. Interview, David Gergen.

18. Anderson, *Revolution,* p. 78.

19. Bruce Parrott, *The Soviet Union and Ballistic Missile Defense* (Boulder, Colo.: Westview Press, 1987), pp. 75–76.

20. Mikhail Gorbachev, *Perestroika: New Thinking for Our Country and the World* (New York: Harper and Row, 1987), p. 234.

21. Rosy Nimroody, *Star Wars: The Economic Fallout* (Cambridge, Mass.: Ballinger, 1988), pp. 180, 186.

22. Andrei Sakharov, *Moscow and Beyond: 1986 to 1989* (New York: Alfred A. Knopf, 1991), pp. 21–22.

23. Interview, David Cortright with Michael Deaver, July 16, 1990.

24. Parrott, *Soviet Union and Ballistic Missile Defense,* p. 56.

25. Lakoff and York, *Shield in Space?* p. 176.

26. Strobe Talbott, *Deadly Gambits: The Reagan Administration and the Stalemate in Nuclear Arms Control* (New York: Vintage Books, 1985), p. 356.

27. Matthew Evangelista, "Sources of Moderation in Soviet Security Policy," in *Behavior, Society, and Nuclear War,* ed. Philip Tetlock et al. (New York: Oxford University Press, 1991), p. 323.

28. Talbott, *Master of the Game,* pp. 261–262.

29. Quoted in ibid., p. 206.

30. Quoted in ibid., p. 284.

31. *Wall Street Journal,* July 22, 1986, p. 1.

32. Quoted in Talbott, *Master of the Game,* p. 312.

33. John Newhouse, *War and Peace in the Nuclear Age* (New York: Alfred A. Knopf, 1989), pp. 363, 382.

34. Bundy, *Danger and Survival,* p. 574.

35. Lakoff and York, *Shield in Space?* p. 171.

36. Talbott, *Deadly Gambits,* p. 3.

37. Interview, Michael Deaver.

38. "Detailed Tabulations of Survey Results: Prepared for SANE, Inc.," #74146, Opinion Research Corporation, Princeton, N.J., March 1986.

39. Mark Hertsgaard, *On Bended Knee: The Press and the Reagan Presidency* (New York: Shocken Books, 1989), p. 291.

Chapter 11

1. Elizabeth Drew, "Letter from Washington," *The New Yorker,* October 27, 1986, p. 124.

2. Strobe Talbott, *The Master of the Game: Paul Nitze and the Nuclear Peace* (New York: Vintage Books, 1989), p. 315.

3. Donald Regan, *For the Record: From Wall Street to Washington* (San Diego, Calif.: Harcourt Brace Jovanovich, 1988), p. 341.

4. "The Political Campaign: Reagan Emphasizes 'Star Wars' Plan on Stump," *New York Times,* October 27, 1986, p. 19.

5. Interview, David Cortright with Tom Downey, August 29, 1991.

6. Interview, David Cortright with David Cohen, August 23, 1991.

7. *Congressional Quarterly Almanac,* 99th Congress, Second Session (Washington, D.C.: Congressional Quarterly, Inc., 1986), Volume 42, p. 478.

8. Kenneth Adelman, *The Great Universal Embrace: Arms Summitry—A Skeptic's Account* (New York: Simon and Schuster, 1989), p. 44.

9. *Congressional Quarterly Almanac,* Volume 42, p. 478.

10. Adelman, *Great Embrace,* p. 31.

11. Ibid., p. 32.

12. Dunbar Lockwood, "U.S. Begins Testing Moratorium," *Arms Control Today* 22 (October 1992): 33.

13. Interview, David Cortright with Caspar Weinberger, September 23, 1991.

14. "Star Wars: Budgeting Big for University Science," *Science and Government Reports,* April 15, 1985, p. 1.

15. David Meyer, *A Winter of Discontent: The Nuclear Freeze and American Politics* (New York: Praeger, 1990), pp. 98–99.

16. Caspar Weinberger, *Fighting for Peace: Seven Critical Years in the Pentagon* (New York: Warner Books, 1990), p. 300.

17. Ibid., p. 308.

18. All quotations from David Parnas, unless otherwise noted, are from an interview by Robert K. Musil with David Parnas for the "Consider the Alternatives" radio program of the SANE Education Fund, 1985, program 679.

19. David Parnas, letter of resignation to James Offut, SDIO, June 28, 1985.

20. Interview, David Parnas.

21. Robert Jastrow, "The War Against Star Wars," *Commentary* 78 (December 1984): 19–20.

22. Quoted in Sanford Lakoff and Herbert York, *Shield in Space? Technology, Politics, and the Strategic Defense Initiative* (Berkeley: University of California Press, 1989), p. 15.

23. Quoted in Jastrow, "The War Against Star Wars," p. 20.

24. Lakoff and York, *Shield in Space?* pp. 270–271.

25. *Chemical and Engineering News*, July 21, 1986, p. 18.

26. William Sweet, "Scientists Shoot Down Star Wars," *Bulletin of Atomic Scientists* 43 (July/August 1987): 7.

27. Ibid.

28. "Summary and Current Results of the Boycott of Star Wars Research Funds by University Scientists and Engineers," September 15, 1987, available from Lisbeth Gronlund, Center for International Security Studies, University of Maryland.

29. Interview, David Cortright with Lisbeth Gronlund, March 13, 1991.

30. As rated by the Conference Board of Associated Research Councils, published in *The Chronicle of Higher Education*, September 29, 1982.

31. "6,500 College Scientists Take Anti-SDI Pledge,"*Washington Post*, May 14, 1986, p. 3; *Boston Globe*, May 14, 1986, p. 1; and *Nature* 323 (October 30, 1986): 747.

32. Letter to Nobel Institute from Representative Barbara Boxer et al., December 1, 1986.

33. Tim Carrington, "Shaky Launch: Politics of Star Wars Misfire," *Wall Street Journal*, July 22, 1986, p. 1.

34. Lakoff and York, *Shield in Space?* pp. 293–294.

35. Quoted in Carrington, "Shaky Launch," p. 1.

36. Weinberger, *Fighting for Peace*, pp. 308–309.

37. Lakoff and York, *Shield in Space?* p. 29.

38. Weinberger, *Fighting for Peace*, p. 309.

39. Ibid., p. 313.

40. Ibid., p. 316.

41. Lakoff and York, *Shield in Space?* pp. 293–294.

42. Adelman, *Great Embrace*, pp. 225–226.

43. Ibid., p. 171.

44. *Congressional Quarterly Weekly Report*, October 25, 1986, p. 2654.

45. Talbott, *Master of the Game*, p. 304.

46. See *Congressional Record* 133, March 11, 1987, p. S 2967; March 12, 1987, p. S 3090; and March 13, 1987, p. S 3171.

47. Talbott, *Master of the Game*, pp. 248, 334.

48. Interview, David Cohen.

49. Interview, David Cortright with John Isaacs, March 21, 1991.

50. *Congressional Quarterly Weekly Report,* May 9, 1987, p. 904; September 19, 1987, pp. 2228–2229.

51. *Congressional Quarterly Weekly Report,* September 19, 1987, p. 2228.

52. Ibid., p. 2229.

53. Bruce Parrott, *The Soviet Union and Ballistic Missile Defense* (Boulder, Colo.: Westview Press, 1987), pp. 63, 114.

54. Andrei Sakharov, "Of Arms and Reforms," *Time,* March 16, 1987, p. 42.

55. Adelman, *Great Embrace,* pp. 225, 227.

56. See Theodore Postol, "Lessons of the Gulf War Experience with Patriot," *International Security* 16 (Winter 1991–1992): 119–171.

57. Pat Towell, "A New Rationale for SDI," *Congressional Quarterly Weekly Report,* February 9, 1991, p. 376.

58. Office of the White House Press Secretary, "Joint U.S.-Russian Statement on a Global Protection System," June 17, 1992.

59. Quoted in Dunbar Lockwood, "The Pen-chant for Peace," *Bulletin of Atomic Scientists* 48 (October 1992): 45.

60. Quoted in Matthew Bunn, "The ABM Talks: The More Things Change ...," *Arms Control Today* 22 (September 1992): 21.

Chapter 12

1. "On the Mississippi: Cruising Peaceful Waters," *Time,* August 18, 1986; "Peace Cruise Ends with St. Louis Serenade," *New York Times,* August 3, 1986.

2. The sponsoring group, Promoting Enduring Peace, produced a booklet documenting the news coverage in 1986.

3. Mikhail Gorbachev, *Perestroika: New Thinking for Our Country and the World* (New York: Harper and Row, 1987), p. 214.

4. Interview, David Cortright with Karen Jacob, September 15, 1991.

5. Ibid.

6. "Gorbachev Gets Nobel Peace Prize for Foreign Policy Achievements," *New York Times,* October 16, 1990, p. 1.

7. Statement of Colin Powell, *Hearings Before a Subcommittee of the Committee on Appropriations, Department of Defense Appropriations,* February 8, 1990, House of Representatives, 101st Congress, 2d Session, Part 1, p. 13.

8. *New York Times,* December 5, 1989, p. 35.

9. Georgi Arbatov, *The System: An Insider's Life in Soviet Politics* (New York: Times Books/Random House, 1992), p. 189.

10. Matthew Evangelista, "Sources of Moderation in Soviet Security Policy," in *Behavior, Society, and Nuclear War,* ed. Philip Tetlock et al. (New York: Oxford University Press, 1991), p. 283.

11. Daniel Deudney and G. John Ikenberry, "International Sources of Soviet Change," manuscript, March 1990, p. 10.

12. A. N. Shevchenko, *Breaking with Moscow* (New York: Alfred A. Knopf, 1985), p. 78.

13. *Pravda,* January 15, 1960.

14. Evangelista, "Sources of Moderation," p. 295.

15. Thomas Risse-Kappen, "Did 'Peace Through Strength' End the Cold War?" *International Security* 16 (Summer 1991): 174.

16. Bruce Parrott, *The Soviet Union and Ballistic Missile Defense* (Boulder, Colo.: Westview Press, 1987), pp. 46–47, 55–56; Bruce Parrott, "The Soviet Debate on Missile Defense," *Bulletin of Atomic Scientists* 43 (April 1987): 11.

17. Evangelista, "Sources of Moderation," p. 303.

18. George F. Kennan, "The G.O.P. Won the Cold War? Ridiculous," *New York Times,* October 28, 1992, p. 15.

19. Mary Kaldor, "Taking the Democratic Way," *The Nation,* April 22, 1991, p. 516.

20. *Moscow News,* October 23–30, 1988.

21. Deudney and Ikenberry, "International Sources," p. 17.

22. Ibid, pp. 15–17.

23. Gorbachev, *Perestroika,* p. 132.

24. "Gorbachev Avows a Need for Peace to Pursue Reform," *New York Times,* February 17, 1987, p. 1.

25. See Evangelista, "Sources of Moderation," p. 330; see also Marshall Goldman, *Gorbachev's Challenge: Economic Reform in the Age of High Technology* (New York: W. W. Norton, 1987), pp. 11–12; Ben Eklof, *Soviet Briefing: Gorbachev and the Reform* (Boulder, Colo.: Westview Press, 1989), p. 100.

26. Benjamin Lambeth and Kevin Lewis, "The Kremlin and SDI," *Foreign Affairs* 66 (Spring 1988): 766.

27. Evangelista, "Sources of Moderation," p. 330.

28. Moshe Lewin, *The Gorbachev Phenomenon* (Berkeley: University of California Press, 1988), pp. 15, 31.

29. Ibid., p. 47.

30. Ibid., p. 44.

31. Ibid., pp. 53–54.

32. Ibid., p. 49.

33. Ibid.

34. Lewis Coser, "The Intellectuals in Soviet Reform," *Dissent* (Spring 1990): 183.

35. Lewin, *Gorbachev Phenomenon,* p. 80.

36. Personal correspondence, Max Watts to David Cortright, June 25, 1991.

37. Interview, David Cortright with Sergei Plekhanov, April 1988.

38. Ibid.

39. Quoted in Antony Astrachan, "Perestroika from Below," *The Nation,* July 9, 1990.

40. Quoted in Strobe Talbott, *Deadly Gambits: The Reagan Administration and the Stalemate in Nuclear Arms Control* (New York: Vintage Books, 1985), p. 81.

41. Risse-Kappen, "Did Peace Through Strength End the Cold War?" p. 186.

42. Pam Solo, *From Protest to Policy: Beyond the Freeze to Common Security* (Cambridge: Ballinger, 1988), pp. 44–45.

43. Talbott, *Deadly Gambits,* p. 279.

44. Interview, David Cortright with Daniel Ellsberg, September 1989.

45. "An Interview with Tair Tairov," *Disarmament Campaigns* (The Hague, Netherlands), December 1988/January 1989, p. 31.

46. Interview, David Cortright with Gene LaRocque, July 11, 1991.

47. Ibid.

48. Interview, David Cortright with Marcus Raskin, July 22, 1991.

49. Andrei Sakharov, *Sakharov Speaks* (New York: Alfred A. Knopf, 1974), pp. 33–34.

50. Evangelista, "Sources of Moderation," p. 312.

51. Strobe Talbott, *The Master of the Game: Policy and the Nuclear Peace* (New York: Vintage Books, 1989), pp. 247–248.

52. "Interview with Tair Tairov," p. 31.

53. Kaldor, "Taking the Democratic Way," p. 518.

54. Vaclav Havel, "Peace: The View from Prague," *New York Review of Books,* November 21, 1985, p. 30.

55. E. P. Thompson, "END and the Beginning: History Turns on a New Hinge," *The Nation,* January 19, 1990, p. 121.

56. Mary Kaldor, "Taking the Democratic Way," p. 518.

57. Ibid.

Chapter 13

1. Interview, David Cortright with Helen Seidman, November 20, 1991.

2. Excerpted from the script for "The Peace Therapist," written by Ira Shorr, performed by Ira Shorr and Gene Carroll at the nuclear freeze national conference, December 6, 1986, Chicago, Ill.

3. Roger C. Peace III, *A Just and Lasting Peace: The U.S. Peace Movement from the Cold War to Desert Storm* (Chicago, Ill.: Noble Press, 1991), p. 73.

4. Peace, *Just and Lasting Peace,* p. 81.

5. Peace, *Just and Lasting Peace,* p. 104; for detailed treatments see Ann Crittendon, *Sanctuary: A Story of American Conscience and the Law in Collision* (New York: Weidenfeld and Nicolson, 1988); Renny Golden and Michael McConnell, *Sanctuary: The New Underground Railroad* (New York: Orbis Books, 1986); Susan Bibler Coutin, *The Culture of Protest: Religious Activism and the U.S. Sanctuary Movement* (Boulder, Colo.: Westview Press, 1993).

6. Ed Griffin-Nolan, *Witness for Peace: A Story of Resistance* (Louisville, Ky.: Westminster/John Knox Press, 1991); see also Van Gosse, "North American Front: Central American Solidarity in the Reagan Era," in *Reshaping the American Left: Popular Struggles in the 1980s,* ed. Mike Davis and Michael Sprinker (London: Verso, 1988).

7. Peace, *Just and Lasting Peace,* p. 88.

8. Interview, David Cortright with Richard Allen, December 4, 1991.

9. Alexander Haig, *Caveat: Realism, Reagan, and Foreign Policy* (New York: Macmillan, 1984), p. 123.

10. Ibid., p. 130.

11. Caspar Weinberger, *Fighting for Peace: Seven Critical Years in the Pentagon* (New York: Warner Books, 1990), p. 31.

12. Ibid.

13. Haig, *Caveat,* p. 123.

14. Weinberger, *Fighting for Peace,* p. 31.

15. A comprehensive analysis of adverse public opinion trends for the White House is contained in William Leo Grande, *Central America and the Polls: A Study of U.S. Public Opinion Polls on U.S. Foreign Policy Toward El Salvador and Nicaragua Under the Reagan Administration* (Washington, D.C.: Washington Office on Latin America, March 1987).

16. Ibid., p. 6.

17. *Washington Post,* March 4, 1982, pp. 18, 19.

18. Haig, *Caveat,* p. 127.

19. Interview, Richard Allen.

20. Haig, *Caveat,* p. 125.

21. *El Salvador, 1979–1989: A Briefing Book on U.S. Aid and the Situation in El Salvador,* Congressional Research Service, Library of Congress (Washington, D.C.: CRS, 1989), p. 42.

22. *Bankrolling Failure: United States Policy in El Salvador and the Urgent Need for Reform, A Report to the Arms Control and Foreign Policy Caucus,* U.S. Congress, Washington, D.C., November 1987; documentation provided by the National Agenda for Peace in El Salvador, Washington, D.C.

23. Interview, David Cortright with Angela Sanbrano, December 2, 1991.

24. Interview, David Cortright with Bill Callahan, November 4, 1991.

25. Ibid.

26. See Patrick Tyler and Bob Woodward, "U.S. Approves Covert Plan in Nicaragua," *Washington Post,* March 10, 1982; see also "The Secret War in Nicaragua," *Newsweek,* November 5, 1982.

27. Interview, Bill Callahan.

28. Ibid.

29. Ibid.

30. Ibid.

31. Ibid.

32. Ibid.

33. Quoted in Roy Gutman, *Banana Diplomacy: The Making of American Policy in Nicaragua 1981–1987* (New York: Simon and Schuster, 1988), p. 21.

34. Cindy Buhl, notes from remarks delivered at the annual meeting of the Latin American Studies Association (LASA), Washington, D.C., April 1991.

35. Ibid.

36. Ibid.

37. William LeoGrande, "Did the Public Matter? The Impact of Opinion on Congressional Support for Ronald Reagan's Nicaragua Policy," a paper presented at the conference on Public Opinion and Policy Toward Central America, Princeton University, May 1990, pp. 23–24.

38. Buhl, notes from LASA.

39. Ibid.

40. LeoGrande, "Did the Public Matter?" pp. 36–37.

41. Mark Hertsgaard, *On Bended Knee: The Press and the Reagan Presidency* (New York: Shocken Books, 1989), p. 272.

42. Quoted in Gutman, *Banana Diplomacy,* p. 274.

43. Peace, *Just and Lasting Peace,* p. 83.

44. See LeoGrande, *Central America and the Polls,* passim.

45. Ibid., p. 27.

46. Jane Mayer and Doyle McMannus, *Landslide: The Unmaking of the President, 1984–1988* (Boston: Houghton Mifflin, 1988), p. 15.

47. LeoGrande, *Central America and the Polls,* Table 25.

48. Ronald Reagan, *An American Life* (New York: Simon and Schuster, 1990), p. 479.

49. Memo reprinted in "The Gates Hearings; Text of Gates' 1984 Memo to Casey on 'Straight Talk' About Nicaragua," *New York Times,* September 20, 1991, p. 20.

50. Ibid.

51. See documents on the National Security Planning Group in "The Iran-Contra Affair: The Making of a Scandal, 1983–1987," microfilm collection, published by the National Security Archive, Washington, D.C.

52. Mayer and McMannus, *Landslide,* pp. 86–87.

53. Ibid.

54. "The Gates Hearings; Text of Gates' 1984 Memo to Casey on 'Straight Talk' About Nicaragua," *New York Times,* September 20, 1991, p. 20.

55. Quoted in Gutman, *Banana Diplomacy,* p. 277.

56. Weinberger, *Fighting for Peace,* p. 31.

57. Alexander George, *Forceful Persuasion: Coercive Diplomacy as an Alternative to War* (Washington, D.C.: U.S. Institute of Peace, 1992), p. 73.

58. Testimony of Robert McFarlane, May 11, 1987, *Joint Hearings on the Iran-Contra Investigation,* Washington, D.C., p. 4.

59. Ibid.

60. LeoGrande, *Central America and the Polls,* p. iii.

61. *New York Times,* December 2, 1986, p. 1.

62. LeoGrande, *Central America and the Polls,* p. ix.

63. Interview, David Cortright with Daniel Ellsberg, September 1989.

64. John Newhouse, *War and Peace in the Nuclear Age* (New York: Alfred A. Knopf, 1989), p. 400.

65. Bruce Russett, "Democracy, Public Opinion and Nuclear Weapons," *Behavioral, Society and Nuclear War,* ed. Philip Tetlock, Jo Husbands et al. (New York: Oxford University Press, 1989), p. 242.

66. Interview, David Cortright with Michael Baroody, July 20, 1990.

67. Interview, David Cortright with Richard Wirthlin, September 5, 1990.

68. John Deutsch, Brent Scowcroft, and R. James Woolsey, "The Danger of the Zero Option," *Washington Post,* March 31, 1987, p. 21.

69. Kenneth Adelman, *The Great Universal Embrace: Arms Summitry—A Skeptic's Account* (New York: Simon and Schuster, 1989), p. 201.

70. Tom Smith, "Poll Report: Nuclear Anxiety," *Public Opinion Quarterly* 52 (Winter 1988): 560.

71. See Charles W. Ostrom and Brian L. Job, "The President and the Political Use of Force," *American Political Science Review* 80 (June 1986): 541–566.

72. Both quotes from "Americans Laud Result but Differ on the Moral," *New York Times,* February 27, 1990, p. 14.

73. Quoted in Peace, *Just and Lasting Peace,* p. 97.

74. *Congressional Quarterly Weekly Report,* February 6, 1988, p. 237.

Chapter 14

1. Alexander Haig, *Caveat: Realism, Reagan, and Foreign Policy* (New York: Macmillan, 1984), p. 228.

2. Ibid., p. 105.

3. Strobe Talbott, "Buildup and Breakdown," *Foreign Affairs* 62 (Winter 1983–1984): 587.

4. Strobe Talbott, *Deadly Gambits: The Reagan Administration and the Stalemate in Nuclear Arms Control* (New York: Alfred A. Knopf, 1984), p. 279.

5. Ibid.

6. See James Fallows, "The Military Spend-Up," *Atlantic Monthly,* July 1986, pp. 27–31.

About the Book and Author

This book boldly argues that citizen peace activists played a significant role in ending the Cold War and that grass-roots social movements have the power to shape history. Written by the former executive director of SANE, *Peace Works* combines the personal testimony of dozens of peace activists in the United States and Europe with documents, memoirs, and interviews of Reagan-Bush administration officials. The book shows how, when, and where public opinion and U.S. policy were influenced by the actions and ideas of the peace movement.

Anecdotes and personal stories lend vitality to the narrative allowing the reader to sit in on the conversations and plans of peaceworkers and to see how policy decisions on the MX missile, arms control negotiations, and other issues were affected by public pressure. We are given a front-row seat for many historic events, among them Jesse Jackson's meeting with Mikhail Gorbachev at the Geneva Summit in 1985; the making of the film "The Day After"; and the writing of the Catholic bishops' letter on war and peace. We are at the elbows of negotiators as the Reykjavik Summit falls apart, as the Iran-Contra scandal unfolds in Washington, and as Reagan-Bush officials battle with Congress over restrictions on nuclear testing and the Strategic Defense Initiative. Cortright shows the impact of peace activism in events large and small—from the efforts of prominent leaders like Helen Caldicott and William Sloane Coffin to the changes wrought by tens of thousands of everyday people—confirming that citizens played an important role in the remarkable events of the late 1980s.

David Cortright, former executive director of SANE, is president of the Fourth Freedom Forum and a visiting faculty fellow at the Joan B. Kroc Institute for International Peace Studies at the University of Notre Dame.

Index